782.1 WAG

Wagner and his operas

WAGNER
and His Operas

WAGNER
and His Operas

EDITED BY STANLEY SADIE

MACMILLAN REFERENCE LIMITED, LONDON
ST. MARTIN'S PRESS, INC, NEW YORK, NY

Published in Great Britain by
MACMILLAN REFERENCE LTD
25 Eccleston Place, London, SW1W 9NF

Basingstoke and Oxford
Companies and representatives throughout the world

British Library Cataloguing in Publication Data
Wagner and his operas - (Composers and their operas)
1. Wagner, Richard, 1813—1883.   2. Operas.   3. Composers - Germany - Biography
I. Sadie, Stanley, 1930—
782.1′092
ISBN 0-333-790219

Published in the United States and Canada by
ST. MARTIN'S PRESS, INC
175 Fifth Avenue, New York, NY 10010

ISBN 0-312-244320

A catalog record for this book is available from the Library of Congress

Typesetting by The Florence Group, Stoodleigh, Devon, UK

Printed and bound in Britain by Cambridge University Press, Cambridge.

CONTENTS

PREFACE

This volume is one of a series drawn from *The New Grove Dictionary of Opera* (1992). That dictionary, in four volumes, includes articles on all significant composers of opera and on their individual operas (as well as many other topics). We felt that it would serve the use of a wider readership to make this material available in a format more convenient for the lover of opera and also at a price that would make it accessible to a much larger number of readers.

The most loved, and most performed, of opera composers are (in chronological order) Mozart, Verdi, Wagner and Puccini, who form the central topics of these volumes. The volumes each include chapters on the composer's life (with particular emphasis on his operatic activities) and a chapter on each of his operas. In some cases, the availability of additional space has made it possible for us to include, additionally, information that provides a fuller context for the composer and his work. Not for Verdi, who (perhaps unfortunately) composed so many operas that space did not permit any additions. And in the case of Wagner, whose operas demand quite extensive discussion, it was possible to add material only on his original singers and of course on Bayreuth.

For the Mozart volume, however, in which only a relatively modest number of operas call for extensive treatment, we were able to include material on virtually all his singers (excluding only those on whom we are almost totally ignorant) and on his interesting array of librettists, as well as some background on cities in which his music was heard. And for Puccini, there is material not only on librettists and singers but also on the most important composers among his Italian contemporaries, men whose music is still in the repertory (for instance the composers of *Cavalleria rusticana* and *Pagliacci*).

The authors of the chapters in these books are leading authorities on their subjects. The Mozart volume is chiefly the work of Julian Rushton, the Verdi of Roger Parker and the Wagner of Barry Millington, while the Puccini principal author is Julian Budden. Writers of the shorter sections are individually acknowledged within the book. We are grateful to all of them for permitting the re-use of their work.

STANLEY SADIE
London, 1999

ILLUSTRATIONS

Plate 1 – Design by Carl Emil Doepler for a lantern slide for the first complete *Ring* cycle at Bayreuth, 1876, of the *Ride of the Valkyries* [Nationalarchiv der Richard-Wagner-Stiftung, Richard-Wagner-Gedenkstätte]

Plate 2 – Cross section of the stage at Bayreuth showing various positions of the platform in *Die Walküre* in the 1983 production of the *Ring* cycle [Bayreuther Festspiel]

Plate 3 – Backstage view of the dragon in *Siegfried* in the first Paris production (Opéra, 1902): from the *Scientific American* (29 March 1902), supplement 1369

Plate 4 – The Holy Communion enacted during the Grail scene at the end of Act 3 of *Parsifal*: Paul von Joukowsky's design for the original production at the Festspielhaus, Bayreuth, in 1882 [Nationalarchiv der Richard-Wagner-Stiftung, Richard-Wagner-Gedenkstätte]

Plate 5 – Scene from *Das Rheingold* at the Metropolitan Opera, New York, 1988, with sets designed by Günther Schneider-Siemssen [Metropolitan Opera Association Inc./Lincoln Center, New York (photo Winnie Klotz)]

Plate 6 – Design for Brünnhilde in *Die Walküre*, illustrating the influence of contemporary fashion: Amalie Materna in the original production of the complete *Ring* cycle, Bayreuth, 1876, with costumes designed by Carl Emil Doepler. The winged helmet and chain mail had been suggested by Wagner. Her silhouette and draped skirt with a train were fashionable in 1876 [Nationalarchiv der Richard-Wagner-Stiftung, Richard-Wagner-Gedenkstätte]

Plate 7 – Walther's Prize Song from *Die Meistersinger*, Act 3: Wagner's second complete draft or 'orchestral sketch' of between 8 October 1866 and 5 March 1867 [Nationalarchiv der Richard-Wagner-Stiftung, Richard-Wagner-Gedenkstätte]

Plate 8 – Richard Wagner: photograph taken in Vienna during the winter of 1862–63 [Bildarchiv, Osterreichische Nationalbibliothek]

CONTRIBUTORS

A.W.	Arnold Whittall
B.M.	Barry Millington
C.F.	Christopher Field
E.F.	Elizabeth Forbes
F.B.	Friedrich Baser
G.S.	Geoffrey Skelton
J.W.	John Warrack

CHRONOLOGY OF WAGNER'S LIFE AND OPERAS

1813

22 May	Born in the Brühl, Leipzig, the son of Johanna Rosine Wagner and Carl Friedrich Wagner
23 November	Death of Carl Friedrich Wagner; Ludwig Geyer (*d* 1821) offers family assistance

1827

8 April	Wagner confirmed at the Kreuzkirche, Dresden

1828

21 January	Enters the Nicolaischule in Leipzig

1829

First compositions: two piano sonatas and a string quartet (all lost)

1830

16 June	Attends the Thomasschule, Leipzig
July	Revolution in Paris and unrest elsewhere in Europe
25 December	'Drum-beat Overture' performed in Leipzig

1831

23 February	Attends Leipzig University

1833

January	Takes up post as chorus master at the Würzburg theatre; writes text and starts composition for *Die Feen*

1834

July	Becomes musical director of Heinrich Berthmann's travelling music company

1836

29 March	Première of *Das Liebesverbot* in Magdeburg
24 November	Marries Christine Wilhelmine ('Minna') Planer at Königsberg-Tragheim

1837

24 December	Cosima Liszt born at Como

1842

20 October	*Rienzi, der Letzte der Tribunen*, Dresden, Hoftheater

1843

2 January	*Der fliegende Holländer*, Dresden, Hoftheater, conducted by Wagner
2 February	Appointed Kapellmeister at the King of Saxony's court in Dresden

1845

19 October   *Tannhäuser*, Dresden, Hoftheater, conducted by Wagner

1848   'The year of the revolution' – risings in Paris and many German cities
Wagner denounces the monarchy at the Dresden Vaterlandsverein

1849

24–28 May   Following a warrant for his arrest, Wagner flees to Switzerland, and from there to Paris (2 June)

July   Settles in Zürich and writes *Art and Revolution*

1850

28 August   *Lohengrin*, Weimar, Grossherzogliches Hof, conducted by Liszt

Winter   Writes *Opera and Drama*

1853

10 October   Meets Cosima Liszt

1 November   Begins draft of *Rheingold*

1861

March   *Tannhäuser* performed at Paris Opéra

1864

March   Ludwig II ascends to the Bavarian throne and becomes Wagner's patron

Summer   Cosima leaves her husband, the conductor Hans von Bülow, to join Wagner

1865

10 April   Birth of Isolde, Wagner and Cosima's first child

10 June   *Tristan und Isolde*, Munich, Königliches Hof- und Nationaltheater, conducted by Bülow

December   Driven from Munich by scandal, Wagner and Cosima settle at Triebschen on Lake Lucerne, returning to Munich in 1867

1866

25 January   Minna dies in Dresden

1867

17 February   Birth of a second daughter, Eva

1868

21 June   *Die Meistersinger von Nürnberg*, Munich, Königliches Hof- und Nationaltheater, conducted by Bülow

1869

22 September   *Rheingold*, Munich, Königliches Hof- und Nationaltheater, conducted by Wüllner

6 June   Birth of Siegfried, Wagner and Cosima's son

1870

| 26 June | *Walküre*, Munich, Königliches Hof- und Nationaltheater conducted by Wüllner |
| 25 August | Wagner and Cosima marry in the Protestant church in Lucerne |

1876

| 13–30 August | First Bayreuth festival; the complete *Ring* cycle is performed three times, conducted by Richter |

1881

| 5–9 May | First complete performance of the *Ring* cycle in Berlin |

1882

| 26 July | *Parsifal*, Bayreuth, Festspielhaus, conducted by Hermann Levi |

1883

| 13 February | Wagner dies in Venice |
| 18 February | Buried in the garden of Wahnfried |

Biography

Richard Wagner

One of the key figures in the history of opera, Wilhelm Richard Wagner was largely responsible for altering its orientation in the 19th century. His programme of artistic reform, though not executed to the last detail, accelerated the trend towards organically conceived, through-composed structures, as well as influencing the development of the orchestra, of a new breed of singer, and of various aspects of theatrical practice. Born in Leipzig on 22 May 1813, he died on 13 February 1883 in Venice.

THE FORMATIVE YEARS 1813–32   It is both fitting and psychologically congruous that a question mark should hover over the identity of the father and mother of the composer whose works resonate so eloquently with themes of parental anxiety. Richard Wagner's 'official' father was the police actuary Carl Friedrich Wagner, but the boy's adoptive father, the actor-painter Ludwig Geyer, who took responsibility for the child on Carl Friedrich's death in November 1813, may possibly have been the real father. Wagner himself was never sure, though any concern he may have had about Geyer's supposed Jewish origins would have been misplaced: Geyer was of incontrovertibly Protestant stock. Recent research has further established that Wagner's mother Johanna was not the illegitimate daughter of Prince Constantin of Saxe-Weimar-Eisenach, as previously believed, but his mistress.

Wagner's formal education began on 2 December 1822 at the Kreuzschule in Dresden, where his mother and stepfather had moved to enable Geyer to undertake engagements for the Hoftheater. On returning to Leipzig with his mother and sisters he entered the Nicolaischule on 21 January 1828, but school studies were less enthusiastically pursued than theatrical and musical interests, which resulted in a 'vast tragic drama' called *Leubald* and conscientious perusal of Logier's composition treatise. Harmony lessons (initially in secret) with a local musician, Christian Gottlieb Müller (1828–31), were followed by enrolment at Leipzig University (23 February 1831)

3

to study music and a short but intensive period of study with the Kantor of the Thomaskirche, Christian Theodor Weinlig (about six months from October 1831).

In his autobiographical writings Wagner later played down the significance of his musical education in order to cultivate the notion of the untutored genius. But its fruits were evident in a series of keyboard and orchestral works written by spring 1832 and particularly in the Beethovenian Symphony in C major which followed shortly after. A genuine passion for Beethoven, while confirmed by such works and the piano transcription of the Ninth Symphony made in 1830–31, was exaggerated in another typical piece of mythification: Wagner's account of a supposedly momentous portrayal of Leonore by the soprano Wilhelmine Schröder-Devrient in Leipzig in 1829 is undermined by the unavailability of any evidence that the singer gave such a performance. Yet the fable (probably a semi-conscious conflation of two separate events) attests to the young composer's ambition to be proclaimed the rightful heir to the symphonic tradition embodied in Beethoven.

Wagner's first attempt at an operatic project was a pastoral opera based on Goethe's *Die Laune des Verliebten* (probably from early 1830); the work was aborted with only a scene for three female voices and a tenor aria written. His second project, *Die Hochzeit*, was conceived in October or November 1832, while he was visiting the estate of Count Pachta at Pravonin, near Prague. Based on a story from J. G. G. Büsching's *Ritterzeit und Ritterwesen*, *Die Hochzeit* was a grisly tale of dark passions, treachery and murder. The libretto, according to Wagner's autobiography, *Mein Leben*, was destroyed by him as a demonstration of confidence in the judgment of his sister Rosalie. Such music as was completed, between December 1832 and March 1833 – an introduction, chorus and septet – survives.

EARLY CAREER: 1833–42   Wagner's first professional appointment, secured by his brother Albert, was as chorus master at the theatre in Würzburg. There he encountered repertory works by Marschner, Weber, Paer, Cherubini, Rossini and Auber, of which composers the first two influenced him most strongly in his musical setting of *Die Feen* (1833–4), a working by Wagner himself (he was to write all his own librettos) of Gozzi's *La donna serpente*. Returning to Leipzig at the beginning of 1834 he came into contact with the charismatic radical Heinrich Laube (a family friend) and other members of the progressive literary and political movement Junges Deutschland. The writers associated with this uncoordinated grouping, including Karl Gutzkow, Ludolf Wienbarg, Heinrich Heine and Ludwig Börne, rejected not only the classicism of Goethe and Mozart but also what they regarded as the reactionary, socially irrelevant and sentimentally conceived romanticism of Weber and E. T. A. Hoffmann. They turned instead for inspiration to Italy and to the French Utopian Socialists, especially the Saint-Simonians, spurning Catholic mysticism and morality in favour of hedonism and sensuality. It was under these influences that Wagner wrote his essays *Die deutsche Oper* (1834) and *Bellini* (1837), celebrating the italianate capacity for bel canto expressiveness, as well as his next opera *Das Liebesverbot* (1834–6), relocating Shakespeare's *Measure for Measure* in a sun-soaked, pleasure-filled Mediterranean setting; the chief musical models adopted were, appropriately, Bellini and Auber.

It was carnal rather than aesthetic considerations, according to Wagner, that persuaded him to accept a post as musical director of the travelling theatre company run by Heinrich Bethmann: he had fallen instantly in love with one of the leading ladies, Christine Wilhelmine ('Minna') Planer. However, during his term with Bethmann's company (1834–6) he also gained valuable conducting experience and saw *Das Liebesverbot* on to the boards (29 March 1836) for what was to be the only performance in his lifetime.

Minna continued to pursue her theatrical career with engagements at the Königstadt Theater in Berlin and then in Königsberg. Negotiations for Wagner to secure the musical directorship of the opera in the latter city were protracted until 1 April 1837, but in the meantime he had sketched a prose scenario for a grand opera, *Die hohe Braut*, which he sent to Scribe in Paris in the hope that a libretto by him might inspire an Opéra commission. It was Wagner who eventually produced a libretto for *Die hohe Braut* (in Dresden in 1842); it was offered first to Karl Reissiger and then to Ferdinand Hiller, but was finally set by Jan Bedřich Kittl. An already tempestuous relationship with Minna was sealed by their marriage on 24 November 1836. Within months she had abandoned him in favour of a merchant called Dietrich; the rift had been healed only in part when Wagner took up a new post as musical director of the theatre in Riga (the historic capital of Livonia), which was part of the Russian Empire although colonized by Germans. He made the journey alone, arriving on 21 August 1837, but subsequently shared his cramped apartment not only with Minna, but also with her sister Amalie (who had taken up an appointment as singer at the theatre) and a baby wolf. Conditions at the small theatre were similarly constricted and the management unimaginative, though Wagner's enterprise and initiative did result in a series of subscription concerts.

In the summer of 1838 he turned his attention to a comic opera based on a tale from *The Thousand and One Nights*, calling it *Männerlist grösser als Frauenlist, oder Die glückliche Bärenfamilie*. He completed the libretto and began to set it in the manner of a Singspiel, but abandoned it in order to concentrate on a major project that had been simmering since he had read, the previous year, Bulwer-Lytton's novel about the Roman demagogue Rienzi. The poem and some of the music of the five-act grand opera *Rienzi* had been written by August 1838. The Riga appointment turned out to be as precarious for Wagner as his marriage, and after a contractual wrangle he determined to try his luck in the home of grand opera, Paris.

The departure from Riga had to be clandestine; Wagner and his wife were heavily in debt and their passports had been impounded. Under cover of night, Wagner, Minna and their Newfoundland dog, Robber, clambered through a ditch marking the border, under the nose of armed Cossack guards. Then, reaching the Prussian port of Pillau (now Baltiysk), they were smuggled on board a small merchant vessel, the *Thetis*, bound for London. The dangerous, stormy crossing and the crew's shouts echoing round the granite walls of a Norwegian fjord were later represented by Wagner as the creative inspiration for *Der fliegende Holländer*. If any ideas for text or music were jotted down at the time of the sea crossing (July–August 1839), the evidence has not survived. Crossing the channel from Gravesend to Boulogne,

Wagner was received there by Meyerbeer, who listened to Wagner's reading of the libretto of *Rienzi, der Letzte der Tribunen* and promised to provide letters of introduction to Duponchel and Habeneck, respectively the director and conductor of the Paris Opéra.

Wagner spent a dismal, penurious two-and-a-half years (September 1839 to April 1842) in Paris, a victim of the sharp social divisions of Louis-Philippe's July Monarchy which reserved wealth and privilege for a bourgeois élite. He was forced to earn his keep by making hack arrangements of operatic selections and by musical journalism in which he lambasted the mediocrities perpetrated by the Opéra. In March 1840 the Théâtre de la Renaissance accepted *Das Liebesverbot*, but the theatre was forced into bankruptcy two months later. There is no evidence to support Wagner's suggestion (made subsequently in *Mein Leben*) that Meyerbeer, through whose agency the work had been accepted, was aware of the imminent bankruptcy. Nor, apparently, did Wagner so believe at the time: on 20 September 1840 he wrote to Apel, 'Meyerbeer has remained untiringly loyal to my interests'. It is psychologically more plausible that Wagner's shameless obsequiousness before an influential patron was later transmuted by frustration and jealousy into the venomous bitterness seen, for example, in *Das Judentum in der Musik*. In May 1840 Wagner sent Eugène Scribe a copy of his sketch for *Der fliegende Holländer*, and in letters of 3 May and 4 June he mentioned it to Meyerbeer, in the hope that he might use his influence to have the work put on at the Opéra. Meyerbeer introduced him to the new director of the Opéra, Léon Pillet, who bought the story for 500 francs, supposedly to have it made into an opera by one of the composers under contract to him. In fact, the two librettists given the sketch, Paul Foucher and Bénédict-Henry Révoil, did not, as generally stated, base their work *Le vaisseau fantôme* primarily on it but on a variety of sources including Captain Marryat's *The Phantom Ship* and Sir Walter Scott's *The Pirate*. Wagner meanwhile proceeded to elaborate his scenario into a work of his own and initially he worked on the *Holländer* in tandem with *Rienzi*, which was completed in November 1840.

At this time Wagner was threatened with imprisonment for debt, but the available evidence strongly suggests that the threat was never executed. Partly through Meyerbeer's influence, *Rienzi* was accepted by the Dresden Hoftheater. Preparations were under way by April 1842, when Wagner, deeply disillusioned with Paris, began to make his way back to the fatherland.

KAPELLMEISTER IN DRESDEN: 1843–9   The première of *Rienzi* on 20 October 1842 was an immense success, catching as the work did the rebellious spirit of the times. The darker, introspective quality of the *Holländer*, which followed at the Hoftheater on 2 January 1843, was found less appealing. Nevertheless, Wagner was an obvious candidate for the post of Kapellmeister at the King of Saxony's court in Dresden, which had become vacant. The prospect of financial security finally outweighed any doubts he had about accepting a liveried post in the royal service. Contrary to what he had been led to believe, Wagner's status was that of second Kapellmeister, subordinate to that of Reissiger, who since his appointment as Kapellmeister in 1828 had elevated the reputation of the opera house to the highest level, but who by the 1840s was content to rest on his laurels while a younger colleague undertook the more onerous duties.

Those duties included conducting operatic, instrumental and orchestral performances and composing pieces for special court occasions. Among the latter works are numbered *Das Liebesmahl der Apostel* (1843), a biblical scene for male voices and orchestra; *Der Tag erscheint* (1843), a chorus for the unveiling of a monument to the king; *Gruss seiner Treuen an Friedrich August den Geliebten* (1844), another choral tribute to the king; and *An Webers Grabe* (1844), a chorus for the ceremony accompanying the reburial of Weber's remains in his home town (the campaign to effect which Wagner had vigorously supported).

Wagner had begun work on his next major project, *Tannhäuser*, in the summer of 1842, when a detailed prose draft was worked out at Aussig (now Ústí nad Labem) in the Bohemian mountains. It was versified by the spring of the following year and the composition occupied Wagner between July 1843 and April 1845. The first performance took place at the Hoftheater on 19 October 1845. Wagner then spent three months analysing the conditions under which court music was produced at Dresden. His proposals, including a series of winter orchestral concerts, were eminently reasonable, but after a year's delay he was informed that they had been rejected.

Wagner's library in Dresden embraced a broad range of literature, both ancient and modern, from Calderón to Xenophon and Molière to Gibbon. It also contained versions of Gottfried von Strassburg's *Tristan*, editions of the Parzival and Lohengrin epics, and a number of volumes on the medieval cobbler-poet Hans Sachs. The subjects of *Lohengrin* and each of the music dramas to follow the *Ring* are thus likely to have been germinating in his mind during these years. A first prose draft was actually made for *Die Meistersinger von Nürnberg* at Marienbad (now Mariánske Lánskì) in 1845.

An event of major importance for Wagner was his organization in 1846 of a performance of Beethoven's Ninth Symphony (then still considered an unapproachable work) for the traditional Palm Sunday concert in the old opera house. Against considerable opposition from the administration he secured a notable financial and artistic success. The existence of sketches dating from 1846–7 for at least two symphonies bears witness to the inspirational effect the preparations for the Ninth had on Wagner himself.

During these years too he was working on the composition of *Lohengrin*, as well as studying Aeschylus (*Oresteia*), Aristophanes and other Greek authors in translation. In February 1847 he conducted his own arrangement of Gluck's *Iphigénie en Aulide*. His meagre salary (1500 talers per annum) was not enough to cover essential outgoings, but Minna managed the household efficiently and enjoyed the status of Kapellmeister's wife. They remained involuntarily childless (probably as a result of an earlier miscarriage) but in general the marriage was at its most stable at this period.

The insurrectionary outbreaks in Paris in February 1848 and in Vienna the following month were greeted with zealous approbation by the ranks of middle-class German liberals, indignant at the indifference of their princely rulers to social deprivation among the working classes and motivated by fear of their own proletarianization. In Dresden barricades were erected and the king was presented with demands for democratic reform. Wagner's plan for the organization of a German national theatre, which proposed that the director of such an institution be elected, that a drama school be set up, the court orchestra expanded and its administration put under self-management, was a reflection of such democratic principles, and consequently rejected. It is mistaken to see such a proposal – or, indeed, Wagner's involvement in the revolution generally – simply as opportunist. He naturally wished to see the role of the opera house enhanced in a reconstructed society, but such a desire sprang from the conviction that art was the highest and potentially most fruitful form of human endeavour.

He threw in his lot with the insurrectionists when in June 1848 he delivered a speech to the Vaterlandsverein, the leading republican grouping, on the subject of the relation of republican aspirations to the monarchy. The evils of money and speculation were denounced as barriers to the emancipation of the human race, and the downfall of the aristocracy was predicted. The notion that the Saxon king should remain at the head of the new republic, as 'the first and truest republican of all', was not an idiosyncratic one, but in tune with the limited demands of the bourgeois liberals for constitutional government.

Wagner remained for the time being at his post, and began to set down a prose résumé of what was to become *Der Ring des Nibelungen: Der Nibelungen-Mythus: als Entwurf zu einem Drama* (October 1848). A prose draft of *Siegfrieds Tod* (later to become *Götterdämmerung*) was made the same month, followed (not preceded, as previously supposed) by the essay *Die Wibelungen: Weltgeschichte aus der Sage* (probably written in about mid-February 1849). Other projects of the period included *Friedrich I* (in five acts, possibly an opera), *Jesus von Nazareth* (probably also intended as a five-act opera, though only a prose draft was completed), *Achilleus* (probably a three-act opera) and *Wieland der Schmied* (a heroic opera in three acts; prose draft). *Wieland* and, in particular, *Jesus von Nazareth* espouse the ideas of Pierre-Joseph Proudhon and Ludwig Feuerbach: ownership of property as the root of evil, supremacy of love over the law, and a new religion of humanity.

Wagner's assistant conductor, August Röckel, was no less of a firebrand, and the weekly republican journal he edited, the *Volksblätter*, contained various inflammatory tirades by Wagner and others. Through Röckel, Wagner came to know Mikhail Bakunin, the Russian anarchist, who in turn was acquainted personally with Marx and Engels. The fact that no works of Marx were contained in Wagner's library at Dresden provides no proof that Wagner was unfamiliar with his ideas: radical theories would have circulated freely in a major city such as Dresden.

Wagner's active role in the Dresden insurrection obliged him to flee for his life when the Prussian troops began to gain control in May 1849. He was sheltered by Liszt at Weimar before making his way on a false passport, via Paris, to Switzerland. A warrant had been issued for his arrest.

ZÜRICH ESSAYS   Even after the savage crushing of the 1848–9 uprisings, Wagner continued to believe that both social and artistic reform were imminent. In the first years of his exile in Zürich – he was not to enter Germany again until 1860 – he formulated a set of aesthetic theories intended to establish opera in a radically recast form as at once the instrument and the product of a reconstructed society. In the first of this series of Zürich essays, *Die Kunst und die Revolution* (1849), written under the influence of Proudhon and Feuerbach, Wagner outlined the debasement of art since the era of the glorious, all-embracing Greek drama. Only when art was liberated from the sphere of capitalist speculation and profit-making would it be able to express the spirit of emancipated humanity. The vehicle envisaged to effect this transformation process, namely the 'art-work of the future', was elaborated, along with the concept of the reunification of the arts into a comprehensive *Gesamtkunstwerk* ('total work of art') on the ancient Greek model, in two further essays, *Das Kunstwerk der Zukunft* (1849) and *Oper und Drama* (1850–51).

In the former, Wagner argued that the elements of dance, music and poetry, harmonized so perfectly in Greek drama, were deprived of their expressive potential when divorced from one another. In the 'art-work of the future' they would be reunited both with each other (in the 'actor of the future', at once dancer, musician and poet) and with the arts of architecture, sculpture and painting. Allowance was even made for the occasional use of the spoken word. Theatres would need to be redesigned according to aesthetic criteria rather than those of social hierarchy. Landscape painters would be required to execute the sets. Above all, the new work of art was to be created, in response to a communal need, by a fellowship of artists, representative of *das Volk* ('the People').

The philosophical basis of *Das Kunstwerk der Zukunft* is multifaceted. The *völkisch* ideology, which urged a return to a remote primordial world where peasants of pure Germanic blood lived as a true community, had evolved with the rise of national consciousness in the 18th century. Notions such as that of the *Volk*'s creative endeavours arising spontaneously out of sheer necessity – a process of historical inevitability – owe much to Feuerbach and to such revolutionary thinkers as Marx. Nor was the concept of the *Gesamtkunstwerk* new: writers such as Lessing, Novalis, Tieck, Schelling and Hoffmann had previously advocated, either in theory or in practice, some sort of reunification of the arts, while the idea of the regeneration of art in accordance with classical ideals can be identified with Winckelmann, Wieland, Lessing, Goethe and Schiller.

Oper und Drama is an immense discourse on the aesthetics of drama-through-music. A new form of verse-setting (*Versmelodie*) is outlined, in which the melody will grow organically out of the verse. It will use *Stabreim* (an old German verse form using alliteration) and a system of presentiments and reminiscences, functioning as *melodische Momente* ('melodic impulses'). Only rarely will one voice serve as harmonic support for another; choruses and other ensembles will be eliminated. Wagner's claim that the new ideas and techniques had 'already matured' within him before the theory was formulated is something of an exaggeration, as is suggested by his willingness to adapt the theoretical principles in the light of practical experience. Their formulation did, however, enable him to grapple with the central issue: how to reconcile his own fundamentally literary and dramatic inspirations with the Classical symphonic tradition.

Two other important essays of the period should be mentioned. *Das Judentum in der Musik* argues that the superficial, meretricious values of contemporary art are embodied, above all, in Jewish musicians. The rootlessness of Jews in Germany and their historical role as usurers and entrepreneurs has condemned them, in Wagner's view, to cultural sterility. The uncompromisingly anti-semitic tone of the essay was, in part, provoked by repeated allegations that Wagner was indebted artistically, as well as financially, to Meyerbeer. The preoccupations and prejudices of *Das Judentum* also place it in an anti-Jewish tradition, perpetuated by writers often of otherwise impeccably liberal and humanitarian credentials, going back via Luther to the Middle Ages. Even the idea that Jews should, as part of the process of assimilation, undergo a programme of re-education was not novel, though the refinement (stated elsewhere) that that programme should largely consist of the Wagnerian music drama was original.

In 1851 Wagner wrote an extensive preface to accompany the projected publication of the librettos of the *Holländer*, *Tannhäuser* and *Lohengrin*. This autobiographical essay, called *Eine Mitteilung an meine Freunde*, is of interest for the insights it offers into Wagner's own view of his life and works to that date.

COMPOSER IN EXILE: 1849–63   In Zürich Wagner made the acquaintance of a number of cultured individuals, some of whom provided pecuniary as well as intellectual sustenance. A pair of female admirers, Julie Ritter, a widow from Dresden, and Jessie Laussot (*née* Taylor), an Englishwoman married to a Bordeaux wine merchant, jointly offered him an annual allowance of 3,000 francs (equivalent to 800 talers, or approximately half his Dresden salary), for an indefinite period. Such benefactors showed the kind of disinterested generosity and confidence in his artistic endeavours that he found lacking in his wife, Minna, whose constant reproaches he found increasingly hard to bear. A love affair between Wagner and Jessie (who, according to him, was also unhappily married) briefly blossomed. When, after the intervention of Jessie's mother and death threats from her husband, it ended, one source of financial support dried up. But an unexpected legacy then enabled Julie Ritter to confer the full amount herself, which she continued to do from 1851 to 1859.

Lohengrin received its world première at Weimar under Liszt, with the composer necessarily absent. A drastic water cure at nearby Albisbrunn failed to relieve the dual complaints of erysipelas (a skin disease) and severe constipation, and further depression resulted from the failure of the revolution to materialize in France, or elsewhere in Europe. Several of Wagner's letters of the period speak of a love-less, cheerless existence; more than once he contemplated suicide.

By February 1853 he was able to recite the completed text of the *Ring* to an invited audience at the Hotel Baur au Lac in Zürich; 50 copies of the poem were printed at his own expense. Financial assistance from Otto Wesendonck, a retired silk merchant to whom Wagner had been introduced early in 1852, allowed him to present and conduct three concerts of excerpts from his works (May 1853) and to make a trip to Italy. Wagner's account (in *Mein Leben*) of the dream-inspired onrush of inspiration for *Das Rheingold* while he lay half-asleep in a hotel room in La Spezia has been dismissed as a further example of mythification, though it has been argued that the documentary evidence neither supports nor contradicts Wagner's account. The story bears witness, in any case, to the perceived importance of the new artistic phase being entered, and it was indeed in the succeeding months that the music of the *Ring* began to take shape.

In September 1854 Wagner reckoned his debts at 10,000 francs – by this time he was supporting not only Minna and her illegitimate daughter Natalie but also Minna's parents. Wesendonck agreed to settle most of these in exchange for the receipts from future perfor-mances of Wagner's works. Appeals for clemency made on his behalf to the new king of Saxony, Johann, were rejected, no doubt on the advice of the Dresden police, whose agents still had him under surveillance. Several of his acquaintances were regarded as dangerous political refugees, not least Georg Herwegh. Ironically, it was Herwegh who in September or October 1854 introduced him to the quietist, renunciatory philosophy that was to influence his future outlook on life: that of Arthur Schopenhauer.

Schopenhauer's influence was twofold: his Buddhist-inspired philosophy, advocating the denial of the will, and the quest for the state of nirvana (cessation of individual existence), was profoundly to affect the ideological orientation – and even the locution – of each of Wagner's remaining dramatic works. Schopenhauer's aesthetics, which elevated music above the other arts, made a similarly forceful impact. But Wagner's abandonment of the concept of the egalitarian coexistence of the arts should be seen not so much as a wholesale *volte face* from *Oper und Drama* principles as a shift of emphasis from the realization of those principles in *Das Rheingold* and *Die Walküre*.

An invitation from the Philharmonic Society to conduct a series of eight concerts in London resulted in a four-month stay in England in 1855. A hostile press campaign, uncongenial weather and the philistinism of the English combined to make the visit an unhappy one. On returning to Zürich he completed his severely disrupted work on *Walküre* (1856) and made a short prose sketch for an opera on a Buddhist subject: *Die Sieger*. The latter project was never completed, but its themes – passion and chastity, renunciation and redemption – later found a place in *Parsifal*.

Otto Wesendonck put at Wagner's disposal a small house adjacent to the villa he was having built in the Enge suburb of Zürich. Wagner and Minna moved in at the end of April 1857 and Wesendonck and his wife Mathilde to their own home in August. A love affair developed between Wagner and Mathilde, though their love – celebrated and idealized in *Tristan und Isolde* – was probably never consummated. To begin work on *Tristan* (20 August 1857) Wagner abandoned *Siegfried*, returning to sustained work on it only in 1869. An eruption of marital strife necessitated Wagner's move out of the Asyl (as, following Mathilde's suggestion, he had called the little house). In the company of Karl Ritter he travelled to Venice; the second act of *Tristan* was completed there (in draft) on 1 July 1858 and the third act in Lucerne on 16 July 1859.

Preparing another offensive against Paris, Wagner conducted, at the beginning of 1860 in the Théâtre Italien, three concerts of excerpts from his works. Through the intervention of Princess Pauline

Metternich *Tannhäuser* was eventually staged at the Opéra on 13 March 1861; a politically inspired demonstration, combined with Wagner's refusal to supply the customary second-act ballet, caused a débâcle and the production was withdrawn after three severely disrupted performances. A partial amnesty (Saxony remained barred until the following March) allowed Wagner to return to Germany on 12 August 1860.

In February 1862 he took lodgings in Biebrich, near Mainz, and set to work on the composition of *Die Meistersinger von Nürnberg*, for which he had made two further prose drafts (elaborating that of 1845) the previous November. Surrounded as he now was by female admirers, he yet baulked, on compassionate grounds, at putting a decisive end to his irreparably broken marriage. Instead he installed Minna, with a not ungenerous allowance, in Dresden; they last met in November 1862 and Minna died in January 1866. In May 1863 he rented the upper floor of a house in Penzing, near Vienna, furnishing it in luxurious style, heedless of the consequences. His generosity to friends was equally unstinting and by March the following year he was obliged to leave Vienna under threat of arrest for debt.

MUNICH AND BAYREUTH: 1864–77   A plea for pecuniary assistance published by Wagner along with the *Ring* poems in 1863 was answered in spectacular fashion when a new monarch ascended the throne of Bavaria in March 1864. The 18-year-old Ludwig II discharged Wagner's immediate debts, awarded him an annual stipend of 4,000 gulden (comparable to that of a ministerial councillor) and continued his support for many years, making possible the first Bayreuth festivals of 1876 and 1882.

A plea to Mathilde Maier to join him in the Villa Pellet, his new home overlooking Lake Starnberg, was less successful. But by now Wagner was on intimate terms with Cosima von Bülow, unsuitably married to the conductor Hans von Bülow, and their union was consummated some time between the arrival at Starnberg of Cosima (with two daughters and nurserymaid) on 29 June 1864 and that of Hans on 7 July. The child that resulted, Isolde, was born on 10 April 1865.

In October 1864 a more spacious house at 21 Briennerstrasse in Munich was made available to Wagner by Ludwig; it was decked out extravagantly, as was Wagner himself, in silks and satins supplied by a Viennese seamstress. When Ludwig summoned Gottfried Semper to Munich to design a Wagnerian festival theatre, local vested interests opposed the scheme. Difficulties were also encountered with Franz von Pfistermeister and Ludwig von der Pfordten, respectively Ludwig's cabinet secretary and prime minister, and eventually with resentment from the court circles and populace generally. Wagner's proposal for a music school to be established in Munich, appropriate for the nature of German music and drama, was seen as opportunistic, and Ludwig's support of the première of *Tristan* at the Hof- und Nationaltheater merely fuelled the hostility that accompanied the work's unveiling to a bemused public.

Castigation of Wagner for 'cynical exploitation' of Ludwig can be overplayed. It is true that he was as skilled in manipulating people in real life as in his dramas, and that he seized the opportunity to acquire the domestic comforts he had been so long denied. But his overriding concern was to obtain the best possible conditions for his art. And the total amount received by Wagner from Ludwig over the 19 years of their acquaintance – including stipend, rent and the cash value of presents – was 562,914 marks, a sum equivalent to less than one-seventh of the yearly Civil List (4.2 million marks). It is a sum that also compares modestly with the 652,000 marks spent on the bed-chamber alone of Herrenchiemsee, or with the 1.7 million marks spent on the bridal carriage for the royal wedding that never took place.

Ludwig, however, recognized that his close association with Wagner was costing him popular support, and in December 1865 reluctantly instructed him to leave Munich. Accompanied by Cosima, Wagner discovered and acquired a house called Tribschen (or Triebschen, to adopt Wagner's idiosyncratic spelling) overlooking Lake Lucerne. His cohabitation with Cosima (permanent from October 1868) was initially concealed from Ludwig, and a scandal-mongering article in the Munich *Volksbote* drove the couple to blind the king with a charade of lamentable mendacity.

From Tribschen Wagner continued to offer Ludwig the political advice with which he had always been generous. Now that Bavaria was caught up in the war between Prussia and Austria, Wagner's opinion, strongly influenced by the views of the conservative federalist Constantin Frantz, was that Bavaria should remain neutral. Bavaria, however, sided with Austria; its defeat not only enabled Prussian hegemony to be established, but also brought about the collapse of the German Confederation.

The impact on Wagner of Frantz's views was crucial to the ideological background of *Meistersinger* as it took shape during the 1860s. Schopenhauer's ethic of renunciation had by now given way to a more positive, more nationalistic outlook, reflecting the mood of optimism in the country at large arising from Germany's increasing industrial growth, national wealth and social cohesion, coupled with the rise of Bismarck. In *Was ist deutsch?* (1865), written for the private edification of the king, Wagner articulated the concern of many members of the middle class for traditional German values, apparently under threat. The divided religion effected by the Reformation, and the near-collapse of the German race, have led to an invasion by 'an utterly alien element', namely the Jews. The result is a 'repugnant caricature of the German spirit', which, according to Wagner, is beautiful and noble, not motivated by profit or self-interest.

Shortly after *Was ist deutsch?* was written, Wagner received a letter from Frantz telling him that in his music he had recognized 'the fundamental chord of German being'. A subsequent essay, *Deutsche Kunst und deutsche Politik* (1867), endorses Frantz's assertion that it is the 'mission' of Germany to forge a 'nobler culture, against which French civilization will no longer have any power', and goes on to propose that German art is a manifestation of that indomitable 'German spirit' which alone is capable of steering Germany and its politics through these difficult days. *Meistersinger* is the artistic component of Wagner's ideological crusade of the 1860s: a crusade to revive the 'German spirit' and purge it of alien elements.

The première of *Meistersinger* on 21 June 1868 was a triumph for Wagner. At Ludwig's insistence, but to Wagner's dismay when he realized how inadequate the performances would be, *Rheingold* and

Walküre were also staged in Munich in 1869 and 1870 respectively. A second child, Eva, had been born to Wagner and Cosima on 17 February 1867, and a third, Siegfried, on 6 June 1869. Cosima had meanwhile asked her husband for a divorce, and Bülow agreed, though Cosima's marriage to Wagner could not take place until 25 August 1870.

Wagner's anti-Gallic sympathies were given their head when in July 1870 war broke out between France and Prussia (supported by the south German states, including Bavaria). His farce, *Eine Kapitulation*, making tasteless capital out of the suffering endured by the Parisians during the siege of their city, returned to a favourite theme: the swamping of German culture by frivolous French art.

In the essay *Beethoven*, published in 1870 to coincide with the centenary celebrations of the composer, Wagner completed a process of rapprochement, initiated with '*Zukunftsmusik*' ten years earlier, between the aesthetics of *Oper und Drama* and those of Schopenhauer. In '*Zukunftsmusik*' Wagner continued to elevate his own species of text-related musical discourse above pure instrumental music, but the claim is modified by a reappraisal of the worth of symphonic music, particularly that of Beethoven. In *Beethoven* he finally accepts that words and music cannot enjoy totally equal status: with Schopenhauer, he maintains that music is the ultimate vehicle of expression. However, the union of music and words does permit a range of emotional expression far wider than that yielded by each alone. With this formulation, Wagner returned (as Carl Dahlhaus has pointed out) to something akin to the traditional Romantic conception of the aesthetic of music which he had espoused about 1840, long before his encounter with Schopenhauer.

Settling on the Upper Franconian town of Bayreuth for his planned festival enterprise, Wagner began to secure the support both of the local authorities and of 'patrons' across the country. The foundation stone of the theatre was laid on 22 May 1872 (Wagner's birthday); Beethoven's Ninth Symphony was performed. Wagner and Cosima moved to a temporary home in Bayreuth, and then, in April 1874, into 'Wahnfried'. The first festival, announced for 1873, had already been postponed for lack of funds. After an unsuccessful appeal to the

Reich, the enterprise was saved only by a loan of 100 000 talers from Ludwig. Admission tickets would have to be sold, however, in contravention of Wagner's original ideal of free access for the populace.

The score of *Götterdämmerung* was completed on 21 November 1874; rehearsals were initiated in the summer of the following year. The part of Siegfried went not to Albert Niemann, Wagner's Paris Tannhäuser, but to the untried Georg Unger, who required close supervision from a singing teacher. The Brünnhilde, Amalie Materna from Vienna, also had to be coached, though the Wotan, Franz Betz, having sung the Munich Hans Sachs, was more familiar with Wagner's demands. In charge of movement and gesture on the stage was Richard Fricke, with Wagner retaining overall control of the direction; his instructions were recorded in detail by Heinrich Porges. There were three cycles, beginning on 13 August 1876, attended by musicians, critics and notables from all over Europe. The reaction, predictably, was mixed, admiration for the realization of such an enterprise being tempered by criticism of details. Wagner himself was far from satisfied with the staging, which he vowed to revise in future years; nor were the tempos of the conductor, Hans Richter, to his liking.

An intimacy with the French writer Judith Gautier continued from the time of the 1876 festival until February 1878, when it was brought firmly but diplomatically to a halt by Cosima. A scarcely less intense relationship with Friedrich Nietzsche continued from 1869, when the latter first visited Tribschen, until Nietzsche's so-called 'second period' (1876–82), when he turned against art as romantic illusion and excoriated Wagner for betraying what he had identified as his challenging, affirmative spirit.

In the hope of discharging the deficit of the festival (148,000 marks) Wagner undertook a series of concerts in the recently opened Royal Albert Hall in London. He was well received, but the net profits of £700 (approximately 14,300 marks) were disappointingly low, thanks to miscalculations by the inexperienced agents.

'REGENERATION' WRITINGS   In January 1878 the first issue of the *Bayreuther Blätter* appeared, a journal devoted to the

Wagnerian cause, set up by Wagner under the editorship of Hans von Wolzogen. Its viewpoint was described by Wagner as 'the decline of the human race and the need for the establishment of a system of ethics'. That 'system of ethics' was expounded in the series of essays known as the 'regeneration writings', beginning with *Modern* (1878) and ending with *Heldentum und Christentum* (1881). The salient themes are as follows: the human species has degenerated by abandoning its original, natural vegetable diet, and absorbing the corrupted blood of slaughtered animals. Regeneration may be effected only by a return to natural food and it must be rooted in the soil of a true religion. Even the most degenerate races may be purified by the untainted blood of Christ, received in the sacrament of the Eucharist. The miscegenation of the pure Aryan race with the Jews has also contributed to the degeneration of the species.

The last notion Wagner owed to Count Joseph-Arthur de Gobineau, whose acquaintance in these years he greatly valued. Their respective philosophies diverged, however, in as much as Gobineau held that miscegenation was a necessary evil for the continuation of civilization, whereas in Wagner's more optimistic view the human race was redeemable by Christ's blood. Racialist philosophies of this kind were rampant in Wilhelminian Germany. With the unification finally achieved in 1871 had emerged an industrial bourgeoisie that usurped the privileged position of the former liberal nationalists who had struggled for it. Wagner was one of many such whose allegiance shifted from liberalism to a form of romantic conservatism. A new wave of anti-semitic sentiment swept Germany, if anything intensified rather than tempered by the emancipation legislation of the early 1870s. This is the ideological background against which *Parsifal* was written.

THE FINAL YEARS: 1878–83   The Bayreuth deficit was eventually cleared by an agreement, dated 31 March 1878, according to which Wagner confirmed Ludwig's right to produce all his works in the Hoftheater without payment, the king voluntarily setting aside 10 percent of all such receipts until the deficit was discharged. In a further clause, Wagner agreed that the first performance of *Parsifal* (either in Bayreuth or Munich) should be given with the orchestra, singers and artistic personnel of the Hoftheater, after which Munich was to have unrestricted rights over the work. It was this clause that compelled Wagner to accept the Jewish Hermann Levi as the conductor of *Parsifal* in 1882.

In August 1879 Wagner responded to an appeal for his support in a campaign against vivisection by writing a sympathetic open letter to Ernst von Weber on the subject. However, he refused to sign Bernhard Förster's 'Mass Petition against the Rampancy of Judaism', partly out of self-interest and partly out of a preference for addressing the issue in a more theoretical manner. In the early 1880s his health began to deteriorate: cardiac spasms were followed by a major heart attack in March 1882. After the second Bayreuth festival, consisting of 16 performances of *Parsifal* in July and August 1882, Wagner and his family took up residence in the Palazzo Vendramin, Venice. His final, fatal heart attack occurred there on 13 February 1883, following an uncharacteristically bitter row with Cosima, apparently provoked by the announcement of a visit from one of the *Parsifal* flower-maidens, Carrie Pringle, with whom Wagner may have been having an affair. His body was taken in a draped gondola to the railway station, whence it was conveyed to Bayreuth. The burial was a private ceremony held in the grounds of Wahnfrie.

STYLE AND STRUCTURE   Nothing more vividly demonstrates the multiplicity of genres available to composers of opera in the first decades of the 19th century than the stylistic variety of Wagner's first three operas, *Die Feen*, *Das Liebesverbot* and *Rienzi*. In *Die Feen* the model was German Romantic opera, especially as developed by Weber and Marschner: the supernatural subject matter, the enhanced role of the orchestra and the shift away from static, closed forms towards organic growth are all evident to at least some degree. Acts 2 and 3 each contain a fine scene and aria, that in the latter, depicting the mental derangement of Arindal, being a complex in which recitative, arioso and aria are juxtaposed. One of the work's most inventive numbers, the comic duet for Drolla and Gernot in Act 2, is untypical in its *opera buffa*-style patter. *Die Feen* is marked by the return of a few characteristic melodic ideas, but scarcely with a persistence such as to merit the term 'leitmotif'.

Das Liebesverbot has a handful of recurring motifs, of which the most prominent is that associated with Friedrich's ban on love; it occasionally returns to make an ironic comment on the dramatic situation, as when Friedrich himself is tempted by passion (Act 1 finale). Wagner's models in *Das Liebesverbot* were Italian and French opera, especially Bellini, Auber and Hérold; vestiges remain of the *opéra comique* convention of spoken dialogue. German influences should not, however, be overlooked. That Wagner was absorbed at this period in the works of, particularly, Marschner is evident, and there are direct reminiscences of Beethoven, including an imitation of Leonore's 'Töt' erst sein Weib!' at the climax of the trial scene ('Erst hört noch mich').

With *Rienzi, der Letzte der Tribunen* Wagner turned his attention to grand opera, his explicit intention being to gain a popular success at the Opéra in Paris. Meyerbeer, with his spectacular large-scale effects, was naturally a primary model, but the influence of Spontini, Auber and Halévy, all of whom Wagner admired, is also evident. In his desire to 'outdo all previous examples' with the sumptuousness of his own grand opera, Wagner imposed a grandiosity of scale on material scarcely able to support it. The powerful but empty rhetoric that results has been seen both as a reflection of the extravagant pomp with which the historical Rienzi surrounded himself and as an emblem of totalitarianism inherent in the opera. Wagner's resumption of work on *Rienzi* after his move from Riga to Paris coincided with his growing dissatisfaction with the discrete number form of conventional opera. Acts 3 to 5 begin to embody the principles of unified poetry and music enunciated in such Paris essays and novellas as *Eine Pilgerfahrt zu Beethoven* (1840); the change is subtle, but is seen in a more expressive, more poetically aware use of recitative that foreshadows the arioso of the mature style, and in the occasional use of the orchestra to comment independently on the action.

According to *Mein Leben*, Wagner's intention, in *Der fliegende Holländer*, was to sweep away the 'tiresome operatic accessories' altogether. Such an aim was not completely realized, but there is a further shift towards the kind of organic continuity that was already evident in such German Romantic scores as *Euryanthe* (1822–3) and that was to distinguish the mature Wagnerian music drama. Recitative is still present in the score of the *Holländer* and referred to as such. Arias, duets, trios and choruses are also present, but such divisions as, for example, 'scene, duet and chorus' (for Daland and the Dutchman, Act 1) have suggested the designation 'scene opera' in preference to 'number opera'. In the treatment of the duets for Erik and Senta and for the Dutchman and Senta (both in Act 2) there are already signs of the greater precedence to be accorded the setting of words, though quadratic phrase structure (i.e. in regular multiples of two or four bars) is still the norm. As for ensembles, the Sailors' Chorus at the end of Act 1 and the Spinning Chorus in Act 2, despite their clever linking by the orchestra's development of a dotted figure common to both, are not closely integrated into the work's structure; the choruses of the Norwegian and Dutch crews in Act 3, on the other hand, serve a more dramatic function in their vying for supremacy. Significantly, the fidelity to, and departure from, conventional operatic norms is related to the two strikingly contrasted worlds of the *Holländer*: the exterior world of reality to which belong Daland, Erik, the spinning girls and the sailors, and the interior world of the imagination inhabited by Senta and the Dutchman. Erik's two arias, for example, represent the most old-fashioned writing in the work, while the Dutchman's Act 1 monologue frequently manages to break free from the constraints of regular periodic structure.

A similar dualism is evident in *Tannhäuser*, where traditional operatic structures are associated with the sphere of the reactionary Wartburg court while a more progressive style is associated with the Venusberg. To the former belong, for example, the more or less self-contained arias of the song contest, Elisabeth's two set-piece arias, her conventional duet with Tannhäuser and Wolfram's celebrated aria 'O du mein holder Abendstern', highly conservative in its regular eight-bar periods and tonal scheme. Venus's music, by contrast, is more radically advanced: her contributions to the duet with Tannhäuser (Act 1) continually breach the constraints of quadratic periods (notably contrasting with Tannhäuser's own more formal utterances), and both that scene and the preceding Bacchanal are progressive in their harmonic vocabulary and rhythmic structure, especially in the Paris version. The most advanced writing in *Tannhäuser*, however, occurs in the Rome Narration (Act 3), where the expressive demands of the text are satisfied by a flexible form of dramatic recitative or arioso responsive to verbal nuance; the orchestra also assumes a major illustrative role here, bearing the burden of the dramatic argument. Another primary dualism present in *Tannhäuser* (related to that of Venusberg and Wartburg) is the traditional struggle between sensuality and spirituality – a dualism reflected in an 'associative' use of tonality. E major is associated with the Venusberg and $E^\flat$ with the pilgrims, holy love and salvation. Thus Wolfram's $E^\flat$ hymn to 'noble love' (Act 2) is abruptly interrupted by the delayed fourth verse of Tannhäuser's Hymn to Venus in E. Similarly, the Rome Narration reaches $E^\flat$ as Tannhäuser recounts how he stood before the Pope; after a series of modulations the enticements of the Venusberg reappear in E, but the final triumphant return to $E^\flat$ confirms Tannhäuser's salvation.

The 'associative' use of tonality is also evident in *Lohengrin*. Lohengrin himself and the sphere of the Grail are represented by A major, Elsa with $A^\flat$ major (and minor), while Ortrud and her magical powers are associated with $F^\sharp$ minor (the relative minor of Lohengrin's tonality), and the king's trumpeters on stage with C major. In the second and third scenes of Act 1, the tonalities of Lohengrin and Elsa, a semitone apart, are deployed skilfully to symbolic and expressive effect. *Lohengrin*, like the *Holländer* and *Tannhäuser*, contains various motifs associated with characters or concepts, but in general (the motif of the Forbidden Question is an exception) these do not conform to the strict prescriptions to be laid down in *Oper und Drama*; they also tend to be fully rounded themes rather than pithy ideas capable of infinite transformation, and do not therefore serve the vital structural function of the leitmotifs in the *Ring*. For all that *Lohengrin* marks a stylistic advance over the earlier operas, it fails to fulfil several criteria of the fully-fledged music drama. Vestiges of grand opera are still present in the use of diablerie, spectacle and crowd scenes, with minster, organ, fanfares and bridal procession. Traces of old-fashioned number form are still evident, but recitatives, arias, duets and choruses (even those numbers, such as Elsa's Dream or Lohengrin's Narration, which have become celebrated as independent set pieces) are in fact carefully integrated into the musical fabric. The two latter pieces, at least after their conventional openings, display a greater propensity for irregular phrase structure than most numbers in *Lohengrin*. The quadratic phrase patterns that dominate the work, together with the virtual absence of triple time, impart a uniformity of rhythmic impulse that may be perceived as ponderousness.

Several fundamental changes characterize the musical language of the *Ring*, as Wagner began, in *Das Rheingold*, to implement the principles enunciated in the theoretical essays of 1849–51. In the first place, regular phrase patterns give way to fluid arioso structures in which the text is projected in a vocal line that faithfully reflects its verbal accentuations, poetic meaning and emotional content. On occasion in *Rheingold*, the rigorous attempt to match poetic shape with musical phrase results in pedestrian melodic ideas. But in *Walküre* the musico-poetic synthesis is found at its most ingenious, interesting melodic lines registering the finer nuances of the text with no unnatural word stresses. The Forging Song in Act 1 of *Siegfried* gives notice of a shift towards musical predominance, while Act 3 of *Siegfried* and *Götterdämmerung*, for all the fine examples of scrupulous matching of words and music, exhibit a tendency towards quick-fire exchanges, as found in *Die Meistersinger* but modified in accordance with the elevated tone of the tetralogy.

Hand-in-hand with this evolution of musico-poetic synthesis go developments in formal structure and in the use of leitmotif. The excessively rigid symmetries of Lorenz's analyses (an over-reaction to charges of formlessness in Wagner's music) have now been rejected, or rather radically modified to take account also of such elements as period and phrase structure, orchestration and tempo. Lorenz's arch (*A–B–A*) and *Bar* (*A–A–B*) forms are indeed present in Wagner, but like the other traditional forms of strophic song, rondo and variation, they are constantly adapted, often in midstream, creating new, hybrid forms notable for their complexity and ambiguity.

26

The leitmotif (though never actually called that by Wagner) takes on a structural role in the *Ring*, whereas in *Lohengrin* its function was purely dramatic. As Wagner suggested in his 1879 essay *Über die Anwendung der Musik auf das Drama*, motivic transformation provides a key to the analysis of his music dramas; but he went on to say that his transformations were generated according to dramatic imperatives and as such would be incomprehensible in a symphonic structure. It is the dramatic origination of the motifs that is responsible for their frequent association with specific tonalities. The Tarnhelm motif, for example, is associated with $G\sharp$ minor and that of the Curse with B minor. Modulatory passages are common in which the primary tonality of an important motif is engineered. Sometimes, too, the tonality in question becomes the determining key of a whole section or structural unit (the return of B minor for the Curse motif in Scene iv of *Rheingold*, as Fasolt is murdered by Fafner, is an example of this).

The deployment of motifs in the *Ring* underwent a change during the course of composition. In *Rheingold* the identification of motifs with specific objects or ideas is at its most unambiguous. In *Walküre* and the first two acts of *Siegfried*, motivic representation is still made according to reasonably strict musico-poetic criteria, but without quite the literal-mindedness of *Rheingold*. In Act 3 of *Siegfried* and *Götterdämmerung*, however, written after the long break in composition, the motifs frequently aspire to an independent life of their own. They are combined in such profusion and with such contrapuntal virtuosity that it is clear that the principles of *Oper und Drama* are no longer being strictly adhered to. In *Rheingold*, the thematic transformations that take place in the passages that link the scenes are not typical of the work; the score of *Götterdämmerung*, however, is characterized by congeries of motifs drawn on for a brief thematic development.

Just as certain leitmotifs are associated with specific tonalities, so groups of characters (though, unlike the earlier operas, not individual characters) are also identified with particular keys: the Valkyries with B minor, the Nibelungs with $B\flat$ minor. The entire Nibelheim Scene (Scene iii) of *Rheingold*, for example, is dominated by $B\flat$ minor, which even interrupts Loge's A major music as Alberich asserts himself. The B♭ minor of the Nibelheim Scene is framed by the D♭ major in which Scene ii begins and Scene iv ends. The relative key, contrasting but intimately connected, denotes the relationship of Wotan (Light-Alberich) to Alberich. If the first scene of *Rheingold* be excluded (since it is in the nature of a prelude, outside the main action and its time zone), the tetralogy both begins and ends in D♭ major; it should not be regarded as the chief tonality to which all others are related, but it does provide a framework of sorts, and at the end affords a sense of homecoming. *Rheingold* was originally conceived by Wagner as a drama in three acts with a prelude, a structure which replicates not only that of *Götterdämmerung* (three acts and a prologue) but also that of the *Ring* as a whole.

The tendency towards the non-specificity of leitmotifs in the course of the *Ring* is continued in *Tristan und Isolde*. Aptly for a work dealing in metaphysical abstractions, motifs are not used in the latter to symbolize swords and spears; nor can they generally be confined to a single concept (the motifs associated with 'death' and 'day' are exceptions). The elusiveness of the motifs and their associations is reflected in their propensity for interrelation by means of thematic transformation. And if the abstract nature of the motifs in *Tristan* enhances their flexibility, making them more conducive to 'symphonic' development, they are also more closely integrated into the harmonic structure of the work: the melodic line of the motif associated with the words 'Todgeweihtes Haupt! Todgeweihtes Herz!' is a product of the chromatic progression A♭–A, not vice versa.

The elevation of motivic interplay to an abstract level in *Tristan* is accompanied by a further shift in the balance of music and text towards the former. There are still many examples of musico-poetic synthesis that conform to *Oper und Drama* principles, but there is also an increased tendency towards vowel extension, melisma, and overlapping and simultaneous declamation of the singers, not to mention the opulent orchestration with triple wind – all of which conspire to reduce the clarity with which the text is projected. The extended vowels of Brangäne's Watchsong, for example, render her words virtually inaudible; the text is not irrelevant, but has been absorbed into the music to create an intensified line that is then reintegrated into the orchestral fabric.

The temporal values of society represented by King Mark and Melot, and the earthy humanity of Kurwenal, are often matched by four-square diatonicism. Conversely, the neurotic self-absorption of Tristan and Isolde and their unassuageable yearning are reflected in the work's prevailing mode of chromaticism; suspensions, unresolved dissonances and sequential variation are ubiquitous and chromatically heightened. Every element, poetical and musical, is geared to the generation and intensification of tension – the tension of promised but evaded fulfilment.

The vocal line undergoes a further development in *Die Meistersinger*. For much of the time it is little more than recitative, but its bareness is counteracted by the orchestra's richness of detail; the orchestra is by now firmly established as the chief commentator on the dramatic action. The improvisatory nature of the musical texture corresponds to the principle that Wagner was to codify in *Über die Bestimmung der Oper* (1871), whereby the improvisatory element in acting was to be harnessed to the essential improvisatory ingredient in musical composition, resulting in a 'fixed improvisation'.

The subject matter of the music drama – the creation of a mastersong – might seem to lend weight to Lorenz's formal analysis in terms of *Bar*-form. But this would be to reckon without the more flexible, more sophisticated structures that Wagner had been developing throughout his career, and without the element of parody that is central to the work. Aspects of *Bar*-form are indeed present but often in an ironic context: the variation entailed in the *A–A–B* structure of 'Am stillen Herd', for example, is absurdly florid.

A similar distancing tendency is at work in Wagner's persistent use in *Die Meistersinger* of such traditional forms as set-piece arias, ensembles and choruses; all three acts end with a massed finale worthy of grand opera. The forms of Walther's arias or of Beckmesser's Serenade tell us as much about the characters and their dramatic predicament as the notes themselves. The irregular phrase lengths, false accentuations and disorderly progress of the Serenade depict Beckmesser's agitation and supposed artistic sterility, and should not be regarded as symptomatic of an 'advanced' musical style (unlike the Act 3 'pantomime' in Hans Sachs's study, which does look to the future in its graphic musical pictorialism).

Old and new are fused also in the musical language: the work's predominant diatonicism has an archaic tendency, largely as a result of the penchant for second ary triads with their modal flavour. If this challenge to the traditional tonic-dominant hierarchy is a musical metaphor for *Die Meistersinger*'s nostalgic retrospection, it is at the same time a means of rejuvenating tonality.

In *Parsifal*, Wagner the librettist supplied Wagner the composer with some of his freest verse, ranging from sonorous, measured lines to violently expressive ones. The vocal lines which resulted similarly range from more or less melodic arioso (though often the primary idea is in the orchestra and the vocal line functions rather as counterpoint) to a form of recitative-like declamation (for example in Gurnemanz's Act 1 Narration). There are leitmotifs which can be identified with objects or concepts, such as the Spear, the Last Supper or the Grail, but the associations are not rigidly consistent: as in *Tristan*, the function of the motifs is less representational than to provide raw material for 'symphonic' development.

Again as in *Tristan* and *Die Meistersinger*, the modes of chromaticism and diatonicism are counterposed, but whereas in those two works the signification was relatively clear, in *Parsifal* the relationship of the two is more equivocal. The realms of the Grail and of Klingsor are associated with diatonicism and chromaticism respectively, but between these two poles are many cross-currents: Amfortas's suffering, for example, conforms exclusively to neither category, confirming that his experience, while ultimately the catalyst for the redemptive process, is tainted by depravity. The propensity for tonal dissolution in *Parsifal*, for diatonicism to yield to chromaticism, is a potent metaphor for the theme of spiritual degeneration. Tritones, augmented triads and mediant tonal relationships, which all undermine the tonic-dominant hierarchy, contribute to the uncertain nature of a tonal continuum that veers between diatonicism and chromaticism, stable and unstable tonality. Ambiguity also surrounds the polarity of $A^\flat$ major and D (major and minor), which are evidently not to be viewed as irreconcilably opposing forces but as complementary spheres to be brought into resolution. The final stage in that process takes place at the setting of Parsifal's last words, 'Enthüllet den Gral', which effects a modulation from D major to the A♭ with which the work unequivocally concludes.

B.M.

Operas

Die Feen
('The Fairies')

Grosse romantische Oper in three acts, set to Wagner's own libretto after Carlo Gozzi's *La donna serpente*; first performed in Munich, at the Königliches Hof- und Nationaltheater, on 29 June 1888.

The models for Wagner's first completed opera were Weber and Marschner, with whose works the young composer became familiar in his first season as chorus master at Würzburg. He began work on the libretto probably in January or February 1833 and the score was finished on 6 January 1834. An aria for Ada was revised in the spring of 1834. *Die Feen* did not receive its first performance until five years after Wagner's death. It was not staged in Britain until 1969, when it was given by the Midland Music Makers Grand Opera Society at Aston University, Birmingham.

*

Ada (soprano), half fairy, half mortal, agrees to marry Arindal, King of Tramond (tenor), on condition that he refrain from asking her identity. Unable to curb his curiosity, he asks the forbidden question, whereupon Ada's magic realm disappears from view. Arindal returns to his court. Ada wishes to join him on earth, but a fateful decree obliges her to test him with a series of tribulations. He fails and curses her, only to be told that she is now condemned to be turned to stone for a hundred years. Arindal's despair drives him insane, but following Ada into the underworld he finally restores her to life by singing and playing the lyre. His courage is rewarded with immortality and, renouncing his earthly kingdom, he departs to reign with Ada in fairyland.

*

The score, by the 20-year-old Wagner, demonstrates a skilful handling of the conventional operatic forms. Particularly worthy of note are Ada's Act 1 cavatina 'Wie muss ich doch beklagen' with its throbbing appoggiatura dissonances, the masterly final ensemble of the same act, the scene and aria for Ada in Act 2 ('Weh' mir, so nah' die fürchterliche Stunde') and that for the distracted Arindal in Act 3 ('Halloh!').

B.M.

Das Liebesverbot

[*Das Liebesverbot, oder Die Novize von Palermo*]
('The Ban on Love, or The Novice of Palermo')

Grosse komische Oper in two acts set to Wagner's own libretto after William Shakespeare's *Measure for Measure*; first performed in Magdeburg, at the Stadttheater, on 29 March 1836.

Das Liebesverbot was written under the influence of the emancipatory hedonism of Wilhelm Heinse's novel *Ardinghello und die glückseeligen Inseln* (1787), of Heinrich Laube's *Das junge Europa* (1833–7) and of the Young Germans generally. A celebration of free love and a humorous attack on sexual puritanism and bourgeois morality *per se*, it transfers the action of *Measure for Measure* to sunny Palermo. Musically *Das Liebesverbot* is indebted to Italian and French models, in particular Bellini and Auber.

Wagner made his prose sketch for the work in June 1834 and started the versification two months later. The music was begun in January 1835 and completed early in 1836. The single performance in March 1836 was a fiasco: none of the singers had mastered their roles. The work was not given again in Germany until 1923 (in Munich) and not in England until 1965 (in an abridged version at University College, London).

*

The Regent Friedrich (bass) has outlawed all licentious behaviour – even love itself, it seems, certainly that expressed extra-maritally – on pain of death. The young nobleman Claudio (tenor) is the first to be condemned under the new law, and his sister Isabella (soprano), a novice, is persuaded with some reluctance to make a personal appeal to the Regent. It transpires that Friedrich was once married to Isabella's fellow novice Mariana (soprano) but for the sake of ambition repudiated her; in defiance of his own decree, he now offers to set Claudio free in exchange for Isabella's favours. Isabella pretends to agree, but in fact sends Mariana – Friedrich's own wife – to the rendezvous: the fancy-dress carnival forbidden by the Regent himself. Friedrich's lubricious hypocrisy is exposed and although he

37

is willing to accept the penalty, the people set him free and a new era of unfettered sensuality is ushered in by the return of their own king.

*

Das Liebesverbot is characterized by several recurring motifs fore-shadowing the leitmotif principle. Chief among them is the motif associated with Friedrich's ban on love: in the overture it takes the form of a falling minor 6th followed by two rising semi-tones; on subsequent appearances the downward leap may range from a perfect 4th or 5th to a diminished 7th.

B.M.

Rienzi, der Letzte der Tribunen
('Rienzi, the Last of the Tribunes')

Grosse tragische Oper in five acts set to Wagner's own libretto after Edward Bulwer-Lytton's novel of the same name; first performed in Dresden, at the Königlich Sächsisches Hoftheater, on 20 October 1842.

At the première Rienzi was sung by Joseph Tichatschek and Adriano by Wilhelmine Schröder-Devrient.

Cola Rienzi *papal notary*	tenor
Irene *his sister*	soprano
Steffano Colonna *head of the Colonna family*	bass
Adriano *his son*	mezzo-soprano
Paolo Orsini *head of the Orsini family*	bass
Raimondo *papal legate*	bass
Baroncelli *Roman citizen*	tenor
Cecco del Vecchio *Roman citizen*	bass
The Messenger of Peace	soprano

Herald, Ambassadors from Milan, The Lombard States, Naples, Bohemia and Bavaria, Roman nobles and attendants, followers of Colonna and Orsini, priests and monks of all orders, senators, Roman citizens (male and female), messengers of peace

Setting Rome, about the middle of the 14th century

Wagner's reading of Bulwer-Lytton's novel *Rienzi, the Last of the Roman Tribunes* in Blasewitz, near Dresden, in the summer of 1837 confirmed his intention of writing an opera on the subject (the idea had apparently been implanted earlier by his friend Apel). He immediately sketched an outline, followed by a prose draft and then, the following summer, a verse draft. A series of fragmentary composition sketches preceded a continuous composition draft, the first two acts of which were completed by 9 April 1839. After a short gap, Act 3 was begun in February 1840 and the work completed in draft,

39

with the overture being written last, in October 1840. In the course of Wagner's dismal, penurious sojourn in Paris he was helped by Meyerbeer, who was influential in having *Rienzi* accepted by the Dresden theatre.

The première lasted, according to *Mein Leben*, more than six hours (including intervals), but the work was received with immense enthusiasm, catching as it did the rebellious spirit of the times, and Tichatschek and Schröder-Devrient scored personal successes in the roles of Rienzi and Adriano. The work was subsequently given both over two evenings and in a truncated version prepared by Wagner himself. The absence of the autograph score (which was in the possession of Hitler) and of any original printed score without cuts has bedevilled the preparation of an authoritative complete edition.

In spite of the practical problems it posed, and somewhat to the composer's embarrassment on account of its stylistic nature, *Rienzi* was one of Wagner's most successful works in the latter years of his life and up to the end of the century. In Dresden alone, 100 performances had been given by 1873 and 200 by 1908. The first production in the USA was at the Academy of Music, New York, in 1878, and in England at Her Majesty's Theatre, London, in 1879.

*

The overture is notable chiefly for the majestically eloquent theme that returns in Act 5 as Rienzi's Prayer and which is succeeded by a vigorous military march.

ACT 1 *A street in Rome* Rienzi's sister Irene is about to be abducted by Paolo Orsini and his followers when they are confronted by their rivals, the Colonnas. Adriano Colonna, in love with Irene, attempts to protect her in the ensuing brawl. The commanding presence of Rienzi, when he arrives on the scene (with a sudden shift of tonality from D to E$\flat$), quells the fighting; his friends and the crowd all urge him to take power and bring order to the city.

Alone with Irene and Adriano (terzet, 'O Schwester, sprich'), Rienzi tells how he has sworn to avenge his brother, murdered by a Colonna; the motif (sometimes called the Vengeance motif) first heard here is a forerunner of the motif of reminiscence as used in the *Ring*. Adriano atones for his family's guilt by pledging himself to Rienzi; in return, he is entrusted with Irene and they sing of their love in an impassioned duet ('Ja, eine Welt voll Leiden').

A single sustained note is sounded on a trumpet (first heard at the start of the overture, it returns periodically to symbolize Rienzi's revolutionary authority). An excited crowd gathers and acclaims Rienzi as their liberator and saviour from the tyranny of the nobles ('Gegrüsst'). Refusing the title of king, he tells them that the state should be governed by a senate; he himself will be their tribune.

ACT 2 *A great hall in the Capitol* An effulgent orchestral introduction heralds the Chorus of the Messengers of Peace: a triumphal song by the patrician youths, clad in white silk, celebrating the success of their peace mission throughout Italy. The Colonnas and Orsini, compelled to obey the law just as the plebeians must, conspire together against Rienzi. Rienzi receives the foreign ambassadors and claims for the Roman people the historic right to elect the German emperor.

A ballet, allegorizing the union of ancient and modern Rome, is performed. Orsini stabs Rienzi with a dagger, but his assassination attempt is thwarted by Rienzi's steel breastplate. Colonna's men have meanwhile attempted to seize the Capitol. Senators and people demand death for the traitors. Adriano and Irene plead for Colonna's life and Rienzi pardons the nobles. In a final ensemble Rienzi's clemency is praised by Adriano and Irene but condemned as weakness by his friends Baroncelli and Cecco; the nobles plot vengeance while the people hail their leader.

ACT 3 *The large square in the ancient forum* The nobles are preparing to attack Rienzi, who, with the battle-cry 'Santo Spirito, Cavaliere!' rouses the people to take up arms. Adriano agonizes over his divided loyalty to his father and to the brother of Irene: 'Gerechter Gott!' A grand procession of senators and armed citizens is led by Rienzi, fully armed and on horseback: the battle-cry 'Santo Spirito, Cavaliere!' is re-echoed, and there is some heavily scored military music.

Adriano begs in vain to be sent as an ambassador to his father. He tells Irene that death is calling him, but finally yields to her entreaties to stay and protect her. Irene and the women pray for victory and in due course Rienzi returns in triumph; the bodies of Orsini and Colonna are borne in on litters. Adriano curses Rienzi and vows revenge. Rienzi is borne aloft on a triumphal chariot, crowned with a laurel wreath.

ACT 4 *A square in front of the Lateran church* A series of taps on the timpani open the act in an atmosphere of mystery and conspiracy as Baroncelli, Cecco and some citizens discuss the situation. They deplore Rienzi's arrogance in interfering with the election of the German emperor: the Germans have, as a result, withdrawn their ambassador from Rome. The new emperor, moreover, is an ally of the pope, who was Colonna's protector. Cardinal Raimondo has also turned to the pope for protection. Baroncelli alleges that Rienzi sought an alliance with the nobles, offering his sister Irene in return. The crowd demands evidence of this treachery and Adriano, throwing off his disguise, endorses the charge. The conspirators vow to strike at Rienzi during the victory celebrations later that day. As they turn to go, they see a procession of priests and monks, led, to their surprise, by Raimondo; they assume they are entering the church in preparation for the celebratory *Te Deum*.

Rienzi enters in festal garb. Adriano baulks at assassinating Rienzi in view of Irene, while the other conspirators are won over by his rhetoric. Suddenly Raimondo appears on the steps of the Lateran to proclaim the excommunication of Rienzi. As his followers desert him, Adriano tries to persuade Irene to abandon him too, but she remains, in her brother's embrace.

ACT 5 Scene i–iii *A hall in the Capitol* Rienzi prays to God for strength: 'Allmächt'ger Vater'; the music of his Prayer draws on the dignified, eloquent main theme of the overture. Joined by Irene, he tells her that he has been deserted by everybody; she refuses to leave him for Adriano and they fondly embrace. Rienzi leaves to arm himself and Adriano enters in agitation. As the commotion outside increases, he tries to carry away Irene by force, but she pushes him away and runs out.

ACT 5 Scene iv *A square in front of the Capitol* Deaf to Rienzi's pleas, the people, led by Baroncelli and Cecci, try to stone him. They set fire to the Capitol and Rienzi and Irene are seen on the balcony, clasped in each other's arms. Adriano and the nobles attack the people and try to reach Irene. But as he approaches, the building collapses, burying Adriano as well as Rienzi and Irene.

*

Wagner's conception of *Rienzi* was that of a grand opera, one, moreover, that 'should outdo all previous examples with sumptuous extravagance'. Deliberately planned so that it could not be given in a small theatre, *Rienzi* is generously endowed with marches, processions and ballets. The models of Italian and French grand opera are, however, more evident in Acts 1 and 2 than in the remainder of the work, written after a gap during which Wagner had begun to rethink his stylistic principles.

B.M.

Der fliegende Holländer
('The Flying Dutchman')

Romantische Oper in three acts set to Wagner's own libretto after Heinrich Heine's *Aus den Memoiren des Herren von Schnabelewopski*; first performed in Dresden, at the Königliches Sächsisches Hoftheater, on 2 January 1843.

The première in Dresden was conducted by Wagner, with Wilhelmine Schröder-Devrient as Senta and Johann Michael Wächter as the Dutchman.

Daland *a Norwegian sailor*	bass
Senta *his daughter*	soprano
Erik *a huntsman*	tenor
Mary *Senta's nurse*	contralto
Daland's Steerman	tenor
The Dutchman	bass-baritone

Norwegian sailors, the Dutchman's crew, young women

Setting The Norwegian coast

The supposedly autobiographical inspiration of the *Holländer*, vividly described in *Mein Leben* – according to which the work took shape during the Wagners' stormy sea crossing in July and August 1839 – is in part a fantasy. If any musical sketches were made in the months following the voyage on the *Thetis*, they have not survived. The first numbers to be composed were Senta's Ballad, and the choruses of the Norwegian sailors and Dutchman's crew, some time between 3 May and 26 July 1840. The poem was written in May 1841 and the remainder of the music during the summer, the overture being completed last, in November 1841.

Heine's retelling of the nautical legend provided Wagner with his chief source, but the composer, who identified himself with the persecuted, uprooted, sexually unfulfilled protagonist, introduced what was to become the characteristic theme of redemption by a woman. The purchase of Wagner's original prose scenario in July 1841 by Léon Pillet, the director of the Paris Opéra, led ultimately to a commission not for Wagner (as he had hoped) but for Pierre-Louis Dietsch. Contrary to what is frequently stated, Dietsch's librettists, Paul Foucher and Bénédict-Henry Révoil, based their opera *Le vaisseau fantôme* not primarily on Wagner's scenario but on Captain Marryat's novel *The Phantom Ship*, as well as on Sir Walter Scott's *The Pirate* and tales by Heine, Fenimore Cooper and Wilhelm Hauff. However, the appearance of *Le vaisseau fantôme* on the stage at the Opéra in the same month (November 1842) as rehearsals for the *Holländer* began in Dresden was undoubtedly one reason for the 11th-hour changes in Wagner's score. Until just a few weeks before the première, Wagner's opera was set off the Scottish coast, with Daland and Erik named Donald and Georg respectively. Other factors in the change may have been Wagner's desire to reinforce the autobiographical element and to distance himself at the same time from the Scottish setting of Heine.

Wagner originally conceived his work in a single act, the better to ensure its acceptance as a curtain-raiser before a ballet at the Opéra; his later claim that it was in order to focus on the dramatic essentials rather than on 'tiresome operatic accessories' may be retrospective rationalization. By the time he came to write the music, the first consideration no longer applied, his proposal having been rejected by the Opéra. He therefore elaborated the scheme in three acts, but at this stage to be played without a break. Then, some time after the end of October 1842, when he retrieved his score from the Berlin Opera (and possibly acting on advice from that quarter), he recast it in three seperate acts – the form in which it was given in Dresden and subsequently published. Following Cosima Wagner's example when she introduced it at Bayreuth in 1901, the work is now often given, both there and elsewhere, in the single-act version. There is, however, an ideological element in Bayreuth's preference for the version that presents the work most convincingly as an incipient music drama (as Wagner himself viewed it in retrospect), and both versions have some claim to authenticity.

Wagner made revisions to the score, largely in the orchestration, in 1846 and again in 1852. In 1860 (not, as sometimes stated, in

1852) the coda of the overture was remodelled (and the ending of the whole work accordingly), introducing a motif of redemption; the textures of the 1860 revision also reflect Wagner's recent preoccupation with *Tristan*.

The first performance in London was in 1870 (in Italian); it was given there in English in 1876 and in German in 1882. The American première (1876, Philadelphia) was also in Italian; it was first given in New York the following year and at the Metropolitan in 1889. Notable interpreters of the title role have included Anton van Rooy, Friedrich Schorr, Hans Hotter, Hermann Uhde and George London. Senta has been sung by Emmy Destinn, Maria Müller, Astrid Varnay, Anja Silja and Gwyneth Jones.

*

ACT 1   *A steep, rocky shore*   The curtain rises to a continuation of the stormy music of the overture, but now in B$^\flat$ minor, in contrast to the overture's D minor/major. Daland's ship has just cast anchor. The cries of the Norwegian sailors ('Johohe! Hallojo!') as they furl the sails allude to their chorus first heard in its entirety in Act 3. The crew is sent to rest and the steersman left on watch. His song, 'Mit Gewitter und Sturm aus fernem Meer' begins confidently, but the phrases of its second stanza are repeatedly interrupted by orchestral comments as he succumbs to slumber. Immediately the storm begins to rage again, and open-5th 'horn calls', string tremolos and a shift of tonality (from B$^\flat$ major to B minor) signify the appearance of the Flying Dutchman's ship with its blood-red sails.

The Dutchman's monologue that follows begins with a recitative, 'Die Frist ist um', in which he tells how he is permitted to come on land once every seven years to seek redemption from an as yet unnamed curse. A section in 6/8, marked 'Allegro molto agitato', 'Wie oft in Meeres tiefsten Schlund', projects a powerfully declaimed vocal line against a storm-tossed accompaniment. An earnest entreaty for deliverance is then sung over relentlessly tremolo strings, in a manner criticized by Berlioz, and the monologue ends with a broadly phrased section, 'Nur eine Hoffnung', in which the Dutchman looks forward to Judgment Day. From their ship's hold, his crew distantly echo his last words.

Daland comes on deck, sees the strange ship, and hails its captain, whom he sees on land. The captain introduces himself simply as 'a Dutchman', going on to give a diplomatically compressed account of his voyaging, 'Durch Sturm und bösen Wind verschlagen'. The regular four-bar phrasing of the latter section, contrasted with the freer phrase structures of 'Die Frist ist um', signify what is to become a characteristic of the score: the 'exterior', public world of Daland, Erik and the Norwegian sailors and maidens is represented by traditional forms and harmonies, while the 'interior', self-absorbed world of the Dutchman and Senta frequently breaks out of the straitjacket of conventionality.

The Dutchman offers Daland vast wealth in exchange for a night's hospitality. Daland, who cannot believe his ears, is no less delighted by the wealthy stranger's interest when he tells him he has a daughter, and in the ensuing duet, 'Wie? Hört' ich recht?', the Dutchman's rugged individuality is entirely submerged by Daland's triteness. Daland's greedy, meretricious character is perfectly conveyed both here and in the duet's continuation, with its jaunty rhythms and elementary harmonic scheme. With the Dutchman preparing to follow Daland to his house, the Norwegian sailors steer the tonality back to B$^\flat$ major for a full-chorus reprise of the Steersman's Song.

ACT 2   *A large room in Daland's house*   To cover the scene change in the original continuous version, Wagner wrote a passage in which the virile double-dotted rhythms of the sailors are transformed into the humming of the spinning wheels in the opening chorus of the second act, 'Summ und brumm'. The full dramatic effect of that transition is lost when the work is given in three separate acts, though the repetition of music from the end of Act 1 at the beginning of Act 2 has a deleterious effect only when the opera is heard on recordings, not in the theatre with an intervening interval. (A similar situation arises between Acts 2 and 3.)

The repetitive figures (both melodic and accompanimental) of the Spinning Chorus evoke not only the ceaseless turning of the wheels, but also the humdrum (if contented) existence of the young women. Urged on by Mary, Daland's housekeeper and Senta's nurse, the women spin in order to please their lovers who are away at sea. Senta is meanwhile reclining reflectively in an armchair, gazing at a picture hanging on the wall of a pale man with a dark beard in black, Spanish dress. She is reproached for her idleness by Mary and mocked in onomatopoeic cascades of laughter by the other women. Senta retaliates by ridiculing the tediousness of the Spinning Chorus, asking Mary to sing instead the ballad of the Flying Dutchman. Mary declines and continues spinning as the other women gather round to hear Senta sing it herself.

Senta's Ballad, 'Johohoe! Johohohoe!', begins with the same bracing open 5ths on tremolo strings that began the overture, and with the 'horn-call' figure of the Dutchman heard first as a pounding bass and then in the vocal line itself. The startling effect of these opening gestures is enhanced, in the version familiar today, by the unprepared drop in tonality from A major to G minor; however, the Ballad was originally in A minor, and Wagner transposed it down at a late date (the end of 1842) for Schröder-Devrient. The strophic structure of Senta's Ballad sets it firmly in the early 19th-century operatic tradition of interpolated narrative songs; indeed, there is a direct link with the song sung by Emmy in Marschner's *Der Vampyr*, which Wagner had prepared for performance in Würzburg in 1833. Each of Senta's three turbulent stanzas (in which we learn that the Flying Dutchman's curse was laid on him for a blasphemous oath) is followed by a consolatory refrain featuring the motif associated with redemption; the final refrain is taken by the chorus, but in an abrupt breach of precedent, Senta, 'carried away by a sudden inspiration', bursts into an ecstatic coda expressing her determination to be the instrument of the Flying Dutchman's salvation. Wagner's retrospective account of the genesis of the *Holländer*, representing Senta's Ballad as the 'thematic seed' or conceptual nucleus of the whole work, was designed to depict the opera as an incipient music drama. But although some elements of the Ballad appear elsewhere in the work, and even in some of its central numbers, the use of the various motifs bears little relation to the closely integrated structural organization of post- *Oper und Drama* works such as the *Ring*.

Erik, who is in love with Senta, is horrified to hear her outburst as he enters. He announces that Daland's ship has returned, and the young women busily prepare to welcome their menfolk. Erik detains Senta and launches into a passionate protestation of love, 'Mein Herz voll Treue bis zum Sterben', whose conventionality of utterance and regularity of period scarcely commend themselves to Senta in her present mood. She struggles to get away but is forced to endure another stanza. After an exchange in which Senta alarms Erik by telling of her empathy with the strange seafarer in the picture, the huntsman recounts a dream whose ominous significance he now dimly discerns: 'Auf hohem Felsen'. From several points of view, Erik's Dream Narration represents the most advanced writing in the work. Where in his previous song the regular phrases had frequently forced normally unaccented syllables on to strong beats, in the Dream Narration the length of phrases is determined by the rhythms of the lines. The lack of melodic interest is an indication of how far Wagner had yet to go to achieve the subtle musico-poetic synthesis of his mature works; nevertheless it is a worthy precursor of the narrations of Tannhäuser and Lohengrin. As Erik recounts how he dreamt that Senta's father brought home a stranger resembling the seafarer in the picture, Senta, in a mesmeric trance, relives the fantasy, her excited interjections latterly adopting the rising 4th of the Dutchman's motif.

Erik rushes away in despair and Senta muses on the picture. As she croons the 'redemption' refrain of the Ballad, the door opens and her father appears with the Dutchman. Recognizing him as the seafarer in the picture, Senta is spellbound and fails to greet her father. Daland approaches her and introduces the Dutchman in a characteristically breezy, four-square aria, 'Mögst Du, mein Kind'.

Daland retires and, after a coda based on themes associated with Daland, the Dutchman and Senta, the long duet that occupies most of the rest of the act begins. Its unconventionality is signified by the opening statements of both characters in turn, each absorbed in his and her own thoughts. The voices eventually come together and there is even a quasi-traditional cadenza. A new plane of reality is signalled by a slight increase in tempo and a shift from E major to E minor. The pair now address each other, and in response to the Dutchman's inquiry, Senta promises obedience to her father's wishes. She goes on to express her desire to bring him redemption, and in an *agitato* section he warns of the fate that would befall her if she failed to keep her vow of constancy. Against an accompaniment of repeated wind chords redolent of a celestial chorus, Senta pledges faithfulness unto death, and the final exultant section of the duet is launched with the singers heard first separately and then together. Although not free of the constraints of traditional opera, the duet is the musical and emotional high point of the work.

Daland re-enters to ask whether the feast of homecoming can be combined with that of a betrothal. Senta reaffirms her vow and the three join in a rapturous trio to bring the act to an end.

ACT 3 *A bay with a rocky shore* Daland's house stands in the foreground, to one side. In the background the Norwegian ship is lit up and the sailors are making merry on the deck, while the Dutch ship nearby is unnaturally dark and silent. According to Wagner's account in *Mein Leben*, the theme of the Norwegian Sailors' Chorus, 'Steuermann! Lass die Wacht!', was suggested to him by the call of the sailors as it echoed round the granite walls of the Norwegian harbour of Sandviken, as the *Thetis* took refuge there on 29 July 1839. After the first strains of the chorus, the men dance on deck, stamping their feet in time with the music. The women bring out baskets of food and drink and call out to the Dutch ship, inviting the crew to participate. Men and women cry out in turn, but a deathly silence is the only response. The lighthearted appeals of sailors and womenfolk, again in alternation, become more earnest, and tension is accumulated in the orchestral texture too. A *forte* and then a *fortissimo* cry are both unanswered, and the Norwegians only half-jestingly recall the legend of the Flying Dutchman and his ghostly crew. Their carousing becomes more manic, and the Dutchman's motif in the orchestra, accompanied by sinister chromatic rumblings, builds to a climax. A storm rises in the vicinity of the Dutch ship, and the crew finally burst into unearthly song, the wind whistling through the rigging. The Norwegian sailors attempt to compete, in a powerful piece of writing for double chorus, but they are eventually subdued.

Senta comes out of the house, followed by Erik, who demands to know why she has changed her allegiance. In a cavatina of conventional cut, 'Willst jenes Tags du nicht dich mehr entsinnen', he reminds her that she had once pledged to be true to him. The Dutchman, who has overheard, makes to return to his ship and releases Senta from her vow to him. She protests her fidelity and the Dutchman, Erik and Senta all voice their emotions in a trio (often needlessly cut).

In a recitative, the Dutchman tells of his terrible fate and how he is saving Senta from the same by releasing her. He boards his ship, and Senta, proclaiming her redeeming fidelity in a final ecstatic outcry, casts herself into the sea. The Dutchman's ship, with all its crew, sinks immediately. The sea rises and falls again, revealing the Dutchman and Senta, transfigured and locked in embrace.

*

The first work of Wagner's maturity, *Der fliegende Holländer* brings together several ingredients characteristic of the later works, notably the single-minded attention given to the mood and colour· of the drama, and the themes of suffering by a Romantic outsider and of redemption by a faithful woman. The initial stages of a tendency towards dissolution of numbers and towards a synthesis of text and music also endorse Wagner's assertion that with the *Holländer* began his career as a true poet.

B.M.

Tannhäuser

[*Tannhäuser und der Sängerkrieg auf Wartburg*]
('Tannhäuser and the Singers' Contest on the Wartburg')

Grosse romantische Oper in three acts set to Wagner's own libretto; first performed in Dresden, at the Hoftheater, on 19 October 1845.

The original cast was: Joseph Tichatschek (Tannhäuser), Wilhelmine Schröder-Devrient (Venus), Wagner's niece Johanna Wagner (Elisabeth) and Anton Mitterwurzer (Wolfram).

Hermann *Landgrave of Thuringia*	bass
Tannhäuser	tenor
Wolfram von Eschinbach	baritone
Walther von der Vogelweide	tenor
Biterolf	bass
Heinrich der Schreiber	tenor
Reinmar von Zweter	bass
Elisabeth *the Landgrave's niece*	soprano
Venus	soprano
A Young Shepherd	soprano
Four Noble Pages	soprano, alto

knights and minstrels (Tannhäuser, Wolfram von Eschinbach, Walther von der Vogelweide, Biterolf, Heinrich der Schreiber, Reinmar von Zweter)

> Thuringian knights, counts and nobles, ladies, older and younger pilgrims, sirens, naiads, nymphs, bacchantes. In Paris version, additionally the Three Graces, youths, cupids, satyrs and fauns

Setting Thuringia at the beginning of the 13th century

Wagner's text is a conflation of two separate medieval legends: those concerning Tannhäuser, believed originally to have been a crusading knight from Franconia, and the song contest on the Wartburg – drawing on a number of 19th-century versions, notably those of Ludwig Tieck, E.T.A. Hoffmann, Heinrich Heine, Friedrich de la Motte Fouqué and Joseph Eichendorff.

Wagner worked out a detailed prose draft (28 June–6 July 1842) at Aussig (now Ústí nad Labem) in the Bohemian mountains, and versified it the following spring. After making a number of preliminary sketches for the musical setting, Wagner made his 'fragmentary complete draft' (so called because it survives only in fragmentary form, albeit now largely reconstructed) and a continuous complete draft, the two evolving side by side between the summer or autumn of 1843 and December 1844. The overture was completed on 11 January 1845 and the full score on 13 April. As late as the continuous complete draft, there is evidence of Wagner's conception in terms of traditional numbers, despite his suppression of such designations in the autograph score.

The uncomprehending response of the audience at the first performance on 19 October 1845 was largely due to the inability of Tichatschek, in the leading role, to grasp the principle of *melos* towards which Wagner was progressing. The composer's abnormal vocal demands also took their toll on the other three principal singers. However, by the mid-1850s the work had established itself in the repertory of more than 40 German opera houses. An invitation from Emperor Napoleon III to stage *Tannhäuser* in Paris led to one of the most celebrated débâcles in the annals of operatic history. Revenging themselves on the politically unpopular Princess Pauline Metternich, who had negotiated the invitation, the members of the Jockey Club disrupted three performances at the Opéra in March 1861 with aristocratic baying and dog-whistles before Wagner was allowed to withdraw the production.

Four 'stages' of the work have been identified: (1) the original version as given at the Dresden première in 1845; (2) the edition published by Meser in 1860, incorporating revisions made (notably to the ending of the work) between 1847 and 1852; (3) the version of 1861 (not published), as performed at the Opéra that year; and (4) the version performed under Wagner's supervision in Vienna In 1875, incorporating revisions made subsequent to 1861 (vocal score 1876, full score 1888). There is, however, no reason to abandon the convenient traditional labels of 'Dresden version' (i.e. no.2) and 'Paris version' (no.4), provided it is borne in mind that these terms refer not to what was actually heard in Dresden in 1845 or Paris in 1861 but to revised editions of those performances.

The most noticeable feature of the Paris version (the major differences are described below, and the Paris variants are usefully given in the Dover full score) is the stylistic incongruity arising from the grafting of new sections in Wagner's mature, post-*Tristan* style on to a work of the 1840s. The characterization of Venus was deepened for Paris in a manner prophetic of Kundry in *Parsifal*. Where her somewhat plain declamation was punctuated for Dresden by bare chords, her vocal line for Paris is sensually pliable, with richly scored accompaniments.

The title role in the Opéra performance in 1861 was taken by Albert Niemann, who went on to sing it at the Metropolitan (1886–9). Tannhäuser was the role in which Lauritz Melchior made his Metropolitan début on 17 February 1926; he went on to sing it 51 times in New York, as well as in other major opera houses (144 times in all).

*

ACT 1 Scenes i–ii *Inside the Hörselberg near Eisenach* One of the primary changes for Paris concerned the opening of the opera. The bacchanal in the Venusberg (identified by Wagner and others with the Hörselberg in Thuringia) was extended to provide the ballet demanded by the management and patrons of the Opéra (albeit in the first rather than the traditional second act). In the original version, the stage directions prescribed a rocky grotto with bathing naiads, reclining sirens and dancing nymphs. Venus lay on a couch in a rosy light, with Tannhäuser, half-kneeling, nestling his head in her lap. Urged on by bacchantes, the dancers reached a peak of orgiastic excitement. The Paris version adds the Three Graces and cupids, while satyrs and fauns cause a riotous frenzy by chasing the nymphs. Prompted by the Graces, the cupids quell the riot by raining down love-arrows on all below. The Paris bacchanal is both longer and more frenzied, with the addition of castanets and a third timpani. At the height of the revelry the rising chromatic four-note phrase ubiquitous in *Tristan* is much in evidence. Orchestral textures are richer, more voluptuous, and transitions are negotiated with the assurance of Wagner's mature style.

In scene ii Tannhäuser starts, as though from a dream. He is surfeited with the sensual pleasures of the Venusberg and longs for the simple joys of earthly life. Urged on by the love goddess, he sings his Hymn to Venus, the first stanza in $D^\flat$ with harp accompaniment, the second in D with added strings, both ending with a plea to be released. Venus summons a magic grotto and against an accompaniment of ethereal divided strings tempts him to surrender to ecstasy: 'Geliebter, komm!'. Tannhäuser seizes his harp again and, to a full orchestral accompaniment, drives his plea to a pitch by singing the third stanza in $E^\flat$. Venus angrily releases him ('Zieh hin! Wahnsinniger!'), prophesying that he will in desperation one day return. When Tannhäuser invokes the Virgin Mary, Venus and her domains instantly disappear. In the Paris version, the voluptuous nature of both vocal line and accompaniment is much enhanced, while two additional passages after Venus's slightly reworded outburst ('Zieh hin! Wahnbetörter!') reveal new aspects of her character as she gives vent to first angry mockery and then despair.

ACT 1 Scenes iii–iv *A valley below the Wartburg* Tannhäuser finds himself in a sunlit valley; sheep bells are heard from the heights and a young shepherd is playing his pipe (an irregularly phrased monody started on the clarinet and continued by an english horn on or behind the stage). His simple song, 'Frau Holda kam aus dem Berg hervor', is followed by the chant of the Elder Pilgrims, wafting from the direction of the Wartburg. The second stanza, in which anguished chromaticisms depict the oppression of sin, is a recollection in quadruple time of the corresponding strain of the overture's main theme. As the pilgrims approach, the shepherd greets them and Tannhäuser makes a pious exclamation. The procession passes and Tannhäuser takes up the guilt-oppressed strain of the pilgrims. As the chant dies away, hunting horns are heard, at first in the distance, then closer.

The Landgrave and minstrels approach (scene iv) and, recognizing Tannhäuser, greet him warmly ('Gegrüsst sei uns'). Tannhäuser's rejection of the past leads to a brief seven-part ensemble, terminated by Wolfram's cry of 'Bleib bei Elisabeth', an invocation of talismanic force. Tannhäuser, stopped in his tracks, can only repeat the name. Wolfram goes on to reveal how in their earlier song-contests,

Tannhäuser had won the heart of Elisabeth, who had subsequently retired from their company – 'Als du in kühnem Sange uns bestrittest' – followed by the aria proper, 'War's Zauber, war es reine Macht?'. The aria, though of conventional cut, has inspired many superlative performances both on stage and on record, often eclipsing those of the singer in the notoriously taxing title role. To Wolfram's pleas for Tannhäuser to stay are added those of the other minstrels in a brief sextet. Tannhäuser yields and embraces his former friends (to an orchestral accompaniment made slightly more exultant in the Paris version). He leads them in a final ensemble which brings the act to an end resounding with the blasts of hunting horns.

ACT 2 *The Hall of Song in the Wartburg* The act opens with Elisabeth's joyous greeting to the Hall of Song, abandoned by her during Tannhäuser's absence, 'Dich, teure Halle, grüss' ich wieder'. The aria is conventional in phrase structure, but its introduction effectively uses repeated quaver triplets to portray Elisabeth's agitation; an oboe and clarinet also sound the ominous motif first heard when Tannhäuser was dismissed by Venus. Wolfram and Tannhäuser have entered at the back (scene ii); the former remains there discreetly while the latter throws himself at Elisabeth's feet. The chords on pizzicato strings depict Elisabeth's steps and are followed by a rushing semiquaver figure illustrative of Tannhäuser's gesture.

She begs him to rise and, after regaining her composure, recalls his earlier minstrelsy, 'Der Sänger klugen Weisen', against an accompaniment of sustained, muted strings, with flowing viola and serene wind punctuations. The vocal line becomes disjointed and the accompaniment sparer as she relives the pain of Tannhäuser's departure. Tannhäuser, enraptured, hails the power of love, and the two break into an ecstatic duet in the old-fashioned style, 'Gepriesen sei die Stunde' (often abridged in performance).

Tannhäuser and Wolfram depart, and an abrupt transition introduces scene iii, in which the Landgrave welcomes his niece back to the Hall but finds her unwilling to divulge her thoughts. Trumpets sound from the courtyard, heralding the arrival of the guests (knights, counts, their ladies and retinue) for the song contest (scene iv). March tunes accompany the long procession, eventually with choral parts added, first male, then female, then both together. When everybody has assembled, in a semicircle, the minstrels enter to a more lyrical theme, still in march tempo, but played *sostenuto* on strings alone. In a passage of recitative interspersed with arioso the Landgrave extols the art of song and calls on the minstrels to demonstrate it by singing in praise of love; the worthiest contender will receive his prize from Elisabeth herself. Fanfares and acclamation greet his announcement.

The first contender is Wolfram, who uses the image of a fountain to sing of the purity of love, 'Blick, ich umher'. His simple, unadorned line (which Wagner wanted sung in time, not as free recitative) is accompanied first by harp alone, to which are subsequently added the mellow tones of divided violas and cellos. His song is approved by the assembled company, but not by Tannhäuser, who retorts that the fountain of love fills him only with burning desire. This response was varied in the Paris version, because Wagner also wished to omit the following song for Walther, as the singer assigned the role was inadequate. In the original, Dresden version, Walther picked up the image of the fountain, celebrating it as chastity itself, in an aria similar to Wolfram's in its stiff, formal style and accompaniment, 'Den Bronnen, den uns Wolfram nannte'.

Another minstrel, Biterolf, voices the outraged opinions of the knights and ladies when he challenges Tannhäuser to a combat of more than vocal prowess. He is scorned by Tannhäuser for his inexperience as regards the joys of true love. Wolfram attempts to restore calm with another invocation of pure love, but Tannhäuser responds with what is, in effect, the fourth stanza of his Hymn to Venus from the previous act. The first three stanzas had winched up the tonality successively from $D^\flat$ to D to $E^\flat$. The E major tonality of the fourth stanza both continues that sequence and contrasts sharply with the $E^\flat$ of Wolfram's last utterance.

There is general consternation, and the ladies, with the exception of Elisabeth, leave the hall in shock. The knights round threateningly on Tannhäuser, but Elisabeth steps between them with the cry 'Haltet ein!', a dramatic moment strongly reminiscent of Leonore's 'Töt' erst sein Weib!' in *Fidelio*, as she protects her husband from Pizarro's knife. The knights are taken aback, but Elisabeth urges clemency, first with some forcefulness, then more touchingly as a woman whose heart has been broken, 'Der Unglücksel'ge'. This section, in B minor and marked Andante, gives way to an Adagio prayer in B major whose simple eloquence moves everybody. Tannhäuser himself, overcome with remorse, sinks to the ground with a cry of grief. In a double chorus the minstrels and knights take up the theme of Elisabeth's prayer, hailing this intervention by an 'angel'. Tannhäuser's interjections of 'Erbarm dich mein!' were originally intended to carry over the flood of the entire ensemble; later Wagner allowed the other voices to be omitted if necessary. Finally Elisabeth and the knights take up a melodic idea which is brought to a climax rather in the Italian style; indeed, it has been demonstrated that the whole of scene iv (that is, from the assembly of the guests to the end of the act) follows the typical pattern of a mid-19th-century italianate finale.

The Landgrave steps forward to tell Tannhäuser that his only hope of salvation is to join the band of pilgrims preparing to make their way to Rome. A final chorus, once again in B major, adopts this more optimistic tone and, after the younger pilgrims are heard in the distance, the act ends with Tannhäuser's cry 'Nach Rom!', echoed by Elisabeth, minstrels and nobles.

ACT 3 *Valley below the Wartburg* The introduction, depicting Tannhäuser's pilgrimage, is built from themes already associated with the pilgrims and with Elisabeth's plea for Tannhäuser, to which is added a new, chromatically winding idea soon to form the basis of Tannhäuser's Narration. As the curtain rises, Elisabeth is praying in front of a statue of the Virgin. Both she and Wolfram, who loves her silently and has been observing her from a discreet distance, are alerted by the return of the pilgrims from Rome. Their chorus moves through a stanza of tortured chromaticism (a vulnerable passage in performance) to an exultant climax, after which it recedes again into the distance.

Elisabeth, seeing that Tannhäuser is not among the pilgrims, falls to her knees and sings her Prayer, 'Allmächt'ge Jungfrau' (in effect another set-piece aria). The use once again of the motif form her Act 2 aria, as she sings of 'foolish longing', invests this phrase with something of the force of a motif of reminiscence. Her prayer ended, Elisabeth notices Wolfram but indicates that he should not speak to her. She leaves; Wolfram remains for scene ii. After an introductory section of arioso, he sings his celebrated Hymn to the Evening Star, 'O du, mein holder Abendstern', a number in the old-fashioned style whose conventionality of phrasing and harmony has done nothing to diminish its evergreen popularity.

The pinched tone of stopped horns and a five-note chromatic phrase in the strings herald the third scene and the reappearance of Tannhäuser; Wolfram initially fails to recognize him. On being told that he has returned from Rome impenitent and unshriven, Wolfram demands to hear the full story. Tannhäuser's Narration, 'Inbrunst im Herzen', is notable on several counts. First, it is the most advanced piece of writing in the opera, in terms of musico-poetic synthesis: that is, the vocal line reflects the natural accentuations of the verse and even changes in character as the narrator's emotional state changes. Second, its formal structure is dictated entirely by the narrative. Third, it is a clear example of the composer's growing recognition of the orchestra's potential for expressive, illustrative purposes. The Narration begins with two stanzas making prominent use of the chromatic winding theme from the act's introduction. A whirr of strings lifts the music into $D^\flat$ as Tannhäuser tells how he arrived in Rome, and a celestial wind chorus sounds the 'Dresden Amen'. He describes how he saw the Pope, and the whirring string figure sweeps on into D and $E^\flat$ major, the frenzied modulations and formal dissolution aptly reflecting Tannhäuser's state of mind. The climax is reached as he repeats the Pope's words of condemnation: if he has tasted the hellish delights of the Venusberg, he can no more be forgiven than the Pope's staff can sprout green leaves. At these words, the motif heard at Tannhäuser's return sounds once more, the pinched tone of the stopped horns transmuted into the Pope's condemnation.

To Wolfram's horror, Tannhäuser declares his intention of returning to the Venusberg. The orchestral frenzy increases and

Venus herself appears in a bright, rosy light, reclining on her couch. (In the original 1845 version Venus did not appear at the end, the Venusberg being suggested by a red glow in the distance; similarly, Elisabeth's death was announced only by bells tolling from the Wartburg. These revisions date from spring 1847.) A struggle ensues for Tannhäuser's soul, resolved by another emphatic enunciation of Elisabeth's name by Wolfram. An offstage chorus announces that Elisabeth has died. But her intercession has redeemed Tannhäuser and Venus disappears, vanquished. Elisabeth's bier is carried on, and Tannhäuser, calling on the saint to intercede for him, falls lifeless to the ground. The final strains of the Pilgrims' Chorus tell of a miracle: the Pope's staff has burst into leaf. Tannhäuser's soul is saved.

*

Tannhäuser, with its frequently abrupt contrasts and rudimentary motivic integration, falls well short of the mature Wagnerian music drama. Yet it marks a considerable advance over *Der fliegende Holländer* in the deployment of the orchestra, continues Wagner's preoccupation with the dramatic conception or 'poetic intent', and shows some awareness of what he later referred to as 'the beautiful, convincing necessity of transition'.

B.M.

Lohengrin

Romantische Oper in three acts set to Wagner's own libretto; first performed in Weimar's Grossherzogliches Hoftheater, on 28 August 1850.

The première, under Liszt's direction, included Carl Beck (Lohengrin), Rosa Agthe (Elsa), Hans Feodor von Milde (Telramund), Josephine Fastlinger (Ortrud), and Höfer (King Henry).

Heinrich der Vogler [King Henry the Fowler]	bass
Lohengrin	tenor
Elsa of Brabant	soprano
Duke Gottfried *her brother*	silent
Friedrich von Telramund *a count of Brabant*	baritone
Ortrud *his wife*	mezzo-soprano
The King's Herald	bass
Four Noblemen of Brabant	tenors, basses
Four Pages	sopranos, altos

Saxon and Thuringian counts and nobles, Brabantine counts and nobles, noblewomen, pages, vassals, ladies, serfs

Setting Antwerp; first half of the 10th century

Wagner's acquaintance with the Lohengrin legend dates back to the winter of 1841–2, when he encountered it in the form of a synopsis and commentary in the annual proceedings of the Königsberg Germanic Society. In the summer of 1845 he became engrossed in the legend of the Holy Grail, reading Wolfram von Eschenbach's poems *Parziv,l* and *Titurel* in editions by Simrock and San-Marte, and the anonymous epic *Lohengrin* in an edition by J. Görres.

By 3 August of that year a prose scenario had been outlined and by 27 November the versification completed. Wagner then made his first complete draft, on two staves (completed 30 July 1846), followed by the second draft with elaboration of instrumental and choral parts.

Various changes were made to the poem during composition, especially in Act 3. Probably for this reason the second complete draft for Act 3 was made before those for Acts 1 and 2, but there is no evidence to suggest that the acts were originally composed in anything other than the usual order. The full score was written out between 1 January and 28 April 1848.

Wagner, by 1850 in exile in Switzerland, was unable to be present at the first performance. The work was received well in Germany, but Wagner was unable to hear it until 1861, when it was given in Vienna. The first performance in Bayreuth did not take place until 1894, when Mottl conducted a cast including Ernest van Dyck and Lillian Nordica. The performances at Bologna in 1871 were the first of any Wagner opera to be given in Italy. The work was first performed in Great Britain in 1875 in Italian, in 1880 in English and in 1882 in German; before World War I *Lohengrin* was by far the most popular of Wagner's operas in Britain, Notable exponents of the title role have included Niemann, De Reszke, Slezak, Melchior, Svanholm, Jess Thomas, Peter Hofmann and Domingo. Elsa has been sung by Eames, Melba, Gadski, Destinn, Jeritza, Rethberg, Lotte Lehmann, Flagstad, Varnay, Grümmer, Tomowa-Sintow and Norman.

Unlike *Holländer* and *Tannhäuser*, *Lohengrin* was not subjected to revision by Wagner, except for the excision of the second part of Lohengrin's Narration (Act 3), a cut carried out at his request at the first performance and ever since (a recording under Leinsdorf reinstating the passage bears out Wagner's conviction that it would have an anti-climactic effect). The double male-voice chorus 'In Früh'n versammelt uns der Ruf' in Act 2 is often cut in performance, despite its imaginative antiphony. A cut traditionally made after Lohengrin's Narration (from Elsa's swoon to 'Der Schwan!') is particularly regrettable in that it gives Elsa no chance to express remorse.

*

The prelude opens with the sounds of a body of divided strings high up in their compass, alternating with four solo violins and a chorus of flutes and oboes: a striking aural image for the shimmering of the Holy Grail. In contrast to all Wagner's earlier overtures, it is conceived like a single breath, as a unified movement, rather than in the traditional sections, yet with references to forthcoming thematic ideas. According to Wagner, the prelude represented the descent from heaven of a host of angels bearing the Grail, and their return to heaven.

ACT 1 *A meadow on the banks of the Scheldt near Antwerp* King Henry (the historical Henry the Fowler) has come to Antwerp to exhort the Brabantines to join him in defending Germany against the imminent invasion from the Hungarians in the east. The curtain rises on two groups of people: the king, under the Oak of Justice, surrounded by Saxon counts and nobles, and opposite them the Brabantine counts and nobles headed by Friedrich von Telramund, by whose side stands his wife Ortrud. The Herald summons the Brabantines to arms and they respond with fervour. But there is dissension in the air. Telramund, charged to give account, accuses Elsa, in a quasi-recitative, of murdering her brother Gottfried, the heir to the dukedom of Brabant; he claims the succession for himself.

The king summons Elsa and she comes forward timidly (scene ii). The subdued wind chorus, contrasting with the clashing brass of the previous scene, suggests her vulnerability. At first she is silent, but then she tells how she had prayed to God in her distress, 'Einsam in trüben Tagen', falling into a sweet sleep. The king urges her to defend herself, but her trance-like state gives way only to an exultant account of a vision of a knightly champion. The latter is prefaced by the Grail music on high strings and accompanied with extreme delicacy on wind and strings, with harp arpeggios and a magical touch on a solo trumpet. The king and bystanders are much moved, but Telramund is unimpressed. He demands judgment through combat; Elsa invokes her visionary champion.

Herald and trumpeters twice sound the call. There is no response, but when Elsa sinks to her knees in prayer, a modulation from $A^\flat$ (the tonality associated with her) to A major (that associated with Lohengrin), combined with an increase in tempo and agitated tremolando strings, signifies the distant approach of the knight, in a boat drawn by a swan. The arrival is greeted by excited choral ejaculations, which at the beginning of scene iii coalesce into a hymn of welcome. Lohengrin bids farewell to the swan and, after making his obeisance to the king, offers himself as Elsa's champion. Shifting into her tonality of A^b, he makes her promise that she will never ask his name or origin, sounding a phrase (ex.1) that will act as a motif of reminiscence. They pledge themselves to each other and Telramund, ignoring entreaties to desist, braces himself for battle.

Ex.1

Nie   sollst du mich   be - fra - gen

['Never may you question me']

The ground is measured out and the Herald announces the rules of combat. In a passage in triple time – the only such example in the entire work – the king invokes the blessing of heaven, 'Mein Herr und Gott'. His prayer is taken up by the chorus and built to a climax. Onstage trumpeters sound the call to battle and, after the king has struck three times with his sword on his shield, the two men fight. Lohengrin defeats Telramund but spares his life. Elsa is overcome with joy, while the crowd acclaim Lohengrin victor in a triumphant finale. Ortrud wonders who the stranger is that renders her magical powers useless. Telramund, crushed and humiliated, falls at her feet.

ACT 2 *The fortress at Antwerp* The curtain rises to reveal the palace at the back and the kemenate at the front (the dwellings of respectively the knights and the womenfolk). The minster stands to the right and on its steps are seated Telramund and Ortrud. It is night. A sustained, muted drum roll and a baleful theme given out on the cello evoke the presence of dark, malignant forces. In the 12th bar an ominous-sounding theme based on the traditionally 'supernatural' chord of the diminished 7th, and associated specifically with Ortrud (ex.2), is announced by cellos and two bassoons. The motif of the 'forbidden question' (ex.1) is also heard on the english horn and bass clarinet. Telramund rouses himself, launching into a bitter tirade punctuated by an aggressively dotted string figure and a rushing, rising semiquaver scale in the bass, blaming Ortrud for his disgrace, 'Durch dich musst' ich verlieren'. The underlying eight-bar structure of this 'aria' is only slightly varied. But after a recitative exchange, in which Ortrud promises a way to undermine Lohengrin's heavenly protection, a more freely structured section begins, 'Du wilde Seherin', in which Ortrud tells Telramund that Lohengrin's power would be nullified if Elsa were to ask him about his name and origins. It is this passage in particular that has caused the scene as a whole to be regarded, with justification, as the most stylistically advanced by Wagner to date. A descending chromatic phrase (a pre-echo of the 'magic sleep' harmonies in the *Ring*) sounded at 'Du wilde Seherin' is the first of a nexus of themes (associated with Ortrud, her sorcery and the 'forbidden question') which have more than an ornamental function: they form the substance of the musical argument. Quasi-recitative and arioso here alternate and merge imperceptibly. The scene ends with a dramatically effective if stylistically regressive revenge duet for the two voices in unison over tremolando strings.

An ethereal wind chorus opens the second scene, heralding the appearance of Elsa, dressed in white, on the balcony of the kemenate. Ortrud, dismissing Telramund, calls up to Elsa (oboes and stopped horns producing a sinister sound next to Elsa's flute) and hypocritically appeals to her generous nature. As Elsa disappears to descend to ground level, Ortrud invokes the pagan gods in a powerful outburst. Affectedly prostrating herself before Elsa, Ortrud listens while the bride-to-be sings of her naive matrimonial bliss in a succession of untroubled diatonic harmonies. Gradually Ortrud instils the poison. First her diminished 7th theme (ex.2) sounds on the bassoons, then, to the accompaniment of the 'forbidden question' motif, she comments darkly on Lohengrin's mysterious origins and appearance. Elsa shudders with dread (tremolando diminished 7th chords), but recovers her composure. In a brief duet, both express their feelings, though Ortrud's vengeance is subjugated musically to the ecstasy of Elsa's line, which is also reinforced by mellifluous strings. As day breaks, Elsa and Ortrud go inside; Telramund reappears briefly, gloating over his expected triumph.

Scene iii opens with an antiphonal exchange between two trumpets blowing the reveille from the tower, answered by two in the distance. As the rest of the orchestra joins in, the palace gates open and four royal trumpeters cause a brief, dramatic plunge into C major (from and back into D major) with their onstage fanfares. The filling of the stage is matched by gathering momentum in the orchestra, leading to the double chorus for male voices 'In Früh'n versammelt uns der Ruf'. Though belonging to the grand operatic tradition soon to be abjured by Wagner, this and subsequent choruses show skill in their part-writing and can be exhilarating in performance. The Herald announces that Telramund is banished; anyone who consorts with him suffers the same fate. The stranger sent by God, he continues, wishes to take as his title not Duke, but Protector of Brabant; today he celebrates his wedding, tomorrow he will lead them into battle. These announcements are punctuated by choral acclamations, following which four disgruntled nobles, formerly liegemen of Telramund, detach themselves from the crowd and are recruited by Telramund, who has been skulking in the shadows.

The fourth scene initiates the wedding procession to the minster, but as Elsa reaches its steps, Ortrud interposes herself (on a dramatically interrupted cadence, leading to diminished 7th agitation) to claim precedence. In a regularly phrased 'aria' she goes on to taunt Elsa for her ignorance of her champion's origins, 'Wenn falsch Gericht'. Elsa's reply is forthright and confident, supported by a full wind chorus in exultant sextuplets. Ortrud's next onslaught is interrupted by the arrival of the king, Lohengrin and the Saxon nobles from the palace (scene v). Lohengrin consoles Elsa and begins to lead her to the minster once more. This time the procession is interrupted by Telramund, who vehemently accuses Lohengrin of sorcery. His demand that the knight reveal his name is brushed aside by Lohengrin. No king or prince can command him, he replies, only

Elsa. But as he turns to his bride, he sees with dismay that she is agitated: the motifs of Ortrud and the 'forbidden question' tell us why. The following ensemble ironically juxtaposes Elsa's doubt, expressed to herself, with the unquestioning trust of the onlookers.

The king expresses his satisfaction and, as the nobles crowd round Lohengrin to pledge their allegiance, Telramund prevails on Elsa to allow him to expose the sorcerer by spilling just a drop of his blood. Lohengrin repulses Telramund and Ortrud, and the procession sets off once again. A climax built by sequential means brings the act to a rousing conclusion. But there is a final *coup de théâtre*. As Elsa and Lohengrin reach the top step of the minster, she looks down to see Ortrud raising her arm in a gesture of triumph. The motif of the 'forbidden question' rings out on trumpets and trombones, its F minor colouring casting a menacing shadow over the radiance of the predominating C major.

ACT 3 Scenes i–ii *The bridal chamber* The celebrated orchestral introduction to Act 3, which has become a concert piece in its own right, is notable for its metric displacements – in contradistinction to the regular common-time periods elsewhere, dictated by the conventional poetic metres adopted. The curtain rises on the bridal chamber. To the strains of the even more celebrated bridal march, 'Treulich geführt', two processions enter from behind: Elsa escorted by the ladies, and Lohengrin by the king and nobles. The couple embrace and are blessed by the king. The attendants retire to a repetition of the march.

With an enharmonic modulation from B$\flat$ to E major an atmosphere of tender devotion is immediately established for scene ii, 'Das süsse Lied verhallt'. Muted strings provide the background for a profusion of melodic ideas, launched by first a solo clarinet then a solo oboe. Except for a few brief bars, the voices are heard in succession rather than combination. Elsa's first suggestion that Lohengrin share with her the secret of his name is deflected, but she becomes more and more insistent, despite his alternate warnings and protestations of love. Attempting to reassure her, he says that he renounced glorious and blissful delights to woo her. But Elsa is far

67

from reassured: he may tire of her and return to the joys he left behind. The tempo quickens. Ortrud's theme (ex.2) is ubiquitous: at one point Elsa's line becomes a diatonic version of it, in E minor. Finally, as the motif of the 'forbidden question' rings out, Elsa asks outright who he is. Telramund and his henchmen break into the chamber. With Elsa's assistance, Lohengrin fells Telramund at a stroke; the henchmen kneel before Lohengrin. He orders Telramund's body to be taken to the king's judgment seat; there he will answer Elsa's question.

ACT 3 Scene iii *The banks of the Scheldt; daybreak* Brabantines appear from all sides, stirringly heralded by trumpets. Telramund's covered body is brought in. Then Elsa enters, followed by Lohengrin, who tells the king that he can no longer lead his troops into battle. He explains how he killed Telramund in self-defence and goes on to denounce Elsa for breaking her vow. Now he is forced to reveal his origins. The shimmering Grail music of the work's opening intro-duces Lohengrin's Narration, 'In fernem Land'. He tells how he came as a servant of the Grail; such knights are granted invincible power on condition of anonymity. Now that his secret is revealed, he must return to Monsalvat. His father is Parzival and his name is Lohengrin. The Narration begins with conventionally balanced phrases but develops into a freer structure more appropriate to narrative as the unfolding of the tale seizes the imagination of teller and listener. Elsa momentarily swoons; then to Lohengrin's remonstrations she begs forgiveness. The king and chorus add their pleas, Elsa's voice soaring above them all. But the laws of the Grail are immutable. The swan appears, drawing an empty boat. After addressing the swan, Lohengrin turns to Elsa and tells her that had they lived together for just a year, her brother Gottfried would have been restored to her. He entrusts her with his sword, horn and ring, to be given to Gottfried should he return one day. Ortrud comes forward declaring that she recognizes the swan, by the chain round its neck, as Gottfried, whom she bewitched; now he is lost to Elsa for ever. To the radiant music of the Grail, Lohengrin kneels silently in prayer. A white dove descends and hovers over the boat. Seeing it, Lohengrin loosens the chain round the swan, which sinks. In its place appears a boy in shining silver: Gottfried. Lohengrin lifts him to the bank, proclaiming him Duke of Brabant. Ortrud falls to the ground, while Gottfried advances first to the king and then to Elsa. Her joy turns to sorrow as she watches Lohengrin depart. As the Grail knight vanishes from sight, Elsa falls lifeless to the ground.

*

Lohengrin is the last of Wagner's works that can fairly be described as an opera rather than a music drama. It contains, however, the seeds of future developments and is a powerfully conceived, imaginatively scored work in its own right.

B.M.

Tristan und Isolde
('Tristan and Isolde')

Handlung (drama) in three acts set to Wagner's own libretto; first performed in Munich, at the Königliches Hof- und Nationaltheater, on 10 June 1865.

The conductor at the première was Hans von Bülow; Isolde was sung by Malvina Schnorr von Carolsfeld, and Tristan by her husband Ludwig Schnorr von Carolsfeld, who died only three weeks after the final performance. The cast also included Anna Deinet (Brangäne), Ludwig Zottmayr (King Mark) and Anton Mitterwurzer (Kurwenal).

Tristan	tenor
König Marke [King Mark]	bass
Isolde	soprano
Kurwenal *Tristan's servant*	baritone
Melot *a courtier*	tenor
Brangäne *Isolde's maid*	soprano
A Shepherd	tenor
A Steersman	baritone
A Young Sailor	tenor

Sailors, knights and esquires

Setting At sea, in Cornwall and Brittany during the Middle Ages

The ancient Tristan legend, probably of Celtic origin, achieved its first literary form in the 12th century. The version used by Wagner as the basis for his drama was that of Gottfried von Strassburg (*fl* 1200–20). Wagner conceived the idea of writing an opera on the Tristan subject in the autumn of 1854, but the earliest dated surviving sketch (an elaboration of two fragments) is from 19 December 1856, at which point he was still engaged on Act 1 of *Siegfried*.

Wagner began his prose scenario the following summer, on 20 August 1857, and the poem was completed on 18 September. Like *Siegfried* – but unlike all the other music dramas – each act was drafted and elaborated, in sequence, the full score being reached before the next act was embarked on in sketch. Indeed, because the publishers were eager to have the new work ready for public consumption, the score was actually engraved one act at a time. The fair copy of the full score of Act 1 was completed on 3 April 1858 in Zürich, of Act 2 on 18 March 1859 in Venice, and of Act 3 on 6 August 1859 in Lucerne.

Epoch-making as *Tristan* proved to be, the work had some notable antecedents. There are frequent pre-echoes in the sultry chromaticism of Spohr's *Jessonda*, while the rising chromatic phrase that opens *Tristan* is prominent in Liszt's song *Die Lorelei*. The celebrated '*Tristan* chord' (see ex.1) is presaged (though never given in that precise form) in the Liszt song, as well as by composers as various as Mozart, Spohr and Gottschalk. Berlioz's *Roméo et Juliette*, of which Wagner was a staunch admirer, contains a number of melodic inspirations that found their way into *Tristan*, in particular a theme which was developed into that of the so-called Liebestod; the sighing chromatic phrases and general atmosphere of the Scène d'amour' from *Roméo et Juliette* foreshadow the love scene in Act 2 of *Tristan*. A further remarkable antecedent of *Tristan* is Hans von Bülow's orchestral fantasy *Nirwana*, the score of which Wagner was studying at precisely the time of his conception of *Tristan* (autumn 1854). When he came to compose the opera three years later, he took over from *Nirwana* (possibly unconsciously) several ideas, both general and specific. *Nirwana* provides not only another, more immediate, source for the rising chromatic phrase that opens *Tristan*, but also a parallel sublimation of it at the close.

Ex.1

The prelude to *Tristan* (with Wagner's own concert ending) was included in a series of three concerts in Paris early in 1860, intended to pave the way for a possible performance of the opera in France by German singers. That scheme came to nothing, as did plans to produce the work in Karlsruhe and Vienna. Providentially the young King Ludwig II of Bavaria came to Wagner's aid, embracing his work with almost febrile passion, and his support enabled the production to go ahead. The day eventually fixed for performance in Munich, 15 May 1865, was the day chosen by Wagner's creditors to send in the bailiffs; in the afternoon his Isolde, Schnorr, lost her voice. The long-delayed première finally took place on 10 June, with three subsequent performances. Un-comprehending hostility in some quarters was matched by unbridled enthusiasm in others; the work was to exert an extraordinary influence over future generations.

Felix Mottl conducted the first performance at Bayreuth in 1886, which was also the year of the first production in the USA (Seidl conducting at the Metropolitan, with Niemann and Lilli Lehmann). The first production in England was at the Theatre Royal, Drury Lane, in 1882. Notable exponents of the role of Tristan have included Jean De Reszke, Lauritz Melchior, Max Lorenz, Set Svanholm, Ludwig Suthaus, Ramón Vinay, Wolfgang Windgassen, Jon Vickers, Peter Hofmann and Siegfried Jerusalem. Isolde has been sung by Lilian Nordica, Olive Fremstad, Eva Turner, Frida Leider, Germaine Lubin, Kirsten Flagstad, Astrid Varnay, Martha Mödl, Brigit Nilsson, Caterina Ligendza, Gwyneth Jones, Hildegard Behrens and Waltraud Meier. Notable conductors of the work, in addition to Mottl and Seidl, have included Gustav Mahler, Arthur Nikisch, Bruno Walter, Thomas Beecham, Albert Coates, Erich Kleiber, Wilhelm Furtwängler, Karl Bohm, Rodolf Kempe, Georg Solti, Herbert von Karajan, Reginald Goodall, Carlos Kleiber and Daniel Barenboim.

*

The titles of Prelude and Liebestod for the opening and closing sections of the work are firmly established by tradition, though Wagner referred to them as respectively Liebestod and [Isolde's] Transfiguration. The prelude introduces several of the work's principal motifs. The descending chromatic phrase that begins it (ex. 1x) is typical in that, although it has been given such labels as 'Tristan', 'Tristan's suffering', 'grief' and 'the confession', it ultimately defies categorization. Its inversion, the rising four-note phrase with which it is combined (ex. 1 *y*), is ubiquitous in *Tristan* and a potent musical image of the work's preoccupation with yearning. The chord occurring at their conjunction in bar 2 is known as the '*Tristan* chord'; returning at various points of significance in the drama.

ACT 1   *At sea, on the deck of Tristan's ship, during the crossing from Ireland to Cornwall*   The curtain rises to reveal a construction like a tent on the foredeck of a ship (scene i); Isolde is seen on a couch, her face buried in the cushions. A young sailor sings, 'as if from the masthead', an unaccompanied song about the Irish lover he has left behind in the west ('Westwärts schweift der Blick'). Isolde, who is being brought from Ireland to Cornwall by Tristan to be the bride of his uncle, King Mark, starts up, assuming that the reference to an 'Irish maid' is an insult to her. When her maid and confidante Brangäne tells her that they are soon to land in Cornwall, Isolde launches into a furious outburst against her own 'degenerate race' who have succumbed so easily to the enemy. Brangäne attempts in vain to calm her.

For the second scene the whole length of the ship becomes visible; in the stern stands Tristan, thoughtfully, with folded arms, his faithful retainer Kurwenal reclining at his feet. The young sailor strikes up again, this time accompanied by a tremolando in the bass. Her eyes fixed on Tristan, Isolde sings the enigmatic words 'Mir erkoren, mir verloren' ('Chosen to be mine, lost to me') to motif ex. 1*y*, followed by 'Todgeweihtes Haupt! Todgeweihtes Herz!' ('Death-devoted head! Death-devoted heart!') to a chord change from $A^\flat$ to A major, the poignant effect of which is enhanced by the switch from woodwind to brass (ex.2), a switch repeated on subsequent occurrences of the motif.

Isolde tells Brangäne to instruct Tristan to attend on her. Brangäne's timid request to Tristan is courteously turned aside by him, but when she repeats Isolde's command – to the same imperious chord sequence as her mistress used – Kurwenal makes his own bluntly negative reply, in the firmly diatonic idiom that is to characterize him. He goes on to revel in the slaying by Tristan of Morold, Isolde's betrothed, who came from Ireland to exact tribute from

['Death-devoted head! Death-devoted heart!']

Cornwall. The mockery of Kurwenal's song is reinforced by its self-contained, ballad-like nature; its refrain is picked up by the sailors. Brangäne returns in confusion to Isolde who is barely able to control her anger (scene iii). With both (*x*) and (*y*) of ex.1 repeatedly in attendance, Isolde's Narration tells how the wounded Tristan, disguised as 'Tantris', came to her to be healed and how she recognized him as Morold's killer: 'Wie lachend sie mir Lieder singen'. Isolde's determination to slay Tristan in revenge dissolved as he looked pitifully into her eyes – (*y*) is meltingly transformed here – but now she bitterly regrets that she let the sword drop. With heavy irony she mimics Tristan's 'insulting' offer to Mark to collect her as bride, and (*x*) undergoes an angry metamorphosis as she curses Tristan.

Brangäne's response makes much use of a tender appoggiatura figure – derived from (*y*); after another gnomic utterance from Isolde, Brangäne switches to triple time in an even more lyrical attempt to console her mistress. The opening bars of the prelude are recalled as Brangäne reminds Isolde of her mother's magic potions. But Isolde has only vengeance in mind (ex.2 intervenes) and she selects the draught of death, at which point the tension suddenly rises as the sailors are heard again, preparing to land.

Kurwenal boisterously calls the ladies to make ready (scene iv), but Isolde insists on speaking to Tristan before they land, in order to 'forgive' him. Her excited farewells to Brangäne, however, and the death-portending motif (ex.3) in the bass (heard previously when she selected the draught) betoken her real intention. Brangäne's pleas are in vain, as is confirmed by the close succession of exx.3 and 2.

Tristan's approach is awaited (scene v) with a striking instrumental passage consisting of a new idea (ex.4) answered by a series of *martellato* chords on full strings; this theme has been variously labelled 'Tristan's honour', 'Morold' and 'Isolde's anger' – an indication of the flexibility Wagner allowed himself in the deployment of motifs in *Tristan*. The ominous ex.3 is heard as Tristan approaches. Isolde tells him that she saw through his disguise as 'Tantris' and demands vengeance (exx.2 and 4). Tristan offers her his sword, but Isolde signals to Brangäne for the potion, ex.3 and the offstage sailors' cries again raising the tension. After more ironic mimicry, Isolde hands Tristan the cup (exx.4 and then 2 are prominent). Tristan lifts the cup and drinks. Fearing further betrayal, Isolde wrests the cup from him and drinks in her turn: Brangäne, in desperation, has substituted the love for the death potion. The climactic chord, played by the full orchestra, is the '*Tristan* chord'. Its association with betrayal, as the obverse of faithful love, resonates beyond *Tristan*, occurring at Brünnhilde's discovery of her betrayal by Siegfried; in *Parsifal* the ambivalent properties of the chord are exploited by its dual association with temptation and redemption. After they have both drunk, they are seized with a succession of conflicting emotions, all portrayed in the music: rapt wonderment by the prolongation of the '*Tristan* chord', agitation by tremolando cellos with muffled drum roll, breathless frenzy by a brief, snatched phrase on unison winds and strings, and finally yearning for each other by the music from the beginning of the prelude. Tristan and Isolde embrace ecstatically, offstage salutations to King Mark again raising the emotional temperature, while Brangäne looks on in horror. The lovers express their passion, first in alternating fragments of phrases, then, in defiance of Wagner's earlier theoretical principles, in conjunction. Only half jolted back to reality by Kurwenal's innocent breeziness and by the jubilant shouts of the onlookers, Tristan and Isolde struggle to comprehend what has happened to them. The act comes to an exhilarating end with the impassioned rising chromatic motif, ex.1(*y*), threading its way through exultant brass fanfares.

Ex.3

Ex.4

ACT 2   *In Mark's royal castle in Cornwall*   The orchestral introduction to Act 2 introduces several new principal motifs: exx.5, 6
and 7, each of which resists definitive categorization, though ex.5 is
generally associated in the ensuing act with 'day' (in Schopenhauer's
terms the outer material world of phenomena, as opposed to the
noumenal sphere of inner consciousness represented by 'night').
Ex.1(y) also assumes a more urgent form: the lovers' yearning has
intensified. The curtain rises to reveal a garden with high trees;
Isolde's chamber is to one side and a burning torch stands at the open
door. A volley of horn calls gradually receding into the distance signifies the departing hunt of King Mark and his courtiers. The cautious
Brangäne warns her mistress that the horns are still audible, but all
Isolde can hear are the sounds of the balmy summer night: the horn
calls are transmuted into a shimmering orchestral texture by clarinets,
second violins and violas, a sweet sound to the lovers ('Nicht
Hörnerschall tönt so hold').

Ex.5

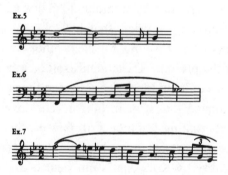

Ex.6

Ex.7

Brangäne further warns Isolde that in her impatience to see Tristan
she should not be oblivious to the devious Melot, Tristan's supposed
friend, who, she alleges, has arranged the nocturnal hunt as a trap.

Isolde brushes these fears aside and requests Brangäne to extinguish the torch: the signal for Tristan to approach. Brangäne demurs, bewailing her fateful switching of the potions. Over glowing orchestral colours, Isolde extols the powers of the love goddess, Frau Minne, which are then celebrated in a new theme (ex.8), the second bar of which includes the shape characteristic of Wagner's main love themes. This new theme is developed sequentially, its ever-intensifying repetitions finally finding release in Isolde's expansive phrase 'dass hell sie dorten leuchte', before her extinguishing of the torch; the climactic power of that phrase is enhanced by the sudden cessation of rhythmic and harmonic motion.

Ex.8

Isolde throws the torch to the ground and, sending Brangäne to keep watch, waits impatiently for Tristan. Her agitated expectation is depicted by ex.6 (with a breathlessly syncopated accompanimental figure); together with another brief figure, that motif is subjected to remorseless sequential repetition, building to a frenzied climax as Tristan finally bursts in (scene ii). They greet each other ecstatically; a breathless exchange follows, in which each brief, snatched phrase (both musical and textual) of Isolde is impetuously appropriated by Tristan: 'Bist du mein?/Hab' ich dich wieder?' After further rapturous effusions, their minds turn to the long-delayed extinction of the torch, a train of thought which soon enters the metaphysical realm of the night–day, noumenon–phenomenon polarity. (An extensive cut (324 bars) is often made at this point, from 'bot ich dem Tage Trutz!' to 'wahr es zu sehen tauge'.) Ex.5, the motif associated with 'day', is prominent here, but most of the others already cited also appear in one form or another.

Tristan draws Isolde to a flowery bank for their central love duet: 'O sink hernieder, Nacht der Liebe', approached by a masterly transition passage that effects a gradual reduction in tension by dynamic, harmonic and rhythmic means. The tonality of $A^\flat$ gradually establishes itself out of the tonal flux of the preceding duet, but the transition to some extent disguises the fact that 'O sink hernieder' has aspects of the traditional operatic duet, the singers sharing phrases of music and text.

An interlude is provided by Brangäne's Watchsong from the tower: 'Einsam wachend in der Nacht'. Ravishingly scored, this passage also exemplifies a trait new in *Tristan*: syllables of the text become so distended that the vocal line is treated as an instrument rather than as the carrier of semantic meaning. The exquisitely prolonged dominant cadence of Brangäne's Watch-song resolves on to ex.9 (an elaboration of an idea heard earlier in the duet) on hushed strings alone, for Isolde's 'Lausch, Geliebter!'. This is much developed, leading to a new melodic idea (ex. 10), taken up first by Tristan, then by Isolde, to the thought of union in death ('So stürben wir, um ungetrennt'); this theme is to provide the main material both for the latter part of this duet and for the Liebestod.

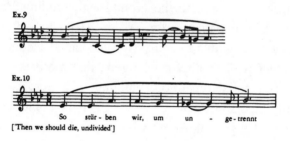

Ex.9

Ex.10

So stür - ben wir, um un - ge - trennt
['Then we should die, undivided']

Brangäne's song returns, in curtailed form. Tristan echoes Isolde's earlier words with 'Soll ich lauschen?'. From this point the duet gathers momentum. The final stage is launched with 'O ew'ge Nacht', the two singing in harmony of eternal night. The long approach to the final climax is shaped by a series of peaks; sequential repetitions and a sustained dominant pedal raise the tension to an unbearable level, which eventually reaches the point of no return.

The cadence, like the coitus, is *interruptus* (scene iii). A savage discord on the full orchestra (topped by shrieking piccolo) is accompanied by a scream from Brangäne, as King Mark, Melot and the courtiers burst in on the scene. The orchestra graphically depicts the subsiding of the lovers' passions as morning dawns (ex.5). King Mark, much moved, addresses Tristan and receiving no direct answer, embarks on his long monologue of questioning reproach: would Tristan do this to him ('Mir dies?')? His new motif, ex.11, announced on his characteristic instrument, the bass clarinet, is an inverted form of the motif sometimes described as 'Tristan's honour' (ex.4). To King Mark's questions there can be no reply, Tristan responds. His feeling that he no longer belongs to this world is captured in a magical enharmonic modulation from the music of the opera's opening to ex.9. He invites Isolde to follow him into the realm of night; she assents and he kisses her on the forehead. At this, Melot, whose actions (according to Tristan) have been motivated by his jealous love for Isolde, draws his sword. Tristan also draws, but allows himself to be wounded. The act ends with King Mark's motif pealing out on brass instruments in D minor.

Ex.11

ACT 3 *Tristan's castle in Brittany* The prelude to the final act opens with a doleful, diatonic transformation of ex.1(y) in a desolate F minor. When the curtain rises, Tristan is seen lying asleep under a lime tree, with Kurwenal bending over him, grief-stricken. A melancholy shepherd's song is heard on the english horn, offstage. The shepherd appears over the castle wall. Kurwenal tells him to play a merry melody if Isolde's ship should come into sight. The sea is empty and desolate ('Öd und leer das Meer!'), responds the shepherd, continuing with his mournful tune. To the joy of Kurwenal, expressed in his characteristically hearty rhythms and melodic lines, Tristan revives and asks where he is. Kurwenal replies that he is in his family castle, Kareol.

Tristan's slow, painful return to consciousness is reflected in his fragmented vocal line. He is dimly aware that he has been brought back from the distant realm of endless night, where he had glimpsed oblivion. Isolde remains in the bright light of day (ex.5) but he looks forward to the final extinction of the torch and their union. This first phase in Tristan's delirium is reflected in the wild lack of control in his music: the complexity of the chromatic harmony, the lurching tempo changes and the undisciplined line.

Kurwenal tells him that he has sent for Isolde, and Tristan, in his fevered imagination, sees the ship approaching; a motif (ex.12) first heard in a sombre form in the prelude to the third act returns here in obsessive sequential repetition. Tristan's frantic cries to Kurwenal to look for the ship are answered by the english horn playing the mournful shepherd's song. In the next phase of his delirium, Tristan remembers how he heard that song ('Du alte ernste Weise') in his childhood, when his mother and father died. The strains of the song are now woven into a fantasy, to be joined by the falling chromatic phrase heard in Act 1 as Isolde recalled her tending of the sick Tristan. Another frenzied climax follows, in which Tristan curses the love potion, for which he senses he is somehow responsible.

Ex.12

He sinks back in a faint. Kurwenal listens anxiously for signs of life. Tristan revives and the music moves to E major for the final, sublime phase of his delirium, in which he imagines Isolde coming to him across the water: 'Wie sie selig'. Tristan's vocal line, introduced by the mellow ex.9 on horns, is now infinitely, ecstatically protracted – sometimes to ten slow-moving bars. Gradually the lines begin to fragment as Tristan again imagines he sees the ship approaching. This time a sprightly C major tune on the english horn confirms that it has been sighted. Kurwenal rushes to the watchtower and reports on its progress. He sees Isolde come ashore and goes down to assist (scene ii). Tristan, meanwhile, anticipates her arrival in feverish excitement, tearing the bandages from his wounds.

Isolde enters in haste (ex.7) but Tristan, to a recapitulation of music from the opera's prelude, expires in her arms. Isolde is distraught, her fragmented line accompanied by various themes including the opening of ex.10, subsequently to form the basis of the Liebestod.

The music becomes reanimated as the shepherd tells Kurwenal that a second ship is arriving (scene iii); they try to barricade the gate. Brangäne appears, and then Melot, whom Kurwenal strikes dead. King Mark and his followers also appear and, oblivious to the king's pleas, Kurwenal sets upon them, sustaining a fatal wound; he dies at Tristan's feet. King Mark, who had come to yield Isolde to Tristan, laments the scene of death and destruction. The Liebestod, or Isolde's Transfiguration, now begins, with ex.10: 'Mild und leise' ('Gently and softly'). In its latter stages, the conclusion of the Act 2 love duet is also recalled, but passion is now sublimated and the climax of the Liebestod is insistent rather than frantic. Isolde sinks, as if transfigured, on to Tristan's body, mystically united with him at last. A final statement of ex.1(y), achieving its long-awaited resolution on to a chord of B major, brings the opera to a radiant close.

*

Tristan und Isolde is regarded as a milestone in the history of music, largely on account of its pervasive emancipation of the dissonance. The far-reaching influence of the work in technical terms is matched by the overwhelming effect the extremity of its emotional expression has had on generations of artists in all media. On one level, *Tristan* is the ultimate glorification of love: 'a monument to this loveliest of all dreams', as Wagner put it. But on another level, the work goes beyond emotional experience and enters a metaphysical realm. Human existence and the outer material world of phenomena are ultimately transcended and salvation found in the embrace of the noumena, the ultimate reality.

B.M.

Die Meistersinger von Nürnberg

('The Mastersingers of Nuremberg')

Music drama in three acts set to Wagner's own libretto; first performed in Munich, at the Königliches Hof- und Nationaltheater, on 21 June 1868.

At the première Franz Betz sang Sachs, Mathilde Mallinger, Eva; Pogner was sung by Kasper Bausewein, Beckmesser by Gustav Hölzel, Walther by Franz Nachbauer.

Hans Sachs *cobbler*		bass-baritone
Veit Pogner *goldsmith*		bass
Kunz Vogelgesang *furrier*		tenor
Konrad Nachtigal *tinsmith*		bass
Sixtus Beckmesser *town clerk*		bass
Fritz Kothner *baker*		bass
Balthasar Zorn *pewterer*	Mastersingers	tenor
Ulrich Eisslinger *grocer*		tenor
Augustin Moser *tailor*		tenor
Hermann Ortel *soapmaker*		bass
Hans Schwarz *stocking weaver*		bass
Hans Foltz *coppersmith*	bass	
Walther von Stolzing *a young knight from Franconia*		tenor
David *Sach's apprentice*		tenor
Eva *Pogner's daughter*		soprano
Magdalene *Eva's nurse*		soprano
A Nightwatchman		bass

Citizens of all guilds and their wives, journeymen, apprentices, young women, people

Setting Nuremberg; about the middle of the 16th century

Wagner conceived *Die Meistersinger* in 1845 as a comic appendage to *Tannhäuser*, in the same way that a satyr play followed a Greek tragedy. His first prose draft for the work was written in Marienbad in July that year, using Georg Gottfried Gervinus's *Geschichte der poetischen National-Literatur der Deutschen* of 1835–42 for historical background. Other relevant volumes in Wagner's Dresden library include Jacob Grimm's *Über den altdeutschen Meistergesang* (1811), J. G. Büsching's edition of Hans Sachs's plays (1816–19) and Friedrich Furchau's life of Sachs (1820). The second and third prose drafts date from November 1861 (the former probably 14–16 November, the latter, containing minor revisions, prepared on 18 November for Schott). At this point, Wagner found J. C. Wagenseil's Nuremberg Chronicle of 1697 a particularly rich source of information on the ancient crafts and guilds and on other aspects of Nuremberg. Also evident are motifs from such contemporary stories as E. T. A. Hoffmann's *Meister Martin der Küfner und seine Gesellen*, which is set in 16th-century Nuremberg. Wagner completed the poem of *Die Meistersinger* on 25 January 1862 and began the composition in March or April. The full score was not completed until October 1867.

Even after the immensely successful première under Hans von Bülow in Munich, *Die Meistersinger* was taken up first by theatres of medium size, such as Dessau, Karlsruhe, Dresden, Mannheim and Weimar (all in 1869). The court operas of Vienna and Berlin followed in 1870. The work was first given at Bayreuth in 1888 under Hans Richter. The first performance in England was also under Richter, at the Theatre Royal, Drury Lane, in 1882, and in the USA under Seidl, at the Metropolitan in 1886. Notable exponents of the role of Hans Sachs have included Edouard de Reszke, Anton van Rooy, Friedrich Schorr, Hans Hotter, Theo Adam, Dietrich Fischer-Dieskau, Karl Ridderbusch, Hans Sotin and Bernd Weikl. Walther has been sung by Jean de Reszke, Max Lorenz, Set Svanholm, Jess Thomas, James King, René Kollo, Jean Cox, Placido Domingo, Peter Hofmann, Siegfried Jerusalem and Ben Heppner. Eva has been sung by Emma Eames, Emmy Destinn, Elisabeth Rethberg, Lotte Lehmann, Elisabeth Schumann, Helen Donath, Hannelore Bode and Eva Marton. Notable conductors, besides Richter and Seidl, have included Carl Muck, Felix Mottl, Erich Leinsdorf, Bruno Walter, Reginald Goodall, Thomas Beecham, Rudolf Kempe, Georg Solti, Herbert von Karajan, Eugen Jochum, Silvio Varviso, and Wolfgang Sawallisch.

*

The prelude opens the work in an emphatic, magisterial C major, with a theme that celebrates the dignity of the Masters, at the same time possibly hinting at their air of self-importance (ex.1). A more pensive idea (ex.2) gives way to a pair of themes (exx.3 and 4), the first, of a fanfare-like nature, standing for the Masters and their guild. An elaborate modulation to E major introduces Walther and the theme of his passion (ex.5), later to form a part of his Prize Song. After an episode in E^b (based on ex.1) depicting the chattering, bustling apprentices, three of these themes (exx.1, 3 and 5) are expansively combined before a grandiloquent coda.

ACT 1 *Inside St Katharine's Church* The act opens with the congregation singing a sturdy C major chorale (of Wagner's invention), the phrases of which are interrupted by ex.2: Walther is urgently trying to communicate with Eva. At the end of the service, the church empties and Walther addresses Eva. He wishes to know whether she is betrothed, and though Eva sends away Magdalene to find first her

handkerchief, then the clasp, and then her prayer-book, she never quite manages to stem Walther's impassioned flow with an answer. Magdalene finally tells him that Eva will marry the mastersinger who wins the song contest to be held the next day. Walther is left to be instructed in the rules of the mastersingers by David, Sachs's apprentice, with whom Magdalene is in love.

In scene ii David, after some ribbing from his fellow apprentices, proceeds to initiate Walther into the secrets of his own master's art: a properly fashioned song is, after all, he says, like a well-made pair of shoes. His catalogue of the tones that have to be learnt ('Mein Herr!'), along with the appropriate rules (mostly taken by Wagner from Wagenseil) overwhelms Walther, but he sees that his only hope of winning Eva is by composing a mastersong in the approved manner. The apprentices, who have erected the wrong stage, put up the right one under David's supervision, to the accompaniment of their bustling semiquavers.

Eva's father, Pogner, now enters with the town clerk, Beckmesser (scene iii). Two tiny motifs are heard here, later much repeated both together and individually (ex.6). Pogner assures Beckmesser of his good will and welcomes Walther to the guild, surprised as he is that Walther wishes to seek entry. Kothner calls the roll, to a contrapuntal working-out of ex.6. Pogner then announces the prize he intends to award to the winner of the song contest the next day ('Nun hört, und versteht mich recht!'). The first part of his address is based entirely on a new motif, ex.7. Then he changes to the style of an old-fashioned recitative, accompanied by sustained chords, to tell how burghers such as they are regarded in other German lands as miserly. Returning to ex.7 and to an important idea derived from fig. x of ex.1, he proposes to counter this slander by offering all his goods, as well as his only daughter, Eva, to the winner of the song contest. His proviso that she must approve the man is not welcomed by all the Masters. Sachs's proposal, however, that the winner be chosen by the populace, as a means of renewing the traditional rules with the good sense and natural instincts of the common people, is laughed out of court.

Walther is introduced by Pogner and asked about his teacher. His reply ('Am stillen Herd') is that he learnt his art from the poetry of

85

Ex.6

Ex.7

Walther von der Vogelweide and from nature itself. In formal terms, the song is a piece of gentle mockery, on the composer's part, of the *Bar* -form so prized by the Masters. Of the three stanzas, *A–A–B*, the last (*Abgesang*) is intended to be a variation of the others (*Stollen*), but in 'Am stillen Herd' the variation is so florid that no one is able to contradict Beckmesser's opinion that it is but a 'deluge of words'.

Beckmesser withdraws into his Marker's box, ready to pass judgment on the young knight's formal attempt to enter the guild. The syncopated motif accompanying him both here and elsewhere is a churlish version of the dotted motif that first introduced Walther, as befits Beckmesser's cantankerous character. The rules of the *Tabulatur* are read out by Kothner in a style that parodies that of Handelian opera, complete with coloratura (given, unusually, to a bass, for comic effect).

For his Trial Song, Walther takes up the command of the Marker: 'Fanget an! So rief der Lenz in den Wald'. A passionate celebration of the joys of spring and youthful love, it again fails to find favour with the Masters. It is, in fact, a complex *Bar*-form in which each *Stollen* is in two parts – *A–B–A'–B'–C* – though Beckmesser interrupts after *A'*, assuming that the form is ternary (*A–B–A*). Beckmesser's critical scratching of chalk on slate provokes Walther's angry outburst about envious Winter lying in wait in the thorn-bush. (That this is intended as a reference to the Grimm brothers' anti-Semitic folktale *Der Jude im Dorn* is clear from the parallel situation: in the Grimm tale a bird flies into the thorn-bush, in Walther's song it flies out again in an image of liberation. The matter is put beyond doubt by Wagner's pun 'Grimm-bewährt', which suggests both 'guarded with anger' and 'authenticated by Grimm'. The identification here of Beckmesser with the stereotypical Jew of folklore has profound implications for the interpretation of the character and of the work as a whole.)

Beckmesser leads the chorus of opposition to Walther; only Sachs admires his originality. Walther mounts the singer's chair (a gross breach of etiquette) to complete his song. The hubbub increases as he does so: the Masters, by an overwhelming majority, reject his application to the guild, while the apprentices revel in the commotion. With a gesture of pride and contempt, Walther strides from the stage, leaving Sachs to gaze thoughtfully at the empty singer's chair.

ACT 2   *In the street in front of the homes of Pogner and Sachs*   The orchestral prelude takes up the main theme of Pogner's Address (ex.7) in a joyous celebration of midsummer's eve: trills and glissandos abound. The curtain rises to reveal a street and a narrower adjoining alley in Nuremberg. Of the two corner houses presented, Pogner's grand one on the right is overhung by a lime tree and Sachs's simpler one on the left by an elder. The apprentices are tormenting David once again.

Magdalene asks him how Eva's paramour fared at the Song School and is vicariously disconsolate at the bad news. Sachs arrives and instructs David to set out his work for him by the window. Pogner and Eva return from an evening stroll and sit on a bench under the lime tree. The new motif (ex.8) to which he expresses his satisfaction with Nuremberg and its customs is reminiscent rhythmically of ex.7. Pogner belatedly realizes that Eva's questions about the knight are no idle curiosity.

Ex.8

As Eva follows her father inside, Sachs has his work bench set up outside his workshop. The tender reminiscences of a phrase from Walther's Trial Song (ex.9) suggest that the knight's celebration of spring and his embodiment of vital youthful passion have made a great impression on him. Sachs's relishing of the scent of the elder in this solo, 'Was duftet doch der Flieder', has given it the name of the 'Flieder Monologue': it develops into an exquisite evocation of the joys of spring.

Eva approaches Sachs's workshop (scene iv) and, in a long, delicately woven exchange, tries to elicit from him the likely winner of the next day's contest. Sachs playfully parries her questions until Magdalene enters to tell her that her father is calling, and that Beckmesser intends to serenade her.

Walther now turns the corner (scene v) and an impassioned duet ensues, based largely on a demonstrative variant of one of the themes from the previous scene. They are at a loss as to how to obviate her father's conditions for obtaining her hand. Walther suggests eloping, but he gets carried away by his loathing of the Masters' pedantry until he is interrupted by the sound of the Nightwatchman's horn: a single blast on an F♯ that launches an exquisite transition to the B major of the Midsummer Magic music. Eva has meanwhile followed Magdalene into the house and now re-emerges, having changed clothes with her. Eva and Walther are about to make their escape when Sachs, who has realized what is afoot, allows his lamp to illuminate the alley they are in. They hesitate and are then pulled up short by the sound of Beckmesser tuning his lute. Walther is for settling his score with the Marker and has to be restrained by Eva: 'What trouble I have with men!', she sighs. She persuades him to sit quietly under the lime tree until Beckmesser has finished his song. But Sachs has other ideas, launching into a noisy, vigorous song of his own ('Jerum! Jerum!'). A simple, ballad-like structure with augmented harmonies spicing the basic B♭ major, Sachs's song is permeated with references to the biblical Eve and to shoemaking that are not entirely lost on the listeners. Beckmesser has less time for the poetic subtleties; seeing what he believes to be the object of his wooing come to the window (in fact Magdalene in Eva's clothes), he begs Sachs to stop his clattering. Reminding him that he had been critical of his workmanship earlier in the day, Sachs suggests that both would make progress if Beckmesser were to serenade while he, Sachs, marked any faults with his cobbler's hammer. (The coloratura of Beckmesser's Serenade 'Den Tag seh' ich erscheinen' is a parody of an old-fashioned bel canto aria. It is also notable for its obvious and stilted rhymes and its grotesque violations of metre and misplaced accents. Clearly Beckmesser provided a target for Wagner's ill-will towards what he perceived as hostile, insensitive critics – not least Eduard Hanslick, whose name was commandeered for the Marker in the 1861 prose drafts – and other reactionary practitioners. But Beckmesser's artistic failings are also precisely those ascribed to the Jews in *Das Judenthum in der Musik*, and it may be argued that the serenade is also a parody of the Jewish cantorial style.)

The commotion caused by Sachs's hammering and Beckmesser's attempts to make himself heard above it brings the populace out on to the streets. A riot ensues (scene vii), during which David, under the impression that Beckmesser is courting Magdalene, cudgels him. The music of the Riot Scene, which takes up the theme of Beckmesser's Serenade, and which contains more than a dozen polyphonic lines, is notoriously difficult to perform; a simplified version, initiated by Toscanini, is used in many houses. At the height of the pandemonium, the Nightwatchman's horn is heard again. Everybody disperses, and by the time he arrives on the scene the streets are empty; he rubs his eyes in disbelief.

ACT 3 Scenes i–iv *Sachs's workshop* The prelude to the third act, familiar as a concert item, opens with a broadly phrased theme on the cellos, taken up contrapuntally by the violas and, in turn, second and first violins; the theme (ex.10) has earlier been heard as a countermelody to Sachs's 'Jerum! Jerum!' in Act 2. The horns and bassoons then intone the solemn chorale that is to become the ode of homage to Sachs sung by the assembled townsfolk at the end of the opera.

Announced by the characteristic semiquavers of the apprentices, David enters the workshop. Sachs, deep in thought, at first ignores him but then asks him to sing the verses he has learnt for the festival of St John, celebrated on midsummer's day. His mind still on the events of the previous evening, David begins his ditty to the tune of Beckmesser's Serenade and has to start again: 'Am Jordan Sankt Johannes stand'. David belatedly realizes that it is also his master's name-day (Hans = Johannes). When the apprentice has left, Sachs resumes his philosophical meditation on the follies of humanity: 'Wahn! Wahn! Überall Wahn!' (The concept of *Wahn*, which includes the notions of illusion, folly and madness, lies at the heart of *Die Meistersinger*: by the 1860s, Wagner had come to believe that all human endeavour was underpinned by illusion and futility, though art, he considered, was a 'noble illusion'.) The 'Wahn Monologue', as it is often known, begins with ex.10; ex.8 is heard as Sachs's thoughts turn to Nuremberg and its normally peaceful customs. The memory of the riot returns, but the agitated quavers are banished by the serene music of the Midsummer Magic. The last part of the Monologue, the dawning of midsummer's day, brings back ex.7.

Ex.10

The end of Sachs's reverie, and the beginning of scene ii, is signified by a modulation with harp arpeggios, rather in the manner of a cinematic 'dissolve'; similar gestures occur later too in connection with dreams and reveries. Walther appears and tells Sachs of a wonderful dream. Sachs urges him to recount it as it may enable him to win the Master's prize. (Wagner had readily become a convert to the Schopenhauerian view that creativity originates in the dream-world.) Walther's resistance to the demands of the Masters is overcome in the name of love, and he embarks on his Morning Dream Song – what is to become the Prize Song: 'Morgenlich leuchtend in rosigem Schein'. He produces one *Stollen* and then, at Sachs's bidding, another similar, followed by an *Abgesang* (ex.5). Under Sachs's instruction, Walther goes on to produce another three stanzas.

The last part of the overall structure (*A–A–A*), each section of which is in *Bar*-form (*A–A–B*), is not supplied until scene iv.

In the third scene, Beckmesser appears alone in the workshop. After his beating the night before, he is limping and stumbling, and prey to nightmarish memories and imaginings. All this is depicted in a 'pantomime' notable for its anarchically progressive musical style. Picking up Walther's freshly penned song, he pockets it on Sachs's re-entry. He adduces it as proof that Sachs means to enter the song contest, but Sachs denies such a plan and offers him the song. Beckmesser's suspicions are eventually allayed, and he delightedly retires in order to memorize the song.

Eva enters (scene iv) and under the cover of a complaint about the shoes Sachs has made for her, she expresses her anxieties about Walther and the coming contest. Sachs affects not to understand, and pretends not to notice Walther's arrival, in spite of Eva's passionate cry and the orchestra's thrilling tonal shift. Walther delivers the final section of his song and Eva, moved to tears, sobs on the shoulder of Sachs, until the latter drags himself away, complaining about the lot of the cobbler. Eva, emotionally torn between the avuncular shoemaker and her younger lover, draws Sachs to her again. Sachs reminds her of the story of Tristan and Isolde and says he has no wish to play the role of King Mark; the themes of the opening of Wagner's *Tristan* and of King Mark are recalled here.

Magdalene and David arrive, and Sachs, with a cuff on his ear, announces David's promotion to journeyman, in time to witness the baptism of 'a child' (the themes of the Masters and of the opening chorale are heard at this point). The progeny turns out to be Walther's new song. The music moves to a plateau of G$^\flat$ major, a tritone from the C major of the surrounding scenes, for Eva's introduction to the celebrated quintet, 'Selig, wie die Sonne'.

ACT 3 Scene v *An open meadow on the Pegnitz* The themes associated with Nuremberg (ex.8) and midsummer's day (ex.7), along with fig. *x* of ex.1, effect a transition to the fifth scene. The townsfolk are all gathered and, to the accompaniment of fanfares on stage, greet the processions of the guilds: first the shoemakers, then the tailors and bakers. A boat brings 'maidens from Fürth' and the apprentices begin dancing with them; David, at first reluctant, is drawn in.

At last the Masters arrive, to the music of the first-act prelude. Sachs is hailed by the populace with the chorale from the third-act prelude to the words with which the historical Sachs greeted Luther and the Reformation: 'Wach auf, es nahet gen den Tag'. Sachs modestly acknowledges the homage and exhorts people and Masters to accord the coming contest and prize their due worth. Beckmesser, who has frantically been trying to memorize Walther's song, is led first to the platform. His rendering of the song, to the tune of his own Serenade, is marked by grotesque misaccentuations and violations of metre, but it is his garbling of the words, producing an absurd, tasteless parody of the original, that provoke a crescendo of hilarity in the audience. He presses on in confusion, but only makes a greater fool of himself. Finally he rushes from the platform, denouncing Sachs as the author.

Sachs refutes that honour and introduces the man who will make sense of it for them. Walther's Prize Song, 'Morgenlich leuchtend in rosigem Schein', compresses his earlier dry run into a single *Bar*-form of three stanzas (*A–A–B*) but with each stanza expanded. In several details, including the heartwarming plunge into B major (from a tonic of C) in the second stanza, Walther's prize-winning entry is a greater infraction of the rules than ever. But the Masters are evidently swept away by Walther's artistic integrity and impassioned delivery, for he is awarded the prize by general consent.

When Pogner proffers the Master's chain to Walther, he impetuously refuses, and Sachs delivers a homily (to exx.1 and ex.3, together with the Prize Song) about the art that the Masters have cultivated and preserved throughout Germany's troubled history: 'Verachtet mir die Meister nicht'. Sachs's address concludes with a celebration of the sovereignty of the German spirit – a theme dear to Wagner's heart in the 1860s; that spirit, it is proposed, can never be exterminated so long as the great German art that sustains it is respected. The salient themes of the opera's prelude, notably ex.4, are recalled for the final choral apostrophe to Sachs and 'holy German art'.

*

On one level, *Die Meistersinger* is a glorious affirmation of humanity and the value of art, as well as a parable about the necessity of tempering the inspiration of genius with the rules of form. The work may also be regarded, however, as the artistic component in Wagner's ideological crusade of the 1860s: a crusade to revive the 'German spirit' and purge it of alien elements, chief among which were the Jews. It can further be argued that anti-Semitism is woven into the ideological fabric of the work and that the representation of Beckmesser carries, at the very least, overtones of anti-Semitic sentiment.

The only comedy among Wagner's mature works, *Die Meistersinger* is a rich, perceptive music drama widely admired for its warm humanity but regarded with suspicion by some for its dark underside. Its genial aspect is immensely enhanced by the technical mastery displayed by Wagner at the height of his powers.

B.M.

Der Ring des Nibelungen
('The Nibelung's Ring')

Bühnenfestpiel ('stage festival play') for three days and a preliminary evening set to Wagner's own libretto. *Der Ring des Nibelungen*
was first performed as a cycle at the Festspielhaus in Bayreuth: *Das
Rheingold*, 13 August 1876; *Die Walküre*, 14 August 1876; *Siegfried*,
16 August 1876; *Götterdämmerung*, 17 August 1876.

The principals in the first three cycles included: Franz Betz (Wotan/
Wanderer), Amalie Materna (Brünnhilde), Georg Unger (Siegfried),
Albert Niemann (Siegmund), Josephine Schefsky (Sieglinde), Karl
Hill (Alberich), Friederike Sadler-Grün (Fricka) and Luise Jaide
(Erda). The conductor was Hans Richter.

Contrary to Wagner's claim that he turned away from historical subjects
on discovering the potentialities of myth for his future music dramas,
myth and history were interwoven in the *Ring* from the beginning. Not
only was he working on his historical drama *Friedrich I*, begun in 1846,
as late as 1848–9, but he was also making speculative connections
between the stories of the Hohenstaufen emperor and the Nibelung
hoard. Those supposed connections were formulated in the essay *Die
Wibelungen: Weltgeschichte aus der Sage*. And although it was previously supposed that *Die Wibelungen* preceded the initial prose résumé
and libretto for what became the *Ring*, it is now considered more likely
that it succeeded them, probably about mid-February 1849.

The chief sources Wagner drew on for the *Ring* are as follows:
the Poetic (or Elder) Edda, the *Völsunga Saga* and the Prose Edda
by Snorri Sturluson (all three of which were compiled in Iceland,
probably in the first half of the 13th century); *Das Nibelungenlied*,
an epic poem written in Middle High German *c*1200; and *Thidreks
Saga af Bern*, a prose narrative written *c*1260–70 in Old Norse.
Wagner also read copiously around the subject and was indebted to
the work of such scholars as Karl Lachmann, Franz Joseph Mone,
Ludwig Ettmüller and the Grimm brothers.

Greek drama was also a major influence, not least in its use of
mythology, its life-affirming idealism and the religious aura sur-

rounding its performance. The *Oresteia* suggested not only the structure of a trilogy (*Das Rheingold* was merely a 'preliminary evening'), but also the confrontations of pairs of characters, the possibility of linking successive episodes with the themes of guilt and a curse, and perhaps even the leitmotif principle (in Aeschylus's use of recurrent imagery). There are also important parallels between the *Ring* and the *Prometheus* trilogy, especially as reconstructed by its German translator, Johann Gustav Droysen.

Wagner outlined a prose résumé for his drama, dated 4 October 1848, which in his collected writings he called *Der Nibelungen-Mythus: als Entwurf zu einem Drama* (the original manuscript is headed *Der Nibelungensage (Mythus)*). In this résumé the drama centres on Siegfried's death, and, at the conclusion, Brünnhilde purges the guilt of the gods by an act of self-immolation, allowing them to reign in glory instead of perishing. The story at this stage largely follows the order familiar from the finished work, but in autumn 1848 Wagner next compiled a libretto for *Siegfrieds Tod*. This created so much back-narration of earlier events, however, that he subsequently, in 1851, wrote *Der junge Siegfried*, and finally *Die Walküre* and *Das Rheingold* (1851–2). Returning to revise *Der junge Siegfried* and *Siegfrieds Tod* in the light of the whole cycle, Wagner replaced Siegfried as the central figure by Wotan, and altered the ending so that the gods and Valhalla are all destroyed by fire. *Der junge Siegfried* and *Siegfrieds Tod* were eventually renamed *Siegfried* and *Götterdämmerung*. Thus the librettos of the constituent parts of the *Ring* cycle were written in reverse order, though the original conception was in the 'correct' order, as was the composition of the music.

After its première the tetralogy was not heard again at Bayreuth until 1896, when it was conducted by Richter, Felix Mottl and Siegfried Wagner. Complete cycles were given in Munich in 1878, Vienna in 1879 and Hamburg in 1880. Following the success of his production in Leipzig in 1878, Angelo Neumann took it on a Europe-wide tour with his travelling theatre, beginning in 1882. The first complete cycle in Britain was given at Her Majesty's, London, in 1882, in German, with Anton Seidl conducting, Emil Scaria as Wotan/Wanderer and Albert Niemann as Siegmund. Not until 1908 was it given in London in English, in uncut performances under the baton of Hans Richter. The first complete cycle in the USA was given at the Metropolitan in 1889, with Lilli Lehmann as Brünnhilde; the conductor was Seidl.

Notable Wotan/Wanderers have included Anton van Rooy, Friedrich Schorr, Rudolf Bockelmann, Hans Hotter, Theo Adam, Donald McIntyre, Norman Bailey, James Morris and John Tomlinson. Brünnhilde has been sung by Lilli Lehmann, Lilian Nordica, Eva Turner, Florence Austral, Frida Leider, Germaine Lubin, Kirsten Flagstad, Astrid Varnay, Brigit Nilsson, Rita Hunter, Gwyneth Jones and Hildegard Behrens. Interpreters of Siegfried have included Jean de Reszke, Lauritz Melchior, Max Lorenz, Wolfgang Windgassen, Jess Thomas, Ludwig Suthaus, Alberto Remedios, René Kollo, Manfred Jung and Siegfried Jerusalem. Siegmund has been sung by Niemann, Set Svanholm, Ramón Vinay, James King, Windgassen, Jon Vickers, Alberto Remedios, Peter Hofmann and Jerusalem. Sieglinde has been sung by Lilli Lehmann, Nordica, Milka Ternina, Maria Jeritza, Lotte Lehmann, Flagstad, Varnay, Leonie Rysanek, Régine Crespin, Jessye Norman, Cheryl Studer and Nadine Secunde. Notable conductors of the *Ring* have included Richter, Mottl, Seidl, Mahler, Arthur Nikisch, Artur Bodanzky, Albert Coates, Bruno Walter, Thomas Beecham, Wilhelm Furtwängler, Georg Solti, Herbert von Karajan, Reginald Goodall, Karl Böhm, Pierre Boulez, Colin Davis, Daniel Barenboim, Bernard Haitink and James Levine.

Interpretations of the *Ring*, both literary and dramaturgical, have ranged from those that explore the work's social and political context to those that focus on its imagery and mythological content, denying any political ramifications. Shaw's classic interpretation of the *Ring* (1898) as a socialist allegory has been hugely influential, as has Donington's radically different analysis of the work in terms of Jungian psychology (1963). Taking their cue perhaps from Shaw, a series of radical stagings in the 1970s and 80s attempted to demythologize the work, emphasizing the corruption and debased moral values by which the gods, and in particular Wotan, are tainted. Recent productions have also dwelt on feminist and ecological aspects of the *Ring*.

B.M.

Das Rheingold
('The Rhinegold')

Vorabend (preliminary evening) of *Der Ring des Nibelungen*, in four scenes, set to Wagner's own libretto; first performed in Munich, at the Königliches Hof- und Nationaltheater, on 22 September 1869. The first performance as part of the Ring cycle, was at Bayreuth's Festspielhaus, on 13 August 1876.

The first Wotan was August Kindermann; Fricka was sung by Sophie Stehle. Loge was Heinrich Vogl; Froh, Franz Nachbauer; Mime, Max Schlosser; and Fafner, Kaspar Bausewein. For the 1876 cast, see *Der Ring des Nibelungen*.

Gods	
Wotan	bass-baritone
Donner	bass-baritone
Froh	tenor
Loge	tenor
Fricka	mezzo-soprano
Freia	soprano
Erda	contralto
Nibelungs	
Alberich	bass-baritone
Mime	tenor
Giants	
Fasolt	bass-baritone
Fafner	bass
Rhinemaidens	
Woglinde	soprano
Wellgunde	soprano
Flosshilde	mezzo-soprano

Nibelungs

The first prose sketch for *Das Rheingold*, at that time conceived in three acts, dates from autumn (probably October) 1851. The sketch

97

was then developed into a prose draft (23–31 March 1852) entitled *Der Raub des Rheingoldes/Vorspiel (oder: das Rheingold)?*. The verse draft was made between 15 September and 3 November 1852 and the final poem was incorporated into the private printing of the entire *Ring* text in February 1853.

According to Wagner's account in *Mein Leben*, the initial musical inspiration for *Rheingold* – rushing arpeggio figures in $E^\flat$ major – came to him as he lay in a trance-like state in an inn at La Spezia. Doubt has been cast on the likelihood of such a 'vision' but it has also been argued that the documentary evidence neither supports nor contradicts Wagner's account. Discounting a handful of musical jottings, the composition of *Rheingold* was begun on 1 November 1853, with the first complete draft, a continuous setting of the poem that occupied him until 14 January 1854. In view of the unprecedented problems of writing for the *Ring*'s expanded forces (including quadruple woodwind), Wagner elaborated the orchestration in a draft of a full score (a procedure he was not to repeat), between 1 February and 28 May 1854. The fair copy of the full score was written out between 15 February and 26 September 1854.

*

Scene i *At the bottom of the Rhine* The simple, protracted $E^\flat$ chords that open the tetralogy do more than depict the depths of the Rhine: they also suggest the birth of the world, the act of creation itself. Eight double basses sound a low octave $E^\flat$, to which is added the $B^\flat$ a 5th higher on bassoons. Eight horns introduce the Nature motif (ex.1), one by one, building up a complex polyphonic texture. The motion is increased by first flowing quavers and then rushing semiquavers, both rising through the strings from the cellos. The curtain rises towards the end of this orchestral introduction – 136 bars of unadulterated $E^\flat$ – to reveal the three Rhinemaidens swimming in the water. Maintaining the $E^\flat$ harmony, but now with pentatonic colouring, the sisters enunciate the first lines of text: an alliterating assemblage of primitive-sounding syllables chosen for aural effect rather than linguistic sense, 'Weia! Waga!'. The falling-tone motif, heard again a little later in the ensemble cry of the Rhinemaidens (ex.2), is one of the most frequently recurring motifs, in its many different forms, in the cycle. Flosshilde chides her sisters for failing to watch over the 'sleeping gold'.

Ex.1

Ex.2

Rhein - gold!

From a dark chasm lower down emerges the hunchbacked dwarf Alberich, his crabbed nature and ungainly movements suggested by stabbing semiquavers accented off the beat and by acciaccaturas. The Rhinemaidens decide to reward his lubricious advances by teaching him a lesson. Woglinde leads him on, and his slithering on the rocks and sneezing are graphically portrayed in the music (accented demisemiquaver slides and more acciaccaturas). Both Woglinde and Wellgunde in turn elude him. Flosshilde too seems to offer him love and consolation (against a harmonic background redolent of a traditional love scene), but she also turns out to be mocking him. Alberich's cry of rage and misery (ex.3) turns the Rhinemaidens' motif (ex.2) from major to minor, the form in which it is to make by far the greater number of appearances.

Ex.3

We - he!   ach   we - he!
['Woe! oh woe!']

Failing in a last desperate bid to seize hold of the Rhinemaidens, Alberich sees a bright light illuminating the large rock in the centre. Against a background of shimmering strings, the announcement of the Gold motif (perhaps symbolically a brass fanfare) anticipates the Rhinemaidens' joyous hymn to the treasure they guard. To a motif in 3rds tracing the outline of an ellipsis, known as the Ring or World Inheritance motif, Wellgunde tells that a ring conferring limitless power can be fashioned from the Rhinegold. Only he who forswears the power of love can fashion the ring, adds Woglinde, to the solemn Renunciation of Love motif – in which case they have nothing to fear from the lascivious dwarf. But as they watch, Alberich climbs to the top of the central rock, declares his curse on love, and wrests the gold away with terrible force. He scrambles away with it, deaf to the lamenting cries of the Rhinemaidens.

This primeval first scene lies outside the time zone of the main action, just as it lies outside its tonal structure: the chief tonality of *Rheingold* can be seen as D^b (the beginning of scene ii and end of scene iv, as of the *Ring* as a whole). Thus the formal structure of *Rheingold* (three scenes and a prologue) replicates that of *Götterdämmerung* and of the entire *Ring*.

Scene ii   *An open space on a mountain height, near the Rhine*   A pair of horns take over the Ring motif, elongating it into something more noble and visionary; this is the transition into the second scene, where Wotan and Fricka are lying asleep on a mountain height. The vision is that of Valhalla, Wotan's newly built fortress, and its grand motif is given out by a chorus of brass instruments, including the Wagner tubas. Fricka, waking first, rouses her husband, who sings a paean to the completed work: 'Vollendet das ewige Werk!' Fricka reminds him that it was her sister, Freia, the goddess of love, who was rashly offered to the giants in payment for the work. Wotan brushes aside her fears. She chides him for trading love and the virtues of woman (echoes of the Renunciation of Love motif) in exchange for power and dominion. Reminding her that he once pledged his only remaining eye to court her (a pledge he was not called upon to fulfil), Wotan says that he never intended to give up Freia.

Even as he speaks, Freia enters in terrified haste, followed closely by the giants Fasolt and Fafner. The second part of the accompanying motif (*x* of ex.4), for long mislabelled that of Flight, has been described as Wagner's 'basic love-motive', a theme central not only to the *Ring* but to all his works. When Wotan refuses to hand over Freia as payment, Fasolt indignantly reminds Wotan that the runes on his spear symbolize his contractual agreements and it is they that legitimize his power. This exchange is punctuated by the measured, stepwise-descending motif (ex.5) that represents Wotan's spear, his authority and the bargains he has struck. Fasolt's eloquent music alternates between anger at Wotan's behaviour and the tenderness he feels towards Freia. Fafner is interested in Freia only as a possible ransom: he knows that without her youth-perpetuating apples the gods will wither and die.

As the giants prepare to take Freia away, her brothers Froh and Donner (the god of thunder) rush in to protect her. Wotan prevents Donner from exercising force and is relieved to see Loge arrive at last. The flickering chromatic semiquavers that accompany him remind us that he is the god of fire; his motif, artfully combining both the falling tone and semitone, hints at his moral ambivalence (ex.6). Pressed by Wotan, Loge relates how he has circled the world to find out what men hold dearer than the virtues of womankind ('So weit Leben und Weben'). His account begins like a conventional aria in D major, but as he tells of Alberich's capture of the gold, the motifs of the Rhinemaidens and their treasure become coloured by minor tonalities. As Loge repeats the Rhinemaidens' plea for the gold to be returned to the water, the same motifs are heard in their original bright C major.

Loge's explanation of the power of the ring forged from the gold sets everybody thinking. Wotan determines to acquire it and Fafner demands that it then be handed over in payment. The giants trudge away, dragging behind Freia as hostage. A mist descends on the gods who, denied Freia's golden apples, begin to wilt; a sense of suspended animation is created by muted tremolando strings and a slow tempo. Wotan, accompanied by Loge, descends through a sulphur cleft in pursuit of the gold. A masterly transition passage for orchestra depicts the descent to Nibelheim. Ex.5 alternates with the motif of the Renunciation of Love. As the tempo quickens, the falling semitone (ex.4) suggests the proximity of greed, evil and servitude, while an obsessively repeated perversion of the Love motif (ex.3) warns of the dangerous forces unleashed in Alberich by sexual frustration. B$^\flat$ minor gradually emerges through the sulphurous mists as the primary key, which is then reinforced by a symphonic working of the motifs associated with the Nibelungs and servitude. Eighteen anvils behind the scenes thunder out the dotted rhythm of the Nibelungs' motif. The F they sound is not an arbitrary note, but part of a gigantic dominant preparation for the Nibelheim scene.

Scene iii *The subterranean caverns of Nibelheim* B$^\flat$ minor is to dominate this scene, as it does others featuring the Nibelungs later in the *Ring*. In the depths of Nibelheim, Alberich is tormenting his weaker brother Mime, and demands the magic Tarnhelm that he has forced him to make. The Tarnhelm (represented by a mysterious-sounding motif on muted horns) renders its wearer invisible, and Alberich proves its efficacy by disappearing and raining blows on the defenceless Mime. Alberich eventually leaves, and Wotan and Loge arrive. Loge, offering to help Mime, hears from him (against a background of first the Ring and then the motif of the Nibelungs, with the falling semitone now identified with servitude) how the carefree race of Nibelung blacksmiths has been held in thrall by Alberich since he forged a ring from the Rhinegold.

Alberich returns, driving his slaves with whiplashes to pile up the gold. He brandishes the ring, in a climactic eight-bar passage of immensely compressed power, and they scatter in all directions. Alberich now turns his attention to the strangers. Scornfully dismissing Loge's reminders of their earlier friendship, Alberich boasts about his newfound power and threatens one day to vanquish the gods and force his favours on their women. The threat is made in a stark recitative-like passage following a striking appropriation by Alberich of the sumptuous Valhalla music. Loge pretends to flatter him, but asks how, mighty as he is, he would protect himself against a thief in the night. Alberich shows him the Tarnhelm and Loge asks for a demonstration. To a coiling serpentine theme Alberich turns himself into a dragon. Loge feigns terror and goads Alberich into turning himself into something small like a toad. Alberich duly obliges and is trapped by the gods. Each of Alberich's transformations switches the tonality briefly to G$\sharp$ minor (the key associated with the Tarnhelm) within a broader context of A major. The latter is the closest the tonally unstable Loge comes to having a key; the chief tonality of the scene remains B$\flat$, that of the Nibelungs. Wotan and Loge tie Alberich and drag him to the surface to the accompaniment of another transition passage in which many prominent motifs are subjected to symphonic development.

Scene iv *An open space on a mountain height, near the Rhine* Wotan and Loge deride Alberich's pretensions to world domination: if he wants to be free, they tell him, he will have to give up the gold. Intending to keep the ring to generate more gold, Alberich agrees to hand over the treasure. His right hand is untied – a series of demisemiquaver slides illustrate the rope slipping away – and he summons the Nibelungs with the ring. To the obsessive accompaniment of their dotted figure, the Nibelungs drag in the gold; the continually repeated falling semitone alludes both to the servitude of the Nibelungs and to Alberich's fuming disgrace at being seen in captivity by his slaves. Loge adds the Tarnhelm to the pile of gold, and to Alberich's horror, Wotan demands the ring on his finger too. It is eventually wrested from him by force, at which Alberich delivers, against a single, sinister drum roll, his fateful curse, 'Wie durch Fluch er mir geriet': the ring will bring anxiety and death to whoever owns it; those who possess it will be racked with torment, those who do not will be consumed with envy.

Alberich vanishes, the atmosphere clears and, to the sound of divided violins soaring and descending together, it gets lighter. Donner, Froh and Fricka welcome back Wotan and Loge, who show them Freia's ransom: the pile of gold. Freia returns with the giants, but Fasolt, reluctant to relinquish her, insists that the gold be stacked so as to hide her from sight. Loge and Froh pile up the treasure, filling all the gaps. But Fafner can still see Freia's hair: the Tarnhelm has to be thrown on the heap. Fasolt too can see her shining eyes through a chink, and Fafner demands that the ring on Wotan's finger be used to stop the gap. The Rhinemaidens' falling tone (ex.2) is heard as Loge suggests that Wotan will be returning the ring to them. But Wotan refuses to yield the ring, remaining impervious both to the giants, who threaten to take away Freia again, and to the other gods, who beg him to relent. Finally Erda, the earth goddess, appears in a blue light from a rocky cleft. Her motif (ex.7), intoned initially on bassoons and Wagner tubas, is a minor variant of the Nature motif (ex.1). The new tonal area (C♯ minor), slow tempo and sombre colouring of the Erda scene mark it out as one of considerable individuality and importance: 'Weiche, Wotan! weiche!'. Erda warns Wotan that possession of the ring condemns him to irredeemable dark perdition. A dark day is dawning for the gods: he should yield up the ring. The prophecy evokes an inversion of Erda's theme, the descending form being known as the Twilight of the Gods (ex.8).

Erda disappears from sight and Wotan decides to heed her advice. He tosses the ring on the pile, but the joyfully expansive phrases greeting Freia's release give way to nagging figures of worry and greed as Fasolt and Fafner bicker over the treasure and Fafner kills his brother. This passage also effects a large-scale modulation to B minor, for the sole purpose of allowing the Curse motif to ring out in its original tonality, on a trio of trombones, at the killing. Thus the tonality of a single motif sometimes determines the key of an entire structural unit. A proliferation of motifs – associated with the curse, the Nibelungs, the ring and Erda – conveys Wotan's agitation.

The gods prepare to enter the fortress. Donner swings his hammer to gather the mists ('Heda! Hedo!'), with brass fanfares over an exhilarating background of swirling string arpeggios. There is thunder and lightning; the clouds lift and a rainbow bridge is visible, stretching across the valley to the fortress. Yet more shimmering effects on strings and winds accompany the theme of the Rainbow Bridge (a radiant transformation of the Nature motif). Wotan greets Valhalla, as a motif later to be associated with the sword rings out on a trumpet. The gods walk in procession to the bridge, though Loge looks on nonchalantly. The wail of the Rhinemaidens, lamenting their lost gold, rises poignantly out of the valley. Wotan ignores it and as the curtain falls he leads the gods over the bridge to the triumphant strains of the Valhalla motif. The dramatic situation suggests that the triumph will be a hollow one, but there are few intimations of that in the blaze of $D^\flat$ major with which the work ends.

*

Das Rheingold, the first dramatic work to be written according to the theoretical principles laid down in *Oper und Drama* (1850–51), also represents the most rigorous application of those principles – an extreme position which Wagner subsequently modified. If melodic distinction is occasionally sacrificed in the process, there are nevertheless many memorable and accomplished passages in the work, both involving word-setting (Loge's narration in scene ii, for example) and in purely orchestral writing (notably the transitions between scenes ii and iii, and iii and iv). Though described as a 'preliminary evening' to the *Ring* tetralogy, *Das Rheingold* is a substantial work in its own right, with characteristics not shared by other works in the cycle.

B.M.

Die Walküre
('The Valkyrie')

First day of *Der Ring des Nibelungen* in three acts set to Wagner's own libretto; first performed in Munich, at the Königliches Hof- und Nationaltheater, on 26 June 1870.

The first Wotan was, as in *Das Rheingold*, August Kindermann; the first Brünnhilde, Sophie Stehle (Fricka in *Rheingold*). Siegmund and Sieglinde were sung by Heinrich and Therese Vogl. For the 1876 cast, see *Der Ring des Nibelungen*.

Siegmund	tenor
Hunding	bass
Wotan	bass-baritone
Sieglinde	soprano
Brünnhilde	soprano
Fricka	mezzo-soprano
Helmwige	
Gerhilde	
Ortlinde	
Waltraute	
Schwertleite *Valkyries*	sopranos and contraltos
Siegrune	
Grimgerde	
Rossweisse	

The first prose sketch for *Die Walküre* dates from autumn (probably November) 1851. In a letter to Uhlig of 11 November 1851 Wagner referred to the new work as *Siegmund und Sieglind: der Walküre Bestrafung*, but by 20 November (letter to Liszt) he had renamed it with the familiar title *Die Walküre*. The sketch was developed into a prose draft (17–26 May 1852) and then into a verse draft (1 June–1 July 1852). The final poem was incorporated into the private printing of the entire *Ring* text in February 1853.

The first musical sketches for *Die Walküre* date from the summer of 1852 and include an early version of the Spring Song. The first complete draft was made between 28 June and 27 December 1854. Unlike the comparable draft for *Das Rheingold*, which for the most part consisted of one vocal staff and one instrumental, that for *Walküre* shows some degree of orchestral elaboration, often with one vocal staff and two instrumental. In spite of the difficulties he experienced – on account of many delays and interruptions – in expanding that first draft into score, Wagner did not find it necessary to make a second draft as for *Rheingold* since he was now familiar with the expanded orchestral forces. Instead he went straight into a draft of the full score (January 1855–20 March 1856); the fair copy was made in parallel between 14 July 1855 and 23 March 1856.

*

ACT 1 *Inside Hunding's dwelling* The turbulent prelude that opens the work depicts at once a raging storm and the mental convulsions that are soon to shake the participants in the drama. A tremolo on a single repeated note is maintained by the second violins and violas for 60 bars, while underneath cellos and double basses rampage up and down a series of notes clearly intended to recall the motif of the spear: that symbol of Wotan's power and authority is evoked because this entire act is contrived, in a sense, at the instigation of his will. The motif sung by Donner, the god of thunder, at the end of *Rheingold* to the words 'Heda! Hedo!' rings out on the brass, first on the Wagner tubas. Despite the different harmonic context it begins in B$^\flat$, exactly as in *Rheingold*; however, it is winched up sequentially through a series of modulations until the tension breaks in a thunderclap, after which the storm begins to subside.

As the curtain rises and Siegmund, collapsing with exhaustion, bursts into the forest dwelling, a cello takes up the Spear motif but turns its end accommodatingly back on itself (ex.1): a hint that an alternative to sheer naked power is being proposed. Sieglinde enters, and as she bends over Siegmund's sleeping figure that idea is taken up again in conjunction with a phrase expressive of her tenderness (ex.2). The two melodic ideas are worked to a small climax as Sieglinde fetches him water. Then ex.1 opens out into a fully-fledged

107

Love theme, ex.3 (derived from Freia's theme in *Rheingold*), the music as yet anticipating events on the stage.

Sieglinde now fetches a horn of mead for Siegmund, to the accompaniment of an effusively lyrical passage in A major, bassoons, horns and clarinets lending a bloom to the strings. The pair gaze at each other in unspoken affirmation of love, the two halves of the Love motif sounding in reverse order. The minor triad of the motif (ex.4) for the Volsungs (the children of Wälse or Wolfe) evokes the ill luck that dogs Siegmund; the motif is combined with ex.2 as he decides to stay and await his fate.

The arrival of Hunding (scene ii) is heralded by a sharp, abrupt motif on the Wagner tubas. He roughly extends his hospitality and asks where Siegmund has come from and what is his name. Siegmund says he should be called Woeful, describing how one day he returned from hunting with his father, Wolfe, to find their home burnt down, his mother murdered and his twin sister brutally abducted. At Sieglinde's prompting he then narrates how he went to the aid of a young woman forced into a loveless marriage, killing her savage kinsmen in the fight. Hunding now realizes that he is harbouring his kinsmen's foe. The laws of hospitality compel him to give Siegmund shelter for the night, but in the morning he will have to fight for his life.

As she prepares Hunding's night drink, Sieglinde drugs it. She leaves the room with a lingering gaze, first at Siegmund and then at a spot in the trunk of the ash tree that stands in the middle of the hut: the Sword motif sounds presciently on the bass trumpet.

In the third scene Siegmund, left alone, meditates on the fever of excitement stirred up by Sieglinde and on his weaponless plight, recalling that his father had promised that there would be a sword for him in his time of need ('Ein Schwert verhiess mir der Vater'). He calls on his father: 'Wälse! Wälse!' (the octave leaps of the Sword motif without the tail-piece are traditionally regarded, by singers and listeners alike, as a test of virility). They launch Siegmund on a heart-warming soliloquy, richly orchestrated, the rippling harp arpeggios mirroring the gleaming of the sword in the ash tree.

Sieglinde enters. She tells how an old man dressed in grey had thrust the sword into the tree at the wedding ceremony of herself and Hunding. This narration, 'Der Männer Sippe sass hier im Saal', is a choice example of the musico-poetic synthesis – the practical application of Wagner's principles of word-setting – that finds its most consistent expression in *Die Walküre*. Particularly noteworthy are the low-lying vocal line depicting the old man's low-brimmed hat, the shape of the melodic line portraying the flash of his eye and then its 'threatening glance', the falling chromatic intervals for his lingering look of yearning, the expressive appoggiatura on 'Tränen' ('tears') and the final rise to a top G for the physical act of implanting the sword in the tree. The sounding of the Valhalla motif by horns and bassoons, announcing the real identity of the stranger, is one of the classic uses of leitmotif to comment on the action.

With startling suddenness the door of the hut flies open, letting in the spring night (and solving the problem of how the two will escape). Their duet, true to Wagner's theoretical principles, does not allow the couple to sing together. Even Siegmund's Spring Song, 'Winterstürme wichen dem Wonnemond', celebrated as a tenor song extracted from its context, is not as conventional as at first appears.

It begins like a ternary aria, but after only nine bars of the middle section the continuation of the Love motif bursts in and disrupts the form. Incomplete and hybrid structures of this kind are typical in Wagner's music dramas. Siegmund speaks of Spring and Love as brother and sister, to which Sieglinde replies that he is the spring for whom she has so longed. The remainder of the act is an ecstatic declaration of their love, with an unashamed acknowledgment that they are also brother and sister. He admits that Woeful is no longer an appropriate name and Sieglinde renames him Siegmund ('guardian of victory'). To her delight he pulls the sword out of the tree, naming it 'Nothung' ('Needful'). They embrace rapturously and the curtain falls with decorous swiftness.

ACT 2 *A wild, rocky, mountain ridge* The music of the prelude anticipates the Ride of the Valkyries in the third act; its vitality is generated by dotted rhythms in 9/8 time, and augmented 5ths heighten the tension. Wotan instructs his daughter Brünnhilde, the Valkyrie of the title, to ensure that Siegmund wins the ensuing battle with Hunding. She revels in the Valkyrie battle cry, but warns Wotan that he has another battle on hand: his wife Fricka is furiously approaching, in a ram-drawn chariot. Brünnhilde disappears as Fricka, angrily but with dignity, tells how, as guardian of wedlock, she has been appealed to by Hunding to punish the adulterous Volsung pair. To her complaint that they have flouted the vows of marriage Wotan replies that he has no respect for vows that compel union without love. Fricka turns her attack to the twins' incest, but Wotan's reply, to the tender accompaniment of the Spring Song and Love themes, indicates that not even this breach of conventional morality shocks him. Fricka continues her indignant protest in an arioso passage in G♯ minor, in which the stock of leitmotifs momentarily gives way to new and distinctive melodic material. At first glance a reversion to an old-style form, 'O, was klag' ich um Ehe und Eid' in fact displays considerable subtlety in its variety of pace and irregular phrase-lengths.

Fricka complains that Wotan has brought disgrace on the gods by fathering these incestuous twins on a mortal woman. He replies that the gods need a hero free from their protection, who will be able to do the deed they are prevented from doing: restore the ring to its owners and thereby institute a new world order. But Fricka devastatingly exposes the flaw in the guilty god's argument: Siegmund is not able to act as a free hero so long as he is protected by Wotan. As Wotan thrashes about in despair without a moral leg to stand on, much use is made of a motif (ex.5) labelled 'Dejection' by Ernest Newman but whose contorted melodic shape and kinship to the Spear motif suggest something more specific: the frustration of Wotan's will. Fricka extracts from him an oath that he will no longer protect his son.

Ex.5

In scene ii Wotan continues to writhe in mental agony (ex.5) and Brünnhilde reappears to receive the full brunt of his outburst of grief and frustration, 'O heilige Schmach!' A powerful climax is generated by the dissonant piling up of motifs, initiated by a new one that is primarily an inversion of ex.5, though also related to that of Wotan's authority (the Spear motif). The notes to which Wotan sings of his endless rage and grief ('Endloser Grimm! Ewiger Gram!') are in fact those of the Love motif (ex.3), a poignant reminder that it is lack of love that is the cause of his troubles.

The ensuing long narration of Wotan, 'Als junger Liebe Lust mir verblich', is a key passage in the work, and one intended not only for the information of Brünnhilde, or even of the audience, but as an act of self-revelation, in which we see Wotan in a new light. He begins by confessing how he attempted to fill the vacuum of lovelessness in his life by acquiring power. His hushed reliving of the story is the closest thing in the whole work to pure recitative, but it is by no means oblivious to Wagner's stated principles of wordsetting and in any case it acquires a special aura of suspense from the accompaniment – double basses alone, *pianissimo*. The characteristic motifs appear as Wotan recalls Alberich's forging of the ring, the building of Valhalla and Erda's prophecy, how in the quest for freedom he sought out Erda again and fathered Brünnhilde on her. The prominence of ex.5 attests to Wotan's sense of frustration, and the motifs of the Curse and the Sword drive the narration to a tremendous climax: he now longs for only one thing – 'das Ende'. He instructs Brünnhilde to protect not Siegmund in the coming battle but Hunding. Aware that his heart is not in this command she tries to change his mind, but he is implacable.

The third scene opens with an orchestral interlude making a symphonic development out of agitated repetitions of the Love motif. Siegmund and Sieglinde enter breathlessly. She, tormented by guilt, begs him to abandon her, but he merely vows to avenge the wrong done her by killing Hunding. Horns are heard echoing round the forest, and Sieglinde, feverishly imagining Hunding's dogs tearing at Siegmund's flesh, falls into a faint.

There follows another scene of key significance in the cycle: the Todesverkündigung (Annunciation of Death). Brünnhilde appears, announcing to Siegmund that he must follow her to Valhalla. The Wagner tubas intone a solemn motif whose interrogatory melodic shape and unresolved dominant 7th have generally earned it a label such as 'Destiny' or 'Fate' (ex.6). It is heard throughout the scene, as is a four-bar theme whose latter half corresponds with it (ex.7). Three distinct brass groupings are used to conjure a mood of quiet, noble heroism: Wagner tubas, trumpets and trombones, horns with bassoons. When Siegmund hears that he cannot take his sister-bride with him to Valhalla, he determines not to go. Brünnhilde tells him that his fate is unalterable but, distressed by his evident devotion to Sieglinde and his threat to kill her rather than be separated, she finally relents and promises to protect him, in defiance of Wotan's command.

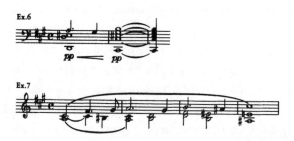

PLATE 1

Design by Carl Emil Doepler for a lantern slide for the first complete *Ring* cycle at Bayreuth, 1876, of the *Ride of the Valkyries* [Nationalarchiv der Richard-Wagner-Stiftung, Richard-Wagner-Gedenkstätte]

PLATE 2

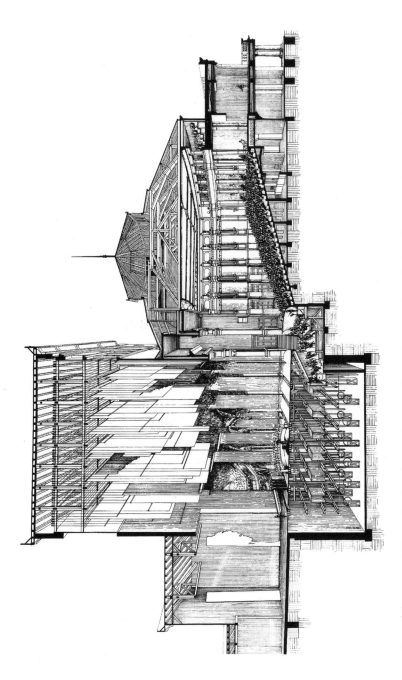

Cross section of the stage at Bayreuth showing various positions of the platform in *Die Walküre* in the 1983 production of the *Ring* cycle
[Bayreuther Festspiel]

PLATE 3

Backstage view of the dragon in *Siegfried* in the first Paris production (Opéra, 1902): from the *Scientific American* (29 March 1902), supplement 1369

PLATE 4

The Holy Communion enacted during the Grail scene at the end of Act 3 of *Parsifal*: Paul von Joukowsky's design for the original production at the Festspielhaus, Bayreuth, in 1882 [Nationalarchiv der Richard-Wagner-Stiftung, Richard-Wagner-Gedenkstätte]

PLATE 5

Scene from *Das Rheingold* at the Metropolitan Opera, New York, 1988, with sets designed by Günther Schneider-Siemssen [Metropolitan Opera Association Inc./Lincoln Center, New York (photo Winnie Klotz)]

PLATE 6

Design for Brünnhilde in *Die Walküre*, illustrating the influence of contemporary fashion: Amalie Materna in the original production of the complete *Ring* cycle, Bayreuth, 1876, with costumes designed by Carl Emil Doepler. The winged helmet and chain mail had been suggested by Wagner. Her silhouette and draped skirt with a train were fashionable in 1876 [Nationalarchiv der Richard-Wagner-Stiftung, Richard-Wagner-Gedenkstätte]

PLATE 7

Walther's Prize Song from *Die Meistersinger*, Act 3: Wagner's second complete draft or 'orchestral sketch' of between 8 October 1866 and 5 March 1867 [Nationalarchiv der Richard-Wagner-Stiftung, Richard-Wagner-Gedenkstätte]

PLATE 8

Richard Wagner: photograph taken in Vienna during the winter of 1862–63
[Bildarchiv, Osterreichische Nationalbibliothek]

Siegmund bends affectionately over the sleeping Sieglinde (scene v). Hunding's horn is heard, and in the ensuing fight Brünnhilde attempts to protect Siegmund with her shield, only for Wotan to appear and shatter Siegmund's sword with his spear. Hunding kills Siegmund, but is himself despatched by Wotan with a contemptuous wave of his hand. Wotan, enraged, then sets off in pursuit of the disobedient Brünnhilde.

ACT 3 *On the summit of a rocky mountain* In the Ride of the Valkyries that opens Act 3, the war-maidens gather, collecting heroes for Valhalla. Although hackneyed, the piece has much to recommend it, especially when sung and staged. The scoring illustrates a characteristic device of Wagner's: a brass theme in unison cutting across a dense texture, in this case of trilling, antiphonal woodwind and swirling string arpeggios. The Valkyries notice that Brünnhilde is missing; eventually she is sighted carrying on her saddle not a hero but a woman. They fearfully refuse to protect her from the fury of Wotan. Sieglinde longs to die, but on being told that a Volsung stirs in her womb, she implores Brünnhilde to protect her. She is urged to make her escape to the forest in the east and is given the fragments of Siegmund's sword from which one day his son will forge a new weapon. This announcement is made with an expansive theme (later to be associated with Siegfried's heroism) whose intrepid ring prompts Sieglinde to react with the work's most enraptured melodic inspiration, 'O hehrstes Wunder!' (ex.8). The motif returns at the end of the cycle, where Wagner referred to it as 'the glorification of Brünnhilde'.

Ex.8

O hehr - - stes Wun - der!

Herr - - li - che Maid!
['Sublimest of wonders! Glorious woman!']

Wotan storms in (scene ii) and the Valkyries in vain try to shield Brünnhilde. She is told that she can no longer be a Valkyrie, and that she is to be confined in sleep on the mountain-top, a prey to the first man to find her. The Valkyries, horror-struck, protest in eight-part counterpoint, but under threat of the same punishment if they interfere, they separate and scatter.

Left alone with Wotan (scene iii), Brünnhilde begs for mercy ('War es so schmählich'); she asks whether it was so shameful if, though contravening Wotan's orders, she was in fact carrying out his inward wishes. The theme she uses is derived from that of the Spear, the symbol of Wotan's authority, but its severity is turned, by octave displacement, into an eloquent melody (ex.9). She recounts how the Volsung touched her heart, and a new melody, similarly derived from the Spear motif, blossoms forth in a transported E major: Brünnhilde's compassionate love thus stands opposed to Wotan's tyrannical wielding of power, but also, in motivic terms, grows organically out of it.

Brünnhilde pleads that at least she be spared the disgrace of an ignoble union: let her be surrounded by a circle of fire that will deter all but the bravest of heroes. Deeply moved, Wotan embraces Brünnhilde and, laying her down on a rock, he kisses her shining eyes closed. Throughout the unfolding of this scene more and more motifs are recalled from the past as emotionally charged memories are brought to the surface. Two new motifs remain to be mentioned: that of the Magic Sleep, evoked by a sinking semitonal melodic line and trance-like mediant progressions, and ex.10, which is heard in an ominous minor key as Brünnhilde dreads being woken by a coward, but which in its major form acquires a luminous, hypnotic quality in the closing pages of the score.

The last part of this scene is a succession of carefully controlled climaxes, none of which is more affecting than that following Wotan's grief-stricken farewells to Brünnhilde: 'Leb' wohl'. Finally the god summons Loge and points with his spear to where he should blaze round the rock. The sea of fire that spreads to enclose the whole mountain in flames is depicted by a richly orchestrated texture created from the themes of Loge and others. Wotan sorrowfully departs.

*

Die Walküre is the music drama that most satisfactorily embodies the theoretical principles Wagner set out in his essay *Oper und Drama*. A thoroughgoing synthesis of poetry and music is achieved without any notable sacrifice in musical expression. Indeed, many of the most powerful passages of the work achieve their effect precisely through the organic relationship of music and text. *Die Walküre* is generally regarded as the most approachable of the *Ring* operas and it has certainly proved the most susceptible to performance in extracts.

B.M.

Siegfried

Second day of *Der Ring des Nibelungen* in three acts set to Wagner's own libretto; first performed at Bayreuth, in the Festspielhaus, on 16 August 1876.

For the original cast see *Der Ring des Nibelungen*.

Siegfried	tenor
Mime	tenor
The Wanderer	bass-baritone
Alberich	bass-baritone
Fafner	bass
Erda	contralto
Brünnhilde	soprano
Woodbird	soprano†

† originally 'boy's voice'

The first sketches for *Jung-Siegfried* (the opera's original title, subsequently changed to *Der junge Siegfried*) date probably from 3–24 May 1851. The prose draft followed between 24 May and 1 June, and two days later Wagner began the versification, ending at midday on 24 June. Following the writing of the poems for *Die Walküre* and *Das Rheingold*, Wagner subjected his texts for *Der junge Siegfried* and *Siegfrieds Tod* (later *Götterdämmerung*) to revision (Nov–Dec 1852). The final poem was incorporated into the private printing of the entire *Ring* text in February 1853. *Der junge Siegfried* and *Siegfrieds Tod* were definitively named *Siegfried* and *Götterdämmerung* in 1856.

Some preliminary musical sketches were made for *Der junge Siegfried* in 1851, but the composition proper was begun in 1856 (probably early September) with the first complete draft. To avoid the problems he had experienced with *Die Walküre*, Wagner took each act through from first draft to score before embarking on the next. He also worked in tandem between the first complete draft (in pencil) and the second (in ink, on at least three staves – two instrumental and

116

one vocal – elaborating details of the orchestral texture). In June 1857 he broke off work on the drafts, with Siegfried resting under the linden tree (Act 2), partly because the *Ring* was becoming a drain on his financial resources, partly because he wished to try out his increasingly chromatic style on the subject of Tristan. Nevertheless, he briefly took up again the composition of Act 2 shortly after, finishing the first complete draft on 30 July 1857 and the second on 9 August. Not until 27 September 1864 was the task of making a fair copy of the score of Act 1 resumed and between 22 December of that year and 2 December 1865 the scoring of Act 2 was undertaken. Work on Act 3 began on 1 March 1869, after the fair copy of the Act 1 and 2 scores had been finished. The scoring of the whole work was completed on 5 February 1871.

*

ACT 1   *A cave in the rocks in the forest*   Opening with a subdued drum roll and a pair of brooding bassoons, the prelude sets the scene in the dark forest, where the dragon Fafner has his lair, at the same time alluding to the crafty scheming of the dwarf Mime. The contrabass tuba joins in with a motif associated (in *Das Rheingold*) with the hoard and then the dotted Nibelungs' motif is introduced as an ostinato accompaniment to it. The tempo becomes more animated and the motifs of the Ring and Sword are heard, the latter on the bass trumpet in its familiar key of C major, though without disturbing the Nibelungs' tonality of $B^\flat$ minor in which the prelude as a whole is set. The curtain rises on Mime hammering away at an anvil (to the rhythm of the Nibelungs' motif), cursing his wearisome labour and his hopeless attempts to forge a sword that the boy Siegfried will be unable to break in two. The giant Fafner has transformed himself into a fierce dragon, Mime tells us (a Dragon motif growls low on tubas), the better to guard the Nibelung treasure. If only he, Mime, could forge together the fragments of Nothung, the sword of Siegfried's father, Siegmund, the boy might kill the dragon with it and the ring would come to Mime.

Siegfried enters to the exuberant strains of his motif (ex.1). He is leading in a huge bear and he laughs all the way to a top C as it chases Mime round the cave. He demands to see Mime's work but on testing it (to the strains of another motif to be associated with his heroism, ex.2), he scornfully smashes it on the anvil; he berates Mime to yet another motif (ex.3). His annoyance with the prattling dwarf is hardly diminished when Mime tells him (to a modified form of the Nibelungs' motif, ex.4) that he should show more gratitude to his guardian. He knocks the proffered meat and soup out of Mime's hands, whereupon the latter embarks upon what Siegfried later calls his 'starling song', 'Als zullendes Kind', telling Siegfried how Mime has nurtured him: one of the several self-contained song forms incorporated into the structure of this act. Siegfried's response, a litany of loathing (exx.3 and 4), inspires only a further attempt at ingratiation, the lyrically tender ex.5. If Mime is his father, Siegfried asks, where is his mother? He forcefully extracts the whole story from Mime, to reminiscences of the themes of the Volsungs and their love. Hearing about the fragments of Nothung, Siegfried excitedly instructs Mime to reforge the sword and rushes off into the forest, leaving Mime sitting dejectedly at the anvil.

The Wanderer (Wotan in disguise) appears and asks for hospitality (scene ii): 'Heil dir, weiser Schmied!'. The textural and motivic contrast between his music, with its noble tread, and Mime's forms the Riddle Scene, as it is sometimes called. The Wanderer stakes his head on answering correctly three questions. Mime asks the name of the races that live in the earth, on the face of the earth and in the cloudy heights. The Nibelungs, the giants and the gods ruled by Wotan, come the answers, duly illustrated with the appropriate motifs, often in their original tonality. To Mime's horror, the Wanderer then demands the same in exchange. His first question concerns the tribe treated harshly by Wotan though dearest to him. The Volsungs, replies Mime confidently. As to the name of the sword to be wielded by the hero Siegfried, he correctly replies Nothung. But when asked who will forge the sword, Mime jumps up in alarm: he has no idea. The answer, the Wanderer tells him against the growls of the Dragon motif, is 'one who has never known fear'. He leaves Mime's head forfeit to the fearless one and departs.

The orchestra paints a dazzling picture of flickering lights and roaring flames as the terrified Mime imagines the dragon looming in the forest (scene iii). Siegfried returns and Mime determines to teach him fear (tremolo strings), but Siegfried's curiosity is only whetted. Mime looks on aghast as Siegfried begins to forge the fragments of the sword himself, to the accompaniment of a transformation of ex.1, its vigour enhanced by augmented triad colouring. On being told the name of the sword, Nothung, Siegfried launches his Forging Song with it: 'Nothung! Nothung! Neidliches Schwert!' This song, also coloured by augmented chords, begins as a strophic structure (the second and third stanzas slightly varied), but after interruptions by Mime, the form dissolves under the pressure of the dramatic momentum. Mime plots how he will offer Siegfried a drugged drink after his battle with the dragon, and then kill him with his own sword. At last the forging is done, and Siegfried crashes the sword down on the anvil, splitting it in two.

ACT 2 *Deep in the forest* Two motifs are dominant in the prelude to Act 2: the growling of the dragon, outside whose cave the scene is set, and the Curse. Alberich is keeping watch over the cave and is surprised by the appearance of the Wanderer. Bitterly recalling how, as Wotan, he stole the ring from him, Alberich taunts him (to frequent repetitions of the Spear motif) with his ambitions for world supremacy. Wotan remains quietly philosophical and even warns Alberich of the approach of Siegfried and Mime. He surprises Alberich further by arousing Fafner on his behalf and asking him to yield up the ring. The dragon, extending the giants' falling perfect 4th to an augmented one, is unmoved.

Mime arrives with Siegfried (scene ii) and describes to him the fearsome dragon; Siegfried is concerned only to know where is the dragon's heart, so that he can plunge in his sword. Mime leaves Siegfried alone and to the mellifluous strains of the Forest Murmurs (shimmering muted strings supporting woodwind solos), the boy expresses his relief that the ugly dwarf is not his father after all. (The rippling movement of the Forest Murmurs is anticipated more than once in the preceding pages of the score, effectively integrating it into the scene as a whole.) He is lonely, though, and would like a friend. Hearing the song of the Woodbird, Siegfried tries to imitate it with a pipe made from a reed, but after several abortive attempts (comically rendered on the english horn) he gives up. He blows his horn instead (exx.1 and 2) and a somnolent Fafner drags himself out of his cave. After an exchange of banter and a battle depicted by the conflict of their motifs, Siegfried stabs Fafner in the heart with Nothung. Fafner, in his last gasp, tells Siegfried his history. Putting his burning hand involuntarily to his mouth, Siegfried tastes the dragon's blood. At last he understands the song of the Woodbird: it tells him to take the Ring and Tarnhelm from the cave.

As Siegfried disappears into the cave, Mime and Alberich appear from opposite sides (scene iii). To a shambling, syncopated accompaniment they argue angrily about the rightful ownership of the treasure. Mime offers to relinquish the Ring, provided he be allowed the Tarnhelm. Their argument is halted by the reappearance of Siegfried with both items; a chorus of horns, wafting the Rhine-maidens' motif, reminds us of the origin of the gold. The Woodbird tells Siegfried to beware Mime, who now approaches and hails him unctuously. As Mime cajoles Siegfried and offers him his drugged drink, thinking he is fooling the boy with his flattery, his actual words keep betraying his intention to make an end of him (a comic device which Wagner apparently borrowed from a 19th-century farce on the Faust legend). Finally, Siegfried, in an access of revulsion, kills Mime with a blow of the sword.

He tosses Mime's body into the cave and drags Fafner's over its mouth. Lying down under the linden tree, he listens again to the song of the Woodbird and asks its advice. The bird tells him of the bride that awaits him on a mountain top surrounded by fire. Siegfried jumps up and follows the bird as it leads the way.

ACT 3 Scene i–ii *The foot of a rocky mountain* The prelude is a symphonic development of a number of major motifs, notably the dotted rhythm pervading the prelude, associated with Wotan, the Valkyries and their riding; the Erda motif and its inversion the Twilight of the Gods; the flattened mediant harmonies of the Wanderer; the falling semitone associated in *Rheingold* with Alberich and the baleful power of his ring; and the Magic Sleep. The Wanderer appears and, summoning Erda (the earth goddess) from her slumber, demands to know more of the earth's secrets: 'Wache, Wala!'. First she refers him to the Norns as they weave the rope of destiny, and then to the daughter she bore him, Brünnhilde. When he tells her that Brünnhilde is being punished for her disobedience, she expresses surprise that the one who taught defiance is now punishing it. The technical advance represented by this scene, written after the long break during which Wagner composed *Tristan* and *Die Meistersinger*, is immediately evident. Powerfully conceived vocal lines completely abandoning recitative in favour of heightened arioso are supported by an orchestral texture of unprecedented richness and motivic density. The scene takes the form of a dialogue between the Wanderer and Erda, in which the characteristic material of each is subjected to variation. The form threatens to disintegrate as the emotional temperature rises, until a climax is reached with the Wanderer's announcement that he now looks forward to the end of the gods. The gravity of the moment is signalled with a noble new motif (ex.6); leitmotifs of such expansiveness and autonomy are henceforth to play a major role in the *Ring*. The Wanderer bequeaths his inheritance to the Volsung hero, Siegfried. Erda, deeply troubled that her wisdom is now ineffectual, sinks back into the earth.

Ex.6

As the Wanderer waits by the cave, Siegfried comes into view, led by the Woodbird which flies off, recognizing the Wanderer as the master of his raven messengers. In answer to the old stranger's questions, Siegfried tells, to the accompaniment of the appropriate motifs, how he killed the dragon, about the deceit of Mime, and how he himself forged the sword. Siegfried, irritated by the stranger, treats him with contempt. In a last attempt to exert his power, the Wanderer is moved to try to block Siegfried's path, but his spear is shattered by a stroke of Siegfried's sword; the motif of the Spear, and hence of Wotan's authority, is symbolically fragmented. The Wanderer vanishes and Siegfried plunges into the flames.

ACT 3 Scene iii *On the peak of Brünnhilde's rock* During an orchestral interlude constructed from motifs associated with Siegfried and the fire, the scene changes to the rocky summit of the end of *Die Walküre*. The first violins, unaccompanied, scale the heights as Siegfried climbs to the top of the rock. He has never seen a woman before and mistakes the form of the sleeping Brünnhilde for that of a man, even after removing her helmet (his doubts and irresolution prompting a brief return to the quasi-recitative style). His eventual realization, on removing the breastplate, that it is a woman causes a frenzy of fear and excitement (depicted in a series of flourishes characteristic of the post- *Tristan* Wagner). Now for the first time he has been taught fear, yet he longs to waken her. In desperation he kisses her on the lips, at which she opens her eyes and raises herself to a sitting position. With a flurry of harps, and in a bright C major, Brünnhilde greets the daylight: 'Heil dir, Sonne!'. She tells him that she has always loved him, even before he was conceived. Siegfried wonders if the woman is in fact his mother, but she tells him how she was confined on the rock for shielding him. This first part of their extended duet introduces a pair of new thematic ideas (exx.7 and 8), which will return to dominate the close of the act.

The confusion engendered by Siegfried's mixed emotions soon gives way to impetuous desire, the excitability of the vocal line being matched by tumescence in the orchestra. These effusions alternate with slower passages of a darker colour as Brünnhilde becomes increasingly conscious of her vulnerability, stripped as she is of her godhead. When Siegfried tries to embrace her, she pushes him away in terror. Now it is she who is prey to conflicting emotions, and motifs associated with Wotan's agony in Act 2 of *Die Walküre* and even the Curse well up from the depths of the orchestra. She begs him not to destroy the purity of their love, embarking on a monologue almost self-contained in its thematic content (the music is familiar from the *Siegfried Idyll*, composed the following year): 'Ewig war ich'. Gradually she is won over by the intensity of Siegfried's passion and is able to accept her new mortal status. To a riotous profusion of themes, including exx.6, 7 and 8, as well as a new one, ex.9, which combines the boyish vigour and falling 4ths of ex.3 with a suggestion of the cycle's principal Love motif, they embrace in ecstasy. Brünnhilde bids farewell to the world of the gods, and, transformed by each other's love, they invoke 'laughing death'.

*

The long span of 15 years over which the composition of *Siegfried* took place accounts for much of the stylistic inconsistency identifiable in the work. Acts 1 and 2 continue the style of *Rheingold* and *Walküre*, but with some interesting experiments in formal structure, while Act 3, written after the composition of *Tristan* and *Die Meistersinger*, demonstrates a new-found flexibility and maturity. The role of Siegfried, in which the singer is required to dominate the stage for the best part of four hours, culminating in a strenuous final scene with the newly awakened Brünnhilde, is one of the most testing in the tenor repertory.

B.M.

Götterdämmerung
('Twilight of the Gods')

Third day of *Der Ring des Nibelungen* in a prologue and three acts set to Wagner's own libretto; first performed in Bayreuth, at the Festspielhaus, on 17 August 1876.

For the original cast see *Der Ring des Nibelungen.*

Siegfried	tenor
Gunther	bass-baritone
Alberich	bass-baritone
Hagen	bass
Brünnhilde	soprano
Gutrune	soprano
Waltraute	mezzo-soprano
First Norn	contralto
Second Norn	mezzo-soprano
Third Norn	soprano
Woglinde ⎫	soprano
Wellgunde ⎬ *Rhinemaidens*	soprano
Flosshilde ⎭	mezzo-soprano

Vassals, women

The first draft of *Siegfrieds Tod* (originally spelt *Siegfried's Tod* and later renamed *Götterdämmerung*) is dated (at the end) 20 October 1848. This draft begins in the hall of the Gibichungs, but having been persuaded that too much background knowledge to the story was presupposed, Wagner added a prologue some time before 12 November. He undertook the versification of *Siegfrieds Tod* between 12 and 28 November, but then put it aside, perhaps unsure how to reconcile the diverging strands of the drama: divine myth and heroic tragedy. In the summer of 1850 he made some preliminary musical sketches for the prologue and began a composition draft, which was discontinued after the opening of the leavetaking scene for Siegfried and Brünnhilde. Having then added a preliminary drama, *Der junge Siegfried* (1851),

and *Die Walküre* and *Das Rheingold* (1851–2), Wagner found it necessary to subject *Siegfrieds Tod* to revision: Siegfried had already been
replaced as the central figure of the cycle by Wotan; the ending was
altered so that the gods and Valhalla are all destroyed by fire; the Norns'
scene was completely rewritten; a confrontation between Brünnhilde
and the rest of the Valkyries was compressed into the dialogue for
Brünnhilde and Waltraute (Act 1 scene iii); and several passages of narrative now rendered superfluous by *Die Walküre* and *Das Rheingold*
were removed. The first complete draft of *Götterdämmerung* was begun
on 2 October 1869 and finished on 10 April 1872. The second complete draft (short score) was made, as with *Siegfried*, in parallel, between
11 January 1870 and 22 July 1872. The full score was finished in
Wahnfried, Wagner's house in Bayreuth, on 21 November 1874.

*

PROLOGUE *The Valkyrie rock (as at the end of 'Siegfried')* The
prologue opens with the two chords heard at the awakening of
Brünnhilde (*Siegfried*, Act 3), but now in the darker, mellower
tonality of E$^\flat$ minor. The Three Norns, daughters of Erda, are
weaving the rope of destiny. The First Norn tells how, long ago,
Wotan came to drink at the Well of Wisdom, sacrificing an eye as
forfeit. He had cut a spear from the trunk of the World Ash Tree,
which had later withered and died. The Second Norn tells how a
brave hero broke Wotan's spear in battle; the god then sent heroes
from Valhalla to chop down the World Ash. The Third Norn
describes how the chopped logs of the World Ash have been piled
round Valhalla; one day they will be ignited and the entire hall will
be engulfed in flames. Gods and heroes are awaiting that day. As
each Norn in turn passes on both rope and narration, the wind and
brass intone the theme of the Annunciation of Death (*Walküre*, Act
2 scene iv). The First Norn sees fire burning round the Valkyrie rock
and is told that it is Loge fulfilling Wotan's command. A vision of
Alberich and the stolen Rhinegold causes the Norns anxiety. To a
baleful statement of the Curse motif on the bass trumpet, followed
by that of the Twilight of the Gods, the rope breaks.

In terror and confusion the Norns descend into the earth and an
orchestral interlude evokes sunrise. A pair of themes, exx.1 (a sturdier

form of Siegfried's horn call) and 2 (a new theme associated with Brünnhilde), are worked into a climax as the lovers come out of the cave to which they retired at the end of *Siegfried*. Brünnhilde sends Siegfried off on deeds of glory ('Zu neuen Thaten'), urging him to remember their love. A rapturous duet follows, constructed from ex.1 and ex.2 and other themes associated with the pair and their love and heroism. The vocal lines continue the new style evolved in Act 3 of *Siegfried*, richly ornamented with figurations and melismas. Siegfried gives Brünnhilde the ring as a token of his faithfulness; in exchange, she offers him her horse, Grane.

Another orchestral interlude (colourfully scored, with the glockenspiel and triangle adding to the gaiety) depicts Siegfried's Rhine Journey. It begins with a variant of ex.1 and the hero's progress is suggested by the appearance of the Fire motif and those of the Rhine and Rhinemaidens. In its latter stages, the dark-hued diminished triad of the Ring motif initiates a change of mood (and tonality).

ACT 1 Scenes i–ii *The hall of the Gibichungs* The action proper begins as Gunther, the chief of the Gibichungs, asks his half-brother Hagen whether his reputation is high: 'Nun hör', Hagen' (Hagen is the son of Alberich from a loveless encounter with Queen Grimhilde). The accompanying motif, that of Hagen (ex.3), is a stunted form of the heroic octave leap of Siegfried's Forging Song (*Siegfried*, Act 1). Hagen replies that it would be higher if Gunther were to find a wife and Gutrune, his sister, a husband. The galloping Valkyrie motif and that of the fire god Loge are heard as Hagen tells them about Brünnhilde lying on a rock encircled by fire. He suggests that Siegfried would win the bride for Gunther if Gutrune had won

127

Siegfried's love first. Hagen reminds them of a potion they have that would make Siegfried forget any other women.

Ex.3

Siegfried's horn is now heard and Hagen calls down to him (scene ii): his 'Heil! Siegfried', with ominous irony, picks out the notes of the Curse motif, sounded simultaneously on a trio of trombones. Such references have become increasingly oblique in the latter part of the *Ring*: a few bars later, the Curse motif sounds again as Siegfried asks whether Hagen knows him – a reminder of what it is that linked their ancestors. Hagen has to tell Siegfried the purpose of the Tarnhelm he is carrying. Gutrune appears, to a tender new motif (ex.4). She offers Siegfried the drugged potion and he, in a gesture pregnant with irony, drinks to the memory of Brünnhilde and their love. An extended trill symbolically shifts the tonality from the A$^\flat$ of Siegfried's memory to the G of Gutrune's presence. Siegfried is immediately drawn to Gutrune and loses no time in offering himself as her husband. He then offers to win Gunther a wife and as he is told about Brünnhilde high on a rock surrounded by fire, it is clear that he has only the faintest recollection of her. (Trills and tremolando strings evoke both the fire and the haziness of his memory.)

Ex.4

Siegfried proposes to use the Tarnhelm to disguise himself as Gunther in order to bring back Brünnhilde. The idea of swearing blood brotherhood brings forth the motifs of the Curse, the Sword (in a fast, energetic variant) and, less expectedly, that of Wotan's Spear: the symbol of the original contracts that have brought such trouble and strife. Siegfried and Gunther swear their oath: 'Blühenden

Lebens labendes Blut', with its duetting in 3rds and 6ths, the first of several reactionary structures in the work. Motivic reference slows down here but does not disappear: the menacing presence of Hagen in the background accounts for both the Ring and Curse motifs and for the effective juxtaposition of falling perfect and diminished 5ths (the former associated with heroism, the latter with evil) at 'blüh' im Trank unser Blut!' Siegfried sets off up the river again, followed by Gunther. The dour Hagen remains guarding the palace, contemplating the satisfactory progress of his scheme to win power: 'Hier sitz' ich zur Wacht'. The falling diminished 5th is now irrevocably associated with him, and the falling semitone, which can be traced back ultimately to Alberich's cries of woe in *Das Rheingold*, here attains its most anguished harmonization.

An orchestral interlude meditating on salient themes effects a transition from Hagen sitting malevolently on watch outside the palace to Brünnhilde sitting in innocent contemplation of Siegfried's ring outside the cave. The introduction of Brünnhilde's ex.2, with lighter scoring, dispels some of the oppressive atmosphere, but there remain enough pungent harmonies to suggest that trouble lies ahead.

ACT 1 Scene iii   *The Valkyrie rock*   There is thunder and lightning and Brünnhilde sees her sister Waltraute approach on a winged horse (much use of the galloping Valkyrie motif). In her delight, Brünnhilde fails to notice Waltraute's agitation: has Wotan perhaps forgiven her? Waltraute explains that she has broken Wotan's command in coming, but sadly he is no longer to be feared. She then narrates ('Seit er von dir geschieden'), to a wealth of motivic reference, how Wotan, as the Wanderer, returned to Valhalla with his spear shattered, how he ordered the heroes to pile up logs from the World Ash Tree, how the gods sit there in fear and dread, and how Wotan longs for the ring to be given back to the Rhinemaidens; it is to persuade Brünnhilde to do this that Waltraute has come. Although stunned by this narration (ex.5 with its anguished leaps is eloquent), Brünnhilde refuses to throw away Siegfried's pledge. The final brief exchange between Brünnhilde and Waltraute is enacted to one of the numerous little groups of allusive motifs which distinguish the score of

Götterdämmerung (in the earlier parts of the *Ring*, motivic references are generally more sparing and explicit).

Ex.5

Waltraute departs in a thundercloud which passes to reveal a calm evening sky. But the peace is illusory. The flames leap up again round the rock and Brünnhilde hears Siegfried's horn. She rushes excitedly to the edge of the cliff and is horrified to find a stranger: Siegfried disguised by the Tarnhelm as Gunther. Her rapturous welcome is abruptly terminated with a discord, remembered from Hagen's Watch, but also identifiable as the '*Tristan* chord' at correct pitch. The significance of the interpolation of that pivotal chord from Wagner's intervening opera at Brünnhilde's cry 'Verrath!' – the point at which the hero's love (under the influence of a magic potion, be it noted) is perceived to be false – need hardly be laboured. No less notable is the fact that the '*Tristan* chord' turns out to be the G$\sharp$ minor of the Tarnhelm motif with the addition of an intensifying diminished 7th (the F). But most extraordinary of all is the fact that the '*Tristan* chord' and Tarnhelm motif – both at their original pitch – effect a return to B minor, the key in which the act will end, as it began: a remarkable example of the interaction of local tonal reference with large-scale structural planning. The disguised Siegfried claims Brünnhilde as wife, violently snatches the ring from her finger and forces her into the cave for the night. He places his sword symbolically between them.

ACT 2 *On the shore in front of the Gibichung hall* Hagen, sitting outside the palace in a half-sleep, is visited by his father, Alberich: 'Schläfst du, Hagen, mein Sohn?'. The syncopations of Hagen's Watch reappear here, but in B$\flat$, the key of the Nibelungs. Hagen is urged to acquire the ring, and intends to do so, but will swear faithfulness only to himself. Dawn breaks in a loosely canonic passage scored for eight horns (scene ii) and Siegfried returns, now in his own form once more. Gunther is following with Brünnhilde, he says, and he tells Hagen and Gutrune how he braved the fire and over-powered Brünnhilde. He secretly changed places with Gunther and, using the Tarnhelm's magic, returned in an instant.

Hagen summons his vassals (scene iii) with blasts on his horn; his cries of 'Hoiho!' make frequent use of the ubiquitous falling semitone. The vassals rush in from all directions and are intemperately amused when they find out that Hagen has summoned them not for battle but for celebration. Their chorus in C major, with augmented-triad colouring influenced by Hagen – 'Gross Glück und Heil' – is another example of stylistic regression in *Götterdämmerung*, exciting as it can be in the theatre.

Clashing their weapons together, the vassals hail Gunther and his bride (scene iv), 'Heil Dir, Gunther!', the switch to B$^\flat$ possibly in recollection of a more celebrated Bridal March in the same key. To a melancholy reminiscence of the galloping Valkyrie motif, Brünnhilde is led forward, her eyes cast down. Gutrune's motif (ex.4) is prominent as she comes out of the hall with Siegfried. The sound of Siegfried's name provokes a violent reaction from Brünnhilde, her mute amazement forcefully depicted in the sustained diminished 7th chord that stops the music in its tracks. It starts up again with the anguished contortions of ex.4 and, less predictably, the Destiny motif from the Annunciation of Death in *Die Walküre*. Has Siegfried forgotten his bride, Brünnhilde asks? She sees the ring on his finger and asks how he got it, as it was seized from her by Gunther. Siegfried states simply that he won it by slaying a dragon. Raging against the gods for allowing Siegfried to betray her, Brünnhilde borrows a broad phrase from the Valhalla motif, in the original key of D$^\flat$. Siegfried tells how he won Brünnhilde for Gunther and claims that his sword lay between them during the night. Brünnhilde asserts that Nothung hung on the wall as its master wooed her. Siegfried, pressed by Gunther and the onlookers to declare his innocence, swears on the point of Hagen's spear that he has kept faith with his 'blood-brother': 'Helle Wehr, heilige Waffe!'. His innocently ringing perfect 5ths (both rising and falling) are tellingly offset by Hagen's diminished 5th sounded in the bass. The enraged Brünnhilde swears on the same spear-point that Siegfried has perjured himself.

Siegfried calls everyone to the wedding-feast and leads Gutrune into the palace.

Brünnhilde, left alone with Gunther and Hagen, laments Siegfried's treachery (scene v). At first she scorns Hagen's offer to avenge her; the hero would soon make him quake, she says. But then she confides that Siegfried's back would be vulnerable; she gave him no protection there as he would never turn it on an enemy. Gunther bemoans his own disgrace, but initially reacts with horror to Hagen's proposal to strike Siegfried dead (the minatory falling semitones on trombones are combined with the tortured ex.5 on bassoons and double basses). He is persuaded by the promise of obtaining the ring and it is decided to tell Gutrune that Siegfried was killed by a boar while out hunting. The trio of the conspirators is a stylistic regression that runs contrary to Wagner's *Oper und Drama* principles (the libretto for *Götterdämmerung* in fact preceded the theoretical essays), though there is some attempt to integrate the passage by means of motivic reminiscence: the new oath of vengeance principally recalls the oaths sworn on Hagen's spear earlier in the act. Siegfried and Gutrune reappear from the palace and a wedding procession forms. The celebratory C major is chillingly darkened in the final bars by the intervention of the falling semitone on trombones in combination with ex.5 a tritone away from the main key.

ACT 3 Scenes i–ii   *Wild woodland and rocky valley by the bank of the Rhine*   Siegfried's horn call is heard first in the orchestra and then in the distance, supposedly sounded by Siegfried out hunting. It is answered by the horn call of the Gibichungs (an inverted form). The ominous falling semitone and tritone from the end of the previous act are heard, but then the lyrical music of the Rhinemaidens supervenes. They are playing in the river, singing of the lost gold. Siegfried, having lost his way, stumbles on them and they playfully ask him for the ring on his finger; he refuses. Then he relents, but when they tell him of the dangers the curse-laden ring brings he says he will not succumb to threats. The Rhinemaidens abandon the 'fool', leaving Siegfried to meditate on the oddity of women's behaviour.

Hagen's voice and falling semitone are heard, and Siegfried calls the hunting party over (scene ii). He tells them that the only game he has seen was three wild water-birds, who told him he would be murdered that day. Siegfried drinks jovially from a horn, but Gunther can see only Siegfried's blood in his. Siegfried is asked to tell the story of his life, and he begins with his upbringing by the ill-tempered Mime (to the ostinato of the Nibelungs' motif): 'Mime hiess ein mürrischer Zwerg'. The dwarf taught him smithing, but it was his own skills that enabled him to forge Nothung, with which he killed the dragon Fafner (the Sword and Dragon motifs are heard). As yet Siegfried has no trouble in recalling the past. Swirling augmented harmonies conjure the enchantment of the world he is describing. He tells how the taste of the dragon's blood enabled him to understand the song of the wood-bird, and the Forest Murmurs are recalled. The bird had warned him of Mime's treachery and he had despatched the scheming dwarf.

Hagen hands him a drugged drink which he says will help him to remember what happened next. The music, recalling the trills of the potion he was given in Act 1, tell us that memories have indeed been stimulated: where the trills previously led to the theme of Gutrune, now they soar into a theme remembered from the prologue duet, closely followed by the Brünnhilde motif, ex.2. To the appropriate motifs, and in an increasingly ecstatic state as he relives the traumatic but forgotten experience, Siegfried relates how he was led to a high rock surrounded by fire; there he found the sleeping Brünnhilde, whom he awoke with a kiss. The expected C major resolution is thwarted by Gunther's tritonal expression of dismay. Two ravens fly overhead and, as Siegfried looks up, Hagen plunges his spear in his back. Brass instruments thunder out the Curse motif and Hagen's falling semitone; one of Siegfried's heroic motifs is hurled out by the entire orchestra, but it reaches its climax on a discord and finally collapses on to the repeated-note, tattoo figure that is to become the basis of the Funeral March. The themes and radiant C major tonality of Brünnhilde's awakening (*Siegfried*, Act 3) are recalled, and Siegfried dies with Brünnhilde's name on his lips.

Siegfried's Funeral March represents a motivic pageant of his life and ancestry, as his body is carried off by vassals in a solemn procession. Themes associated with the Volsungs and their love are followed by a grand statement of the Sword motif in its original C major (on a trumpet), and by the motifs of Siegfried and his heroism, ending with a triumphant transformation, in E♭, of ex.1.

ACT 3 Scene iii   *The hall of the Gibichungs*   Gutrune comes out of her room into the hall. She thinks she hears Siegfried's horn, but he has not returned. She has seen Brünnhilde walking towards the Rhine, and is anxious. Hagen is heard approaching ('Hoiho!', on falling semitones over ex.5) and Siegfried's corpse is brought in. She accuses Gunther of murdering him, but he blames Hagen, who claims – to the music of the oath-swearing – to have killed him for committing perjury; Hagen steps forward to seize the ring and when Gunther stands in his way, he is murdered by Hagen. Hagen tries again to take the ring, but as he approaches Siegfried, the dead man's hand rises into the air, to the horror of all. The Sword motif, in its other primary key of D major, makes a quietly noble intervention, but gives way to the motif of the Twilight of the Gods.

Brünnhilde enters with calm dignity and tells how Siegfried swore her an eternal oath. Gutrune curses Hagen and prostrates herself over Gunther's body, where she remains, motionless, until the end. Brünnhilde orders logs to be gathered to make a funeral pyre worthy of the hero ('Starke Scheite'). Loge's motif blazes in eager anticipation. She sings of her betrayal by this noblest, most faithful of men. Addressing Wotan in Valhalla, she says that Siegfried's death has atoned for his guilt and has brought her enlightenment through sorrow. This quietly reflective passage is rounded off by a statement, no longer threatening, of the Curse motif and a sublime resolution in D♭, the ultimate goal of the cycle ('Ruhe, ruhe, Du Gott!'). She takes Siegfried's ring, promising that it will be returned to the Rhinemaidens, whose carefree music is now heard. She hurls a blazing torch on to the pile of logs, which immediately ignites. Greeting her horse Grane (to recollections of the galloping Valkyrie motif), she mounts it and rides into the flames. The exultant theme sung by Sieglinde in *Die Walküre* on hearing of her future son's destiny ('O hehrstes Wunder') returns now to crown the peroration: Wagner referred to this motif as 'the glorification of Brünnhilde' (ex.6).

Ex.6

The whole building seems to catch fire and the men and women press to the front of the stage in terror. Suddenly the fire dies down and the Rhine bursts its banks, flooding the entire space. On the appearance of the Rhinemaidens, Hagen leaps into the water in pursuit of the ring. To the sound of the Curse motif, they drag him down into the depths and hold up the ring in triumph. The water-level falls again and from the ruins of the palace, which has collapsed, the men and women watch a burst of firelight as it rises into the sky. Eventually it illuminates the hall of Valhalla, where gods and heroes are seen assembled. The Valhalla motif is naturally prominent here, and those of the Rhinemaidens and the Glorification of Brünnhilde are symbolically intertwined. To the sound of the motifs of the Twilight of the Gods and, finally, the Glorification of Brünnhilde in a radiant D$^\flat$ major, Valhalla is engulfed in flames: the long-awaited end of the gods has come to pass.

*

The final opera of the *Ring*, a long evening's performance in its own right, provides an appropriately weighty conclusion to the epic cycle. 26 years elapsed from the time Wagner made his first prose draft for the work to the completion of the full score, with inevitable consequences in terms of stylistic unity. Retrogressive elements of grand opera exist side by side with motivic integration representative of Wagner's most mature style. And yet, the stylistic integrity of *Götterdämmerung* is scarcely compromised, so skilfully are the disparate elements welded together and so intense the dramaturgical conviction. The resources and stamina demanded by the work (from both singers and orchestra), combined with its sheer length and theatrical potency, make it one of the most daunting yet rewarding undertakings in the operatic repertory.

B.M.

Parsifal

Bühnenweihfestspiel in three acts set to Wagner's own libretto; first performed at Bayreuth, in the Festspielhaus, on 26 July 1882.

At the first performances, Parsifal was sung by Hermann Winkelmann, Heinrich Gudehus and Ferdinand Jäger; Gurnemanz by Emil Scaria and Gustav Siehr; Kundry by Amalie Materna, Marianne Brandt and Therese Malten; and Amfortas by Theodor Reichmann. The conductors were Hermann Levi and Franz Fischer.

Amfortas *ruler of the Kingdom of the Grail*	baritone
Titurel *his father*	bass
Gurnemanz *a veteran Knight of the Grail*	bass
Parsifal	tenor
Klingsor *a magician*	bass
Kundry	mezzo-soprano
First and Second Knights of the Grail	tenor, bass
Four Esquires	sopranos, tenors
Voice from Above	contralto
Klingsor's Flowermaidens	6 sopranos

Knights of the Grail, youths and boys, flowermaidens

Setting The Grail castle 'Monsalvat' and its environs, the northern mountains of Gothic Spain, in mythological times

Wagner acquainted himself with the relevant source material for his final opera as early as the summer of 1845, when he read Wolfram von Eschenbach's Parzivâl and Titurel poems, in versions by Simrock and San-Marte. The first prose sketch (now lost) was made in 1857 – not, however, on Good Friday, as Wagner poetically recollected in subsequent years. The first prose draft did not follow until 1865, and the second (written mostly in dialogue form) not until 1877. The poem was written between 14 March and 19 April 1877 and the music between August 1877 and April 1879 (Wagner alternating, in

137

his now customary fashion, between two drafts). He orchestrated the prelude (first version, with concert ending) in autumn 1878 and made his full score of the rest between August 1879 and January 1882.

The first performances were given at Bayreuth on 26 and 28 July 1882 for members of the Society of Patrons, followed by 14 further performances in July and August. In an agreement with his patron, King Ludwig II, designed to pay off the deficit incurred by the first Bayreuth festival, Wagner was obliged to employ the Munich Hoftheater personnel to perform the work, which meant that he had to accept the Jewish Hermann Levi to conduct it. Wagner's intention of consecrating the Festspielhaus with *Parsifal* is indicated by the term *Bühnenweihfestspiel*, which may be translated 'festival play for the consecration of a stage'. In spite of the 30-year embargo placed on performances outside Bayreuth, *Parsifal* was occasionally given elsewhere in those years: Ludwig II had it put on privately in Munich in the years after Wagner's death; it was seen by members of the Wagner Society in Amsterdam in 1905, and again in 1906 and 1908; and in the face of bitter hostility from Bayreuth it was mounted by the Metropolitan in 1903 under Alfred Hertz. Various concert performances were given in Europe during the period of the embargo, including two under Joseph Barnby in London in 1884. The first stage performance in Britain was at Covent Garden in 1914, under Artur Bodanzky.

Parsifal has been sung by Lawitz Melchior, Ramón Vinay, Jess Thomas, Jon Vickers, René Kollo, Helge Brilioth, Manfred Jung, Peter Hofmann and Siegfried Jerusalem; Gurnemanz by Alexander Kipnis, Ludwig Weber, Hans Hotter, Gottlieb Frick, Theo Adam, Martti Talvela, Franz Mazura, Kurt Moll, Hans Sotin and Robert Lloyd; Kundry by Lillian Nordica, Olive Fremstad, Frida Leider, Kirsten Flagstad, Astrid Varnay, Helen Traubel, Martha Mödl, Régine Crespin, Leonie Rysanek, Christa Ludwig, Yvonne Meier and Waltraud Minton; and Amfortas by Anton van Rooy, Clarence Whitehill, Herbert Janssen, Friedrich Schorr, Hans Hotter, George London, Dietrich Fischer-Dieskau, Donald McIntyre, Bernd Weikl and Simon Estes. Notable conductors of the work have included Felix Mottl, Anton Seidl, Carl Muck, Felix Weingartner, Hans

Knappertsbusch, Wilhelm Furtwängler, Rudolf Kempe, Pierre Boulez, Reginald Goodall, Eugen Jochum, Georg Solti, Herbert von Karajan, James Levine and Daniel Barenboim.

*

The prelude begins with a broadly phrased theme (ex.1), containing three elements of significance, of which (*y*) is generally associated with suffering, and (*z*) with the Spear. A shimmering background is built up, against which a trumpet (with oboes and violins) reiterates ex.1, establishing the tonality of A♭ major. The whole process is then repeated in C minor, before two new themes, those associated with the Grail (the 'Dresden Amen': ex.2) and with faith (ex.3) are announced. After some chromatic intensification, especially of ex.1, the curtain rises.

ACT 1 Scenes i–ii *A forest glade* Gurnemanz rouses two of the esquires from sleep and together they kneel and pray (ex.3, as extended in the prelude, followed by ex.2). Gurnemanz bids them prepare the bath for Amfortas, approaching on his sickbed (ex.4 makes its first appearance in the bass here). But first the 'wild woman' Kundry rushes in, her arrival signalled by agitation in the orchestra; she is bringing balsam from Arabia for the sick guardian of the Grail. Amfortas's entrance on his litter is accompanied by ex.4, which

eventually introduces a paragraph in which he looks forward to his relief from pain ('Nach wilder Schmerzensnacht'). The sustained dominant pedal suggests a cadence on B$^\flat$, but the ultimate resolution is on to an evasive G$^\flat$, hinting that the hope of relief is illusory. Amfortas intones the formula of the 'pure fool made wise by suffering' ('durch Mitleid wissend, der reine Thor'), whom he has been promised as a saviour. He is carried away again to the grieving strains of ex.4.

Ex.4

Gurnemanz reprimands the esquires for their harsh words about Kundry; she is perhaps atoning with good deeds for a past sin, he says. Their taunt that she should be sent in quest of the missing Spear draws from Gurnemanz an emotional recollection of how Amfortas was seduced and dealt his terrible wound, losing possession of the sacred Spear to the magician Klingsor ('O, wunden-wundervoller heiliger Speer!': ex.1 *y* and ex.1 *z*). The esquires enquire how Gurnemanz knew Klingsor, and he begins his Narration proper ('Titurel, der fromme Held'). The sacred relics of the cup used at the Last Supper and the Spear that pierced Christ's side on the Cross had been given into the care of Titurel, then guardian of the Grail. ex.1 and a new theme, evolved from ex.3, are developed here in a mystical atmosphere conjured partly by the long, flowing phrases and partly by the radiantly translucent scoring. The brotherhood of the Grail, assembled by Titurel to guard the relics, was closed to Klingsor (his motif, ex.5, is now heard) on account of some unnamed sin. Desperate to quell his raging passions, Klingsor even castrated himself, but was still rebuffed. To avenge himself, he turned to magic and created a garden of delights, where he lies in wait for errant knights, seducing them with 'devilish lovely women' (intimations of the Act 2 flowermaidens' music are heard here). The aging Titurel sent his son Amfortas to defeat Klingsor, with the consequences already described. Gurnemanz ends his narrative with a recollection of the divine prophecy concerning a 'pure fool', echoed homophonically by the esquires.

Ex.5

A flurry of activity is initiated by the opening figure of Parsifal's motif, ex.6. Parsifal has shot down a swan on the holy ground and is dragged in by the knights. Gurnemanz's rebuke fills him with remorse and he breaks his bow. To Gurnemanz's questions about his name and origins, however, he professes ignorance. The two are left alone with Kundry, and Parsifal tells what he knows about himself: his mother's name was Herzeleide (Heart's Sorrow), he had strayed from home in search of adventure and had made his own arms for protection. When Kundry, who clearly knows more about him than he does himself, announces that his mother is dead, Parsifal attacks her and has to be restrained.

Ex.6

In the distance, the knights and esquires are seen bearing Amfortas back to the Grail castle. As the processional music starts, Gurnemanz offers to lead Parsifal there. The change of scene, from forest to castle, is effected during the Transformation Music, which builds the dissonances associated with Amfortas's suffering (ex.7) to an immense climax. Bells ring out with the four-note motif of the procession.

Ex.8

ACT 1 Scene iii *The castle of the guardians of the Grail* Gurnemanz and Parsifal enter the Grail hall and the chorus of knights, 'Zum letzen Liebesmahle', firmly establishes C major as the second primary key of the act. A chorus of youths is heard from mid-height and then one of boys' voices from the top of the dome. Amfortas has been borne in, and the Grail, still covered, placed on a marble table.

Amfortas, reluctant to accede to Titurel's request for him to uncover the Grail, breaks into his monologue of torment, 'Wehvolles Erbe'. He seeks atonement for his sin and the motif of his suffering (ex.7) is prominent along with ex.1. His passionate cry for forgiveness ('Erbarmen!') is answered by the chorus repeating the prophecy. At Titurel's insistence, the cover is removed from the golden shrine and the crystal Grail chalice taken from it. Ex.1 returns, as in the prelude, first in A$^\flat$ major and then in C minor, as the voices from above repeat Christ's words offering his body and blood: 'Nehmet hin meinen Leib, nehmet hin mein Blut'. Amfortas consecrates the bread and wine and they are distributed to the knights, who take up a sturdy new theme in E$^\flat$ started by the boys and youths from above. Ex.2 and Ex.3 are heard and then the processional music and ex.7 as Amfortas is borne out again, his wound gaping anew. Parsifal, who had convulsively clutched his heart at Amfortas's cry of agony, is unable to tell Gurnemanz what he has seen and is roughly shepherded out. A voice from above (contralto solo) repeats the prophecy, answered by ex.2 from other voices in the dome.

ACT 2   *Klingsor's magic castle, on the southern slopes of the mountains facing Moorish Spain*   The act opens with a sinister chromatic transmutation of ex.1, introducing a disruptive tritone, followed by Klingsor's theme (ex.5). Klingsor, surrounded by magical and necromantic apparatus, watches over his domains from a tower. Seeing Parsifal approach, he summons Kundry, whose monosyllabic groans are accompanied by unprepared dissonances. Attempting to resist Klingsor's instructions to seduce Parsifal, she taunts her master with his self-enforced chastity. Parsifal's motif (ex.6) announces that he has reached the battlements; Klingsor watches as he fells one guard after another. The tower suddenly sinks and in its place appears a luxuriant magic garden.

Flowermaidens rush in from all sides, their excited questions accompanied by a playful, dotted variant of ex.1 and by a continuous triplet figure in the strings. As Parsifal appears, they squabble over him, but join forces for their alluring, triple-time 'Komm, komm, holder Knabe!'. A number of striking parallels between this scene and the Act 3 finale of Meyerbeer's *Robert le diable* suggest that Wagner may have intended to demonstrate here the superiority of the music drama over conventional opera. The flowermaidens caress Parsifal insistently; a series of modulations recalls the love music of *Tristan und Isolde* and the '*Tristan* chord' itself is heard. Just as he manages to free himself from their attentions, he is stopped in his tracks by the sound of his long-forgotten name. It is Kundry, now transformed into an enchanting beauty, who calls, her voice emerging seductively out of the orchestral texture. At Kundry's command the flowermaidens reluctantly disperse.

She tells, in a flowing, compound-time narrative, how she saw him as a baby on his mother's breast: 'Ich sah das Kind'. His mother watched over him lovingly, but one day he broke her heart by not returning and she died of grief. Parsifal's distress at the news is reflected in the chromatic intensification both of his line and of the orchestral texture. Kundry consoles him, urging him to show her the love he owed his mother. As she kisses him, the '*Tristan* chord' (at pitch, as ever) is outlined by stopped horns and cello. By a clever twist of its tail, the theme associated with sorcery gradually reveals part of the chaste opening theme of the work (ex.8). Parsifal leaps up, clutching his heart. His cry 'Amfortas! Die Wunde!' indicates his first real identification with Amfortas's suffering, and his first step on the road to self-knowledge. Falling into a trance, he hears Christ the Redeemer himself call on him to save him from 'guilt-tainted hands' and cleanse the polluted sanctuary. The flowermaidens' blandishments are chromatically enhanced as Parsifal realizes that it was caresses such as Kundry is conferring on him now that brought about Amfortas's downfall.

Ex.7

He repels her, but she appeals to him to use his redemptive powers to save her: for her blasphemous mockery of Christ she has wandered the world for centuries. One hour with him would bring her release, she says. But Parsifal, recognizing that salvation for them both depends on his withstanding her allurements, resists her. She attempts to block his way to Amfortas and calls to Klingsor. The magician appears and hurls his Spear at Parsifal (an upward glissando on a harp). Parsifal seizes the Spear and as he makes the sign of the Cross with it, the castle collapses and the magic garden disappears.

ACT 3   The years of anguish and wandering that intervene between the second and third acts are depicted by the heightened chromaticism of the prelude. The curtain rises on an open spring landscape in the domains of the Grail. Gurnemanz, grown very old and dressed as a hermit, emerges from his hut and uncovers Kundry, whose groans, as she lies stiff and apparently lifeless in the undergrowth, he has heard. He revives her, but receives no thanks, just two words: she wants only to serve ('Dienen . . . Dienen!'). A man approaches in a suit of armour and bearing a spear. A sober variant, in the minor, of Parsifal's motif (ex.6) tells us both the stranger's identity and that he is a changed man. Gurnemanz welcomes him but bids him divest himself of his weapons: it is Good Friday and this is holy ground. As Parsifal does so, Gurnemanz recognizes the man whom he once roughly turned away.

He also recognizes the Spear (ex.1 is recalled), but his outburst of joy is undercut by the music associated with Amfortas's suffering (ex.7). Throughout his troubled wandering, Parsifal tells him, he has guarded the Spear safely. Gurnemanz hails its return with an impassioned outburst that again recalls each of the elements of ex.1: 'O Gnade! Höchstes Heil!'. The mystical elaboration of ex.3 from Gurnemanz's Act 1 narrative is now recalled. Gurnemanz tells Parsifal that his return with the healing Spear is timely. Amfortas, longing for death, has refused to reveal the Grail, the brotherhood has degenerated, and Titurel has died. The elegiac music of the Act 3 prelude, and its original key of B$^\flat$ minor, accompanies his words.

Parsifal is almost overcome with remorse. His feet are bathed by Kundry, and Gurnemanz sprinkles water from the spring on his head, asking that he be blessed ('Gesegnet sei'). Kundry then anoints his feet and dries them with her hair. The hesitant reminiscence of the flowermaidens' music suggests that Parsifal may now be aware of Kundry's alter ego. To a grandiose statement of Parsifal's theme, ex.6, in B major, Gurnemanz anoints his head. After an unusually emphatic cadence (twice confirmed) in this key, and before the Good Friday Music begins 27 bars later also in B major, there occurs the incident of Kundry's baptism by Parsifal. The inner significance for Wagner of this act – as an expression of a Schopenhauerian pacification of the will, but also, probably, as a symbol of the liberation of the world from impure racial elements – is intimated by the divorcing of this passage from the immediate tonal context.

Gazing on the beautiful meadows, Parsifal says that on Good Friday every living thing should only sigh and sorrow. As the Good Friday Music modulates from B to D major (asserting itself, along with D minor, as a primary tonality of the work) Gurnemanz replies that on this day repentant sinners rejoice at the Redeemer's act of self-sacrifice and nature herself is transfigured. In a transformation scene similar to that in the first act (but in the reverse direction), and underpinned by a processional ostinato rhythm, Gurnemanz now leads Parsifal and Kundry to the Grail hall. There one group of knights bears Titurel in his coffin, while a second group carries Amfortas on a litter. When Titurel's coffin is opened, all break into a cry of woe. The cry establishes D minor for Amfortas's final monologue: 'Mein Vater!'. He refuses to uncover the Grail, and when the knights become threateningly insistent, he merely invites them to plunge their swords into his heart.

Parsifal has meanwhile appeared unobserved; he holds out his Spear and with its point touches Amfortas's wound: 'Nur eine Waffe taugt'. Amfortas is miraculously healed and his theme (ex.4) gives way to Parsifal's (ex.6), now in a triumphant D major, as he yields his office as lord of the Grail to the new redeemer. D major turns to D minor before a momentous modulation to the final tonality of $A^\flat$ major, on the words 'öffnet den Schrein!' ('open the shrine!'). Here the work's central polarity of $A^\flat$/D (major and minor) is resolved by an integration of the two, as of two complementary spheres. Parsifal takes the

Grail from the shrine and it shines softly, then radiantly as light falls from above. Kundry sinks lifeless to the ground, redeemed at last. As the motifs of faith (ex.3) and the Grail (ex.2) make their final, luminously scored appearance, Parsifal waves the Grail in blessing over the worshipping knights. A white dove descends to hover above his head.

*

In as far as it addressed the 'meaning' of *Parsifal* at all, much of the literature on the opera up to World War II dealt with the question of whether or not it could be regarded as a religious work (for a summary, see Beckett 1981). An equally strong claim, based on Wagner's acknowledged sympathies, could be made for a Schopenhauerian/ Buddhist interpretation, taking the concept of *Mitleid* ('compassion') as the ethical centre of the work. Darker undercurrents of racial supremacy and anti-semitism have been revealed (Gutman 1968; Zelinsky 1978), but the notion that the concepts of racial purity and regeneration formulated by Wagner in his last years were woven into the ideological fabric of *Parsifal* (Millington 1984; Rose 1992) was less readily embraced by directors in the 1980s than the theme of sexuality. Progressive stage interpretations in recent years have attempted to rehabilitate Kundry and womankind generally, allowing them a more prominent role in the final act of redemption.

Parsifal is the most enigmatic and elusive work in the Wagnerian canon. No attempt to elucidate its mysteries can afford to ignore any of its elements, whether its Christian, pagan, Buddhist or Schopenhauerian ideas, or its concepts of racial purity and regeneration. The only one of Wagner's music dramas written with direct experience of the Bayreuth Festspielhaus, the text of *Parsifal* is set to a diaphanous score of unearthly beauty and refinement. The score offers frequent clues to an understanding of the text, but Wagner's characteristically ambivalent treatment of consonance and dissonance, as of pleasure and pain, and his interweaving of diatonicism and chromaticism, resists any oversimplified interpretation. The juxtaposition of sublimity with richly ambivalent symbolism and an underlying ideology disturbing in its implications creates a work of unique expressive power and endless fascination.

B.M.

Bayreuth

The town of Bayreuth in Bavaria, southern Germany, is internationally famous as the site of Richard Wagner's Festspielhaus. Dating back to 1231, and in the 17th and 18th centuries the seat of an independent margravate, the town is now the capital of the district of Upper Franconia and since 1975 has had a university. As well as the Festspielhaus it possesses two theatres in which opera is performed, the Markgräfliches Opernhaus and the modern Stadthalle.

THE MARKGRÄFLICHES OPERNHAUS   In virtually all the kingdoms, principalities, dukedoms and margravates constituting Germany up to 1918, the cultivation of opera was an important part of court life. Bayreuth was no exception: the first opera to be performed there (in 1661) was *Sophia*, by an unknown composer, and in the next 55 years about four to six works by German and Italian composers (among them G. H. Stölzel, G. P. Telemann, C. F. Hurlebusch, Attilio Ariosti and Antonio Lotti) were staged each year, either in the Schlosssaal or in a theatre built within the palace grounds. However, it was not until the accession as margravine of Frederick the Great's sister Wilhelmine in 1735 that opera in Bayreuth became something beyond the ordinary. Wilhelmine (1709–58) the consort of Margrave Friedrich, was a skilled composer herself (her opera *Argenore*, performed in 1740, is lost, but some chamber works remain), and her excellent relations with her brother and the Prussian court ensured that eminent composers and musicians were willing to place themselves at her disposal.

Among the works known to have been performed in Bayreuth under the Kapellmeister Johann Pfeiffer (served 1734–61) were Hasse's operas *Ezio* and *Artaserse* and Bernasconi's *festa teatrale* *L'huomo*. These were staged in the new Markgräfliches Opernhaus built in the street now known as Opernstrasse, close to the margrave's palace. One of the finest late Baroque theatres still in existence, this three-storey building was erected by the French architect Joseph Saint-Pierre in 1745–8, and the interior decoration was entrusted to the Italian theatre designer Giuseppe Galli-Bibiena and his son Carlo. The richly decorated auditorium is dominated by the large margrave's box at the back, with three tiers of boxes on either side, the stalls area being separated from the stage by an ornamental balustrade (see fig.1). The elaborate proscenium stage (14 metres wide, 15 metres high), which is slightly raised, is unusually deep (30 metres); it was this feature that first attracted Wagner to Bayreuth in the hope that it might prove suitable for the production of his *Ring* cycle. He at once saw,, after inspecting it, that it would not do for his work as it was, and he wrote on 20 April 1871 to Lorenz Düfflipp, secretary to King Ludwig II of Bavaria: 'This theatre is probably the most fantastic example of rococo to be found anywhere, and not the least thing in it may be changed'.

Following Wilhelmine's death in 1758 and Friedrich's in 1763, the court moved to Ansbach, and Bayreuth reverted to the status of a provincial town. The Markgräfliches Opernhaus continued, however, to be used by travelling companies from neighbouring towns, mainly Bamberg and Coburg. No complete list is available of the operas presented there, but it is recorded that, to celebrate the 50th anniversary of Bayreuth's incorporation into Bavaria, a performance of Wagner's *Tannhäuser* was given on 30 June 1860 in a production from Coburg – an event of which Wagner himself appears to have been unaware. The Opernhaus was in continuous use until 1935, when, after a restoration that carefully preserved its original character, it became little more than a museum. It was brought into use again in 1948 (its bicentenary) as a venue for the Fränkische Festwochen, which take place annually in May/June and are devoted to performances of early operas and ballets in productions by the Bavarian Staatsoper, Munich. It is also used for occasional recitals and other events.

STADTHALLE   The Markgräfliches Opernhaus's former function as the regular venue of entertainment for the people of Bayreuth was taken over by the Stadthalle in Jean-Paul-Platz. It stands on the site of the former margraves' Reithalle (built 1747–8), which was converted into a theatre in 1935–6. The first Stadthalle was destroyed in an air attack in 1945, but the front wall remained intact and was incorporated in the new Stadthalle, opened in 1965. An all-purpose building also used for plays, concerts, congresses and balls, it contains two theatres with seating capacity of 930 (Grosses Haus) and 300 (Kleines Haus). Opera performances are given throughout the year by companies from Nuremberg, Hof, Coburg and other nearby towns.

WAGNER'S FESTSPIELHAUS   The Markgräfliches Opernhaus may have been the factor that first drew Wagner to Bayreuth, but it was by no means the beginning of his vision of a theatre of his own. That was closely connected with the composition of *Der Ring des Nibelungen*, which he early recognized as unsuitable for presentation within the traditional operatic framework. In the preface to the full text of the *Ring* in 1863 he outlined the ideal theatre he had in mind:

I would have to aim at one of the less large towns in Germany, favourably sited and capable of accommodating an unusual number of guests, and in particular a town in which there would be no danger of clashing with a large existing theatre and thus having to compete with large-city audiences and their established customs. Here a temporary theatre would be erected, as simple as possible perhaps merely of wood, its sole criterion being the artistic suitability of its inner parts. I had already worked out in discussions with an intelligent and experienced architect a plan with an auditorium in the shape of an amphitheatre and with the great advantage of an orchestra invisible to the audience. To this theatre singers from German opera houses, chosen for their outstanding acting skills, would be summoned, probably in early spring, to, rehearse the several parts of my work, uninterrupted by any other artistic activity.

Three performances of the complete cycle, Wagner went on to say, would be given at the height of summer on four successive evenings for 'art-lovers from near and far'.

Bayreuth met in all respects the conditions he had laid down in his *Ring* preface for the site of his festival performances. It had the additional advantages of being within the territories of his patron, King Ludwig, and of having civic authorities (in particular the mayor, Theodor Muncker, and the banker, Friedrich Feustel) eager to serve Wagner in the realization of his ambition. They offered him, free of

149

charge, a site on a hill on the northern outskirts of the town (the Grünes Hügel) for the theatre, and he bought at his own expense a plot of land backing on to the grounds of the Neues Schloss (the margraves' former residence, by now the property of King Ludwig) for a family home. (Called Wahnfried, in Richard Wagner Strasse, it was the home of the Wagner family up to the death of Wieland Wagner in 1966, and is now the Richard Wagner Museum.)

After laying the foundation stone of the theatre on 22 May 1872 (a ceremony that included a performance of Beethoven's Ninth Symphony in the Markgräfliches Opernhaus, conducted by Wagner himself), he set out to raise funds for it by conducting concerts and selling certificates of patronage. The response was disappointing, and he was obliged to construct the building with the simplest and cheapest materials. This, as his *Ring* preface shows, is what he had always intended his Festspielhaus to be: a 'sketch of an ideal', a temporary structure that the German nation, if it chose, could eventually turn into a monumental building. It incorporated all his theatrical ideas, which (as mentioned in the *Ring* preface) had been translated into practical terms by the architect Gottfried Semper. Now, working with the architect Otto Brückwald and the stage machinist Karl Brandt, Wagner realized them.

The auditorium (originally 1460 seats with boxes, including a royal box, behind) is on a single raked level converging fan-shaped on a stage 32 metres wide and 23 metres deep (40 metres including the backstage area). A particular feature is the duplication of the stage proscenium arch (13 metres wide, 11.8 metres high) by a wider one just beyond the orchestra and the continuation of this line by 'false'- wooden pillars projecting from the side walls to the back of the auditorium. The orchestra is positioned in a deep well obscured from the audience's sight. Wagner wrote: 'We called this the "mystic chasm", because its task was to separate the real from the ideal', and the result of this arrangement, together with the extended proscenium, was that the spectator has the feeling of being at a far distance from the events on stage, yet perceives them with the clarity of near proximity; in consequence, the stage figures give the illusion of being enlarged and superhuman'. The hood over the orchestra serves the additional function of throwing the orchestral sound on to the stage to blend with the vocal sound before being projected back to the auditorium. All these features, combined with the theatre's wooden ceiling covered with painted canvas, give the performances in the Festspielhaus a visual and acoustical flavour that is unique.

With the aid of a loan from King Ludwig, Wagner was at last able, in August 1876, to produce the *Ring* for the first time in its entirety, having previously travelled through Germany and Austria with his wife Cosima to assemble singers and orchestral players prepared to work more for love than financial gain (a principle to which Bayreuth still adheres). Three complete cycles were given, the first attended by Emperor Wilhelm I of Germany and the last by King Ludwig. But Wagner's triumph was clouded by dissatisfaction with the production itself and dismay at the huge financial deficit remaining. Six years passed before he could afford to stage another festival, this time (1882) devoted exclusively to *Parsifal*, his only work written expressly for the completed Festspielhaus (a fact reflected in its orchestration) and intended by Wagner to be performed nowhere else. In all, 16 performances were given. At the last, Wagner took the baton for the final scene – his only conducting appearance in his own theatre. He died in the following year.

WAGNER'S SUCCESSORS

COSIMA WAGNER (1886–1906)   The task of running the festival devolved on Wagner's widow Cosima, who dedicated herself to carrying out the composer's wishes exactly as she understood them. Wagner had intended that all his works from *Der fliegende Holländer* onwards should eventually be staged in his theatre, and Cosima's first production (1886) was *Tristan und Isolde*, followed by *Die Meistersinger* in 1888, *Tannhäuser* in 1891, *Lohengrin* in 1894, a new production of the *Ring* in 1896, and *Der fliegende Holländer* in 1901. Her achievement was laudable, but her priestess-like devotion to the voice of the master and her refusal to consider new ideas (such as those of the Swiss designer Adolphe Appia) threatened to turn the Festspielhaus into a museum. She did, however, move with the times to the extent of installing electric lighting in 1888 in place of the original gas. Cosima's choice of artists, though widened to include foreign singers, was based not on their star quality (the Bayreuth Festival prides itself on making reputations rather than profiting from them), but on the artists' willingness to submit to her rigid production style, in which prescribed movements were tied closely to musical phrases and clear diction was of paramount importance.

Cosima was assisted by her daughters Daniela and Isolde (for costumes and so on) and by her son Siegfried, who first conducted in the Festspielhaus in 1896 (the *Ring*). After the festival of 1906 Cosima, in failing health, relinquished control in favour of Siegfried, but remained in Wahnfried.

SIEGFRIED WAGNER (1908–30)   Siegfried made no radical changes in the years before 1914, continuing the pattern established by his mother: festivals were held in two consecutive summers, followed by a rest year; *Parsifal* and the *Ring* were presented at all festivals, together with one other work. His impact was more marked after 1924, when the festival was resumed after a ten-year break. A modest, unassuming man, his methods were evolutionary: while not abandoning the basically realistic productions of his father and mother, he gradually replaced painted backcloths with solid sets, extended the stage depth, improved the lighting system and allowed his singers more freedom of movement. His production of *Tannhäuser* in 1930 was the first decisive move away from the conception of the Bayreuth Festival as a museum religiously preserving Wagner's own production style.

WINIFRED WAGNER (1931–44)   Both Cosima and Siegfried died in 1930. Siegfried's successor, his British-born widow Winifred (née Williams, 1897–1980), had no pretensions as a producer, and she appointed the Intendant of the Berlin Staatsoper, Heinz Tietjen, as artistic director. Tietjen's productions, with scenic designs by Emil Preetorius (except *Parsifal*, redesigned in 1934 by Alfred Roller and in 1937 by Wieland Wagner), were lavish. If this period of the Bayreuth Festival's history is to some extent viewed with disapproval, the fault lies not in the productions or the stylized modified realism of Preetorius's sets, but in Winifred Wagner's personal association with Hitler, a frequent visitor to Bayreuth. At his command the festival became a yearly event from 1936 to 1944 (when war events closed it down), and at his request *Parsifal* was dropped from the programme from 1940. Winifred's contribution to the building itself was the erection of an administrative block on the north-west side and (in 1932) a new line of boxes at the back of the auditorium above the royal box.

WIELAND AND WOLFGANG WAGNER (1951–66)   The fact that Winifred Wagner, politically compromised, was still by the terms of her husband's will the sole owner of the festival's assets delayed the reopening after World War II, but eventually her two sons Wieland (1917–66) and Wolfgang (born 1919) were permitted to assume control as lessees. Wieland Wagner's *Parsifal*, with which the festival reopened in July 1951, made a sensational impact, as did his production of the *Ring*. The realism, modified or otherwise, of the previous festivals had disappeared; what little stage scenery there was came mainly from light projections; costumes were simple and stylized; choruses, uniformly dressed, moved in precise formations; and the soloists matched their movements to the words rather than the music. It was a complete rejection of the tradition established by Cosima Wagner, but not, so Wieland Wagner claimed, a rejection of the ideas of his grandfather, whose works he defined as 'mystery plays', concerned more with inner conflicts than outward events.

The 'new Bayreuth style', as it came to be called, may have owed something of its origin to the need to change the festival's image after its Nazi associations, but it soon established an artistic validity, and before long directors everywhere were copying Wieland Wagner's methods. Wieland, whose production experience had been gained outside Bayreuth (in Nuremberg and Altenburg), acknowledged no masters, but his conception of the stage as an 'illuminated space' owes something to Appia as well as to Gordon Craig. In the years 1951–66, during which the festival was again an annual event, he used the Festspielhaus as an 'experimental workshop', bringing out new productions or modifying older ones in a constant search for new aspects. Like Cosima, he chose singers who were willing to follow his ideas: casts, which had been predominantly German under Winifred Wagner, again became international.

Wolfgang Wagner, who served his apprenticeship under Tietjen in Berlin, concentrated mainly on administrative duties until 1966. These included the restoration of the theatre itself. Although Richard Wagner, regarding it as a temporary structure, had set little store on its outward appearance, Wolfgang Wagner decided, in the interests of its unique visual and acoustic qualities, to retain the original form of the building both inwardly and outwardly, and simply to replace weak parts with more solid materials (steel, concrete, brick). He extended the stage still further, modernized technical equipment, increased the seating capacity (now 1925) and built new offices, dressing rooms and rehearsal stages.

WOLFGANG WAGNER (1967–)   During the period of joint control with his brother, Wolfgang Wagner staged his own productions of some of the works. These, though less radical than Wieland Wagner's, adhered in the main to the principles of the new Bayreuth style. Following Wieland Wagner's death in 1966, Wolfgang Wagner, while continuing to stage operas occasionally himself, adopted from 1969 a policy of inviting directors from outside the family to stage one of the works in turn, each production remaining in the repertory for a number of years (usually five). Guest directors up to 1989 were August Everding, Götz Friedrich, Harry Kupfer, Patrice Chéreau, Jean-Pierre Ponnelle, Peter Hall and Werner Herzog. The result of this policy was the disappearance of a recognizable Bayreuth style. Guest directors have been allowed the freedom to interpret the works each in his own way, untrammelled by any pious regard to the composer's expressed intentions. The tendency of most (though not all) of them has been to place a direct stress (through the use of modern clothing or alienation techniques, for instance) on the moral, sociological and political implications of the works rather than on the mythological guise in which Wagner chose more indirectly to present them. Whatever the directors' individual merits, they have served to maintain that spirit of controversy that has been a constant feature of Wagner's Festspielhaus from its very beginning.

The annual festivals run from the last week of July to the end of August; *Parsifal* and the *Ring* are usually given, together with two of the other works, and each festival normally contains one new production.

The festival was financially self-supporting until World War II, but after its postwar reopening it relied to some extent on public subsidies. In May 1973 exclusive family ownership of the festival ended with the creation of the Richard Wagner Foundation Bayreuth which assumed responsibility in perpetuity for the festival and took over its assets, including the Wagner archives in Wahnfried. The trustees of the foundation include members of the Wagner family and representatives of the Federal Republic of Germany, the Bavarian Land, the town of Bayreuth and the voluntary organization Die Freunde von Bayreuth. The foundation does not finance the festival, which continues to receive public subsidies, and sole artistic control remains in the hands of the appointed festival director (Wolfgang Wagner was appointed in 1973). In the choice of future directors the trustees undertake to give preference to members of the Wagner family.

G.S.

Gesamtkunstwerk

The German term Gesamtkunstwerk, meaning 'total work of art', was used by Wagner for his notion, formulated in his theoretical essays of 1849–51, of an art form that combined various media within the framework of a drama. Harking back to ancient Greek drama, he suggested that there the basic elements of dance, music and poetry had been ideally combined. Their division into separate genres had diminished their expressive force; only in the total work of art could they regain their original dignity. Similarly, the arts of architecture, sculpture and painting would recover their classical and authentic stature only as constituents of the 'artwork of the future'.

The architect of the theatre of the future would be guided by the law of beauty and the dictates of intelligibility rather than by the demands of social distinctions. Sets would be executed by landscape painters, and the three sister arts would be reunited in the actor of the future, who would be dancer, musician and poet in one. The new work of art would be brought into being not by a single creative artist but by a fellowship of artists, in response to a communal demand. The artist of the future was thus the *Volk*, and the *Gesamtkunstwerk* the product of necessity or historical inevitability. Wagner's concept was concordant with the prevailing radical philosophical outlook of the 1840s: the reuniting of constituent parts in the *Gesamtkunstwerk* mirrored the socialist aim of restoring integrity to a fragmented, divided society. This utopian element, taken with the practical constraints of producing operas, perhaps explains why the theoretical model was not realized in detail in Wagner's music dramas.

The term 'Gesamtkunstwerk' is used in the essay *Das Kunstwerk der Zukunft* (1849) alongside similar terms such as 'das vollendete Kunstwerk der Zukunft' and 'das *allgemeinsame* Drama'. The notion of the reunification of the arts did not originate with Wagner: others who had previously advocated some sort of unification, either in theory or in practice, include G.E. Lessing, Novalis, Tieck, F.W.J. Schelling and E.T.A. Hoffmann.

Leitmotif

The word 'leitmotif' is from the German *Leitmotiv* meaning 'leading motif'. A term adopted by early commentators on Wagner's music dramas to highlight what they believed to be the most important feature contributing to comprehensibility and expressive intensity in those works. A leitmotif is a theme, or other coherent musical idea, clearly defined so as to retain its identity if modified on subsequent appearances, whose purpose is to represent or symbolize a person, object, place, idea, state of mind, supernatural force or any other ingredient in a dramatic work. The leitmotif may be musically unaltered on its return, or altered in rhythm, intervallic structure, harmony, orchestration or accompaniment, and may also be combined with other leitmotifs in order to suggest a new dramatic situation. A leitmotif is to be distinguished from a reminiscence motif (*Erinnerungsmotiv*), which, in earlier operas and in Wagner's works up to and including *Lohengrin*, tends to punctuate the musical design rather than provide the principal, 'leading' thematic premises for that design.

The earliest known use of the term 'leitmotif' is by the music historian A. W. Ambros, who wrote, in or before 1865, that both Wagner in his operas and Liszt in his symphonic poems 'seek to establish a higher unity across the whole by means of consistent leitmotifs' (*durchgehende Leitmotive*). From Ambros the term gravitated, via F. W. Jähns's study of Weber (1871) to Hans von Wolzogen's thematic guide to the *Ring*, published in 1876 – the year of the cycle's first complete performance. Wagner used it in print in his essay *Über die Anwendung der Musik auf das Drama* (1879), in the course of a complaint that 'one of my younger friends [presumably Wolzogen] . . . has devoted some attention to the characteristics of "leitmotifs", as he calls them, but has treated them more from the point of view of their dramatic import and effect than as elements of the musical structure'.

The use of the term 'motif' in writing about music goes back at least as far as the *Encyclopédie* (1765), and before 1879 Wagner had employed a variety of expressions when discussing thematic elements

157

in his works: 'melodisches Moment', 'thematisches Motiv', 'Ahnungs-motiv', 'Grundthema', 'Hauptmotiv'. As Wagner's comments in 1879 indicate, he sensed that Wolzogen, whose 'guide' was little more than a pamphlet, was in danger of over-simplifying and trivializing his achievements in the interests of a desire to make the music dramas more accessible; his remarks reinforce the fact that 'leitmotif', and its subsequent usage, tells us as much (if not more) about the reception of his works as about his working methods or creative intentions.

Wagner, with his wide experience as a conductor, was undoubt-edly aware of the extensive use of reminiscence motifs in earlier opera from Méhul and Cherubini to Marschner and Spohr, and his close friend, Theodor Uhlig, in writings on *Tannhäuser* and *Lohengrin*, had drawn attention to the role of recurrent thematic elements in Wagner's own work as early as 1850. Indeed, although Wagner was particularly concerned in *Oper und Drama* (written in 1851, before he had begun any extensive compositional work on the *Ring* cycle) to underline the importance of formal units (periods) constructed to ensure that all aspects of the music responded as vividly as possible to the promptings of the text, in practice he still recognized the necessity for a small number of easily identifiable and malleable motifs, along the lines of Beethoven's most pithy and memorable thematic cells. These would, however, originate in a melody quite different from the four-square and often florid vocal phrases of traditional opera, and embody such a power and direct-ness of expression that the emotion concerned would be recalled when the motif itself returned, even if action or text no longer alluded directly to its original associations.

A major problem for motif-labellers has been that this original association is almost always multivalent – the music depicting the grandeur of Valhalla also portrays the nobility of Wotan, for example – and might well be ambiguous. It is now generally accepted that Wolzogen mislabelled the *Ring*'s principal love motif as 'Flight', taking over this designation from an earlier commentary by Gottlieb Federlein (1871). And the motif which, after Wolzogen, is invariably designated 'Redemption through Love' was seen by Wagner himself – at least in a letter of 1875 – as representing the 'glorification of

Brünnhilde'. Such factors indicate why most commentators on Wagner express reservations about motif-labelling while finding it difficult to discard the activity altogether. After all, despite his own reservations about Wolzogen's efforts, Wagner's presentation and manipulation of his thematic material lay at the heart of his musico-dramatic technique, as he made clear in *Über die Anwendung der Musik auf das Drama*.

Discussing the 'simple nature-motif' (ex.1) and the 'equally simple motif' heard 'at the first appearance of the gods' castle Valhalla in the morning sunlight' in *Das Rheingold* (ex.2: Wagner transposed the motif from D♭ to C for ease of comparison), Wagner observes that 'having developed both these motifs in close correspondence with the mounting passions of the action, I was now able [in *Die Walküre*, Act 2] to link them – with the aid of a strangely distant harmonization – to paint a far clearer picture of Wotan's sombre and desperate suffering than his own words ever could' (ex.3). Later in the essay, seeking to emphasize the structural rather than the semantic role of his motivic techniques, Wagner describes how the 'remarkably simple' motif of the Rhinemaidens' innocent jubilation (ex.4) recurs in varied guises throughout the drama until, in Hagen's 'Watch' (*Götterdämmerung*, Act 1), 'it is heard in a form which, to my mind at least, would be unthinkable in a symphonic movement' (ex.5). Wagner's point is that the malevolent, distorted versions of the gold motif that pervade the music at this point would sound like 'empty sensationalism' in a symphony, but the dramatic context justifies the nature of the musical transformation and the structural emphasis which requires its protracted employment in this 'distorted' form.

Ex.3

Ex.4

Rhein - gold!   Rhein - gold!

Ex.5

Wagner himself understandably sought to underline such larger-scale structural concerns. But the concentration of Wolzogen and others on the identification of local motivic associations is no less understandable, since their principal purpose was not to provide the most far-reaching analysis but to defend the composer against charges of illogicality and incomprehensibility. Just as commentaries on symphonies and sonatas can be valuable on all levels, from simple, non-technical programme notes to elaborate analyses (provided the simple and the elaborate are not confused), so there is room, and need, for such variety in commentaries on opera. There is no evidence that the activities of Wolzogen and his followers seriously inhibited attempts at more sophisticated analytical studies of Wagner's harmonic and formal procedures, though these were slower to emerge. And while the more sophisticated anti-Wagnerians were able to use such naive motif-spotting as Wolzogen's to support arguments about the essential crudity of Wagner's compositional principles (Hanslick, for example, wrote in praise of Verdi's *Falstaff* that 'nowhere is the memory spoonfed by leitmotifs'), many Wagner scholars have built on the foundations laid by Wolzogen, and Wagner himself, to refine and elaborate the study of musical meaning in the music dramas, and the role that leitmotifs play in establishing that meaning. It is motivic evolution and development, in the context of large-scale tonal structuring and formal organization, that has become the focus of attention in the attempt to understand the ways in which Wagner's musical language, and his attitude to drama, changed over the years between *Das Rheingold* and *Parsifal*.

From the very beginning of scene i of *Das Rheingold*, motifs 'lead' in the sense that they do not merely pervade the musical fabric but establish its expressive atmosphere and formal processes. They do not invariably originate in the vocal line as *Oper und Drama* had prescribed, and Wagner soon begins to move beyond their exact or varied repetition at textually appropriate moments into the kind of transformation that creates deeper dramatic resonances and larger-scale musical continuities, suggesting that musical thinking itself is beginning to promote dramatic associations. At the end of scene i of *Das Rheingold*, the motif associated with the ring, and with the world's wealth (Wagner's own interpretation of the idea, according to his sketches), is transformed orchestrally into the Valhalla motif at the start of scene ii, a process leading the listener to connect Alberich's precious acquisition with Wotan's no less highly valued possession, and the power they both embody. As the cycle proceeds, a clear contrast emerges between, on the one hand, the immediate connection of word – or visual image – and tone that first fixes important motivic elements and, on the other hand, the consequent power of music to reinforce a connection that text and action may leave implicit: for example, the use of Alberich's curse when Fafner kills Fasolt (*Das Rheingold*, scene iv), and the references to the Siegfried motif when Brünnhilde and Wotan proclaim the need for a fearless hero (*Die Walküre*, Act 3).

The interruption of work on the *Ring* in 1857 brought a significant change of direction. Up to that point, Wagner's aesthetic had centred on the belief that the most profound art work was a theatrical event to which words and music made significant contributions. But it now began to evolve, under the impact of Schopenhauer, and the sheer force of his own musical inspiration, to the point where music became the central feature – however important the initial conception of theatrical event and text remained in relation to the music he eventually composed. The result, in simple terms, is that leitmotifs become even less specific in meaning and even more subject to musical elaboration; in all the later dramas there is a sense in which the motifs 'lead' the music beyond literal and immediate signification while still, inevitably, remaining linked to, and helping to determine, the progress of the drama. Scholars have wrestled with the inherent complexity of this interaction between the 'symphonic' and the 'dramatic'. In particular, Ernst Kurth (1920) proposed a distinction between leitmotifs, which reflect the dramatic situation directly, and 'developmental motifs' (*Entwicklungsmotive*), which achieve independence not only of such representational functions but also of the kind of clearcut shaping that makes a leitmotif easily identifiable. 'Developmental motifs' are figures that promote the ongoing evolution of the music – a process quite distinct from the actual development (by sequential transposition or any other variation procedure) of the leitmotifs themselves.

Kurth recognized that leitmotivic analysis on its own cannot possibly do justice to the significatory power of Wagner's music. More recently, Carolyn Abbate (1989) has declared that his music 'actually projects poetry and stage action in ways far beyond motivic signs'; she has also asserted that 'Wagner's motifs have no referential meaning; they may, and of course do, absorb meaning at exceptional and solemn moments, by being used with elaborate calculation as signs, but unless purposely maintained in this artificial state, they shed their specific poetic meaning and revert to their natural state as musical thoughts'. No doubt an analysis of *Tristan* that doggedly attempted to confine the meaning of every occurrence of the opening cello phrase to 'Tristan's suffering', or any other of the various tags that have been attached to it, would be absurdly naive and literal. But variation and diversity of meaning is not to be confused with meaninglessness; it seems undeniable that the listener 'comprehends' the intense, elaborate developments and derivations in *Tristan* subliminally, sensing meaning through the sheer force and insistence of its evolving musical logic.

One result of the increasing flexibility of motivic signification in the later Wagner is that the motifs themselves seem to invite reduction to a few unifying archetypes. Robert Donington, Deryck Cooke, Carl Dahlhaus and many others have shown how a few 'primal motifs' in the *Ring* – Donington (1974) has four, featuring Broken Chords, Conjunct Motion, Chromatic Intervals, and Changing Notes – may be regarded as generating a great number of offshoots. Robin Holloway (1986) has argued that in *Parsifal*, even more pervasively than in the *Ring* or *Tristan*, the leitmotifs grow from 'a sonorous image-cluster . . . the nucleus that gives life to the work's expressive substance'. Holloway's interpretation illustrates the tendency of leitmotivic analysis to seek out ever more intricate and all-embracing unifying factors. The role of leitmotif in Wagner's compositional design also remains a central topic in discussion of the extent to which his structures are 'tightly' or 'loosely' knit. No less valuable has been the concern of scholars working in the field of German studies to re-examine the significance of Wagner's motivic theory and practice in the light of evolving concepts of drama.

One example of Wagner's importance in the history of music is the difficulty of avoiding the concept of leitmotif in studies of so many of his contemporaries and successors. Roger Parker has found it useful to discuss Verdi's *Aida* in the light of the observation that 'particularly in its treatment of "motive" and "recurring theme", it is the most nearly Wagnerian of Verdi's operas' (1989). Direct influence or attempted imitation are not implied in this case, but with slightly later composers the probability of literal influence is much stronger, whether the composer is relatively close in style to Wagner, as Richard Strauss was in *Salome* and *Elektra*, or strikingly distant, as with Debussy in *Pelléas et Mélisande*. There are in fact very few composers of significance on whom Wagner's stylistic influence was direct and extensive: Humperdinck is one such.

These composers' operas show that, whatever the musical style, through-composition renders some degree of leitmotivic working a useful means of achieving continuity and directedness. Yet discussion of the topic is bedevilled by the problems facing motivic analysis in general: that is, of recognizing the point at which 'connection' and 'derivation' cease to be more convincing than 'contrast' and 'difference'. John Tyrrell (1982) comments on K. H. Wörner's attempt to demonstrate all-embracing thematic connections in Janáček's *Kát'a Kabanová* that 'too wide an interpretation of permissible manipulations allows almost anything to creep in'. By contrast, Peter Evans (1979) has shown how the presence of pervasive motivic working can be plausibly demonstrated in Britten's operas, despite a style that owes more to Verdi than to Wagner.

George Perle (1980) has attempted to argue that Alban Berg, in *Wozzeck*, used the leitmotif principle more effectively – that is, less predictably and mechanically – than Wagner himself had done. In his discussions of *Wozzeck* and *Lulu* Perle also distinguishes between leitmotif and 'Leitsektion': 'a total musical complex' that serves a referential function. The notion of referential musical function may be further elaborated if not only exact or near-exact recurrences but also the equivalences that are revealed by reduction to the unordered collections known as pitch-class sets are admitted: Allen Forte's work on *Wozzeck* (1985) and *Tristan* (1988) represents the most extensive demonstration of that procedure. Such manipulations might appear to have little to do with the leitmotif principle as it relates to Wagner, moving away as they do from the particular profile of the theme on the musical surface. So, too, Schoenberg's *Erwartung*, in its atonal athematicism, might be felt to be more a reaction against Wagner's influence than a celebration of it. Yet Carl Dahlhaus contends that the brief structural segments of *Erwartung*, 'not unlike Wagnerian periods, are not infrequently defined by means of a characteristic musical idea, which constitutes the predominant motif, albeit not the only one' (1987). If motivic elaboration of any kind is seen in terms of the leitmotif principle, then it becomes possible to extend the range of Wagner's 'influence' still further. The most ambitious operatic enterprise of the late 20th century, Stockhausen's *Licht*, could scarcely be less Wagnerian in style, yet the material of the entire seven-opera cycle derives from a 'super-formula', in which melodies representing the three central characters, Michael, Eva and Luzifer, are superimposed. The virtually constant presence, in the background, of these melodies may represent an approach to motivic composition very different from that of Wagner. We might nevertheless sense a genuine bond with those 'plastic nature motifs, which, by becoming increasingly individualized, were to serve as the bearers of the emotional subcurrents within the broad-based plot and the moods expressed therein', to which Wagner referred in 1871, in the *Epilogischer Bericht* on the *Ring*, when he attempted to describe what he believed his first task had been when embarking on the work almost 20 years before.

A.W.

Interpreters

Kasper Bausewein

Kasper Bausewein was born in Aub, near Ochsenfurt on 15 November 1838; he died in Munich on 18 November 1903. He studied in Munich, making his début there in 1854 at the Hofoper, where he was engaged for 46 years. A bass and a fine actor, equally gifted for comic and serious opera, he had a wide repertory ranging from Mozart's Figaro and Leporello and Rossini's Don Basilio to Caspar (*Der Freischütz*) and the three Wagner roles he created: Pogner in *Die Meistersinger* (1868), Fafner in *Das Rheingold* (1869) and Hunding in *Die Walküre* (1870). He retired in 1900 after a farewell performance as Lord Cockburn in *Fra Diavolo*.

E.F.

Franz Betz

Franz Betz was born in Mainz on 19 March 1835; he died in Berlin on 11 August 1900. A baritone, he studied in Karlsruhe and made his début at Hanover in 1856 as Heinrich (*Lohengrin*). In 1859 he sang Don Carlo (*Ernani*) at the Berlin Hofoper and was immediately engaged there, remaining a member of the company until his retirement in 1897. He sang Valentin in the first Berlin performance of Gounod's *Faust* (given as *Margarethe*) in 1863. At the Munich Hofoper he sang Telramund (1863), and Hans Sachs in the première of *Die Meistersinger* (1868), repeating the role in the first Berlin performance (1870). He was also Berlin's first Amonasro (1874) and King Mark (1876).

Betz sang Wotan at Bayreuth in the first complete *Ring* cycle (1876). He took part in a gala performance of Spontini's *Olympie* in Berlin (1879). Returning to Bayreuth in 1889, he alternated as Kurwenal and King Mark, and also sang Hans Sachs. He made guest appearances in Vienna and other cities in Austria and Germany. His vast repertory included the Dutchman, Wolfram, Pizarro, Don Giovanni and Falstaff, which he sang at the first Berlin performance of Verdi's opera (1894), but his favourite role was Hans Sachs, which he sang over a hundred times in Berlin alone; it perfectly displayed the strength, evenness and warmth of his generous voice, and the humanity of his dramatic style.

E.F.

Marianne Brandt

Marianne Brandt [Marie Bischoff] was born in Vienna on 12 September 1842; she died there on 9 July 1921. She studied in Vienna and in Baden-Baden with Viardot, making her début at Olmütz in 1867 as Rachel (*La Juive*). She first appeared in Berlin in 1868 as Azucena, and was engaged there until 1882. After making her London début at Covent Garden in *Fidelio* (1872), she sang Amneris in the first Berlin performance of *Aida* (1874) and Waltraute in *Götterdämmerung* during the first Bayreuth Festival (1876). At Bayreuth she also sang Kundry at the second performance of *Parsifal* (1882). Her other Wagner roles included Brangäne, which she sang at the first Berlin (1876), London (1882) and New York (1886) performances of *Tristan und Isolde*, Ortrud, Fricka (*Die Walküre*), Magdalene, Adriano (*Rienzi*) and Erda (*Siegfried*). The extensive compass (*g* to *d'''*) of her large and well-projected voice enabled her to sing both soprano and mezzo-soprano parts, and at the Metropolitan, where she appeared from 1884 to 1888, her roles included Leonore, Fidès (*Le prophète*), Siébel (*Faust*) and Eglantine, which she sang at the first American performance of Weber's *Euryanthe* (1887).

E.F.

Hans von Bülow

Hans (Guido) Freiherr von Bülow was born in Dresden on 8 January 1830; he died in Cairo on 12 February 1894.

After hearing Wagner conduct in Dresden in 1849 and the première of *Lohengrin* under Liszt at Weimar in 1850, he abandoned the law career chosen for him by his mother. He sought advice from Liszt and practical help from Wagner, now in Zürich, who arranged for him to conduct Donizetti's *La fille du régiment*. Bülow's lack of tact soon led to his dismissal from Zürich, however, and he moved as musical director to the small opera house in St Gall, where he began with *Der Freischütz*. It was well received, not least because he conducted it without the score, a feature of his working method that was to become renowned.

His conducting work was then interrupted by Liszt, who accepted him as a piano pupil. After teaching in Berlin (1855–64) and under-taking concert tours as a pianist, Bülow began an important phase in his career when he was appointed Hofkapellmeister in Munich. Here he gave the premières of *Tristan und Isolde* (1865) and *Die Meistersinger von Nürnberg* (1868). In his meticulous preparation and rehearsal from memory of both operas (for five years he had been preparing a piano score of *Tristan*), Bülow virtually developed the procedure by which operas have since come to be staged in Germany and elsewhere. He began with individual coaching of his répétiteurs so that they in turn could prepare the singers to his satis-faction. He would then rehearse the singers both singly and in ensembles before they began production rehearsals with piano. This schedule of preparation was also used for the orchestra, with sectional and then full orchestral rehearsals before combining players and singers in *Sitzproben* and stage rehearsals (there were eleven pre-dress rehearsals for *Tristan* before the final dress rehearsal).

In 1869 Bülow resigned from Munich, unable to cope when his wife, Liszt's daughter Cosima, left him for Wagner, and when he foresaw the problems of staging the première of *Rheingold* according to demands made by King Ludwig against the composer's wishes.

After more concert tours, he spent the years 1878–80 as Hofkapell-meister in Hanover, but resigned after a quarrel with the tenor Anton Schott (whom he had described during *Lohengrin* as a Knight of the Swine rather than of the Swan). Bülow moved on to Meiningen as Hofmusikdirektor, where from 1880 to 1885 he moulded the orchestra into one of Germany's finest, insisting that they play standing up and from memory. His last years were spent touring, teaching or guest conducting at the Berlin or Hamburg opera houses.

Bülow was a musician of formidable ability, with absolute self-command and an acute intellectual power of interpretation, notably of new German works. But he also possessed an irascible nature; he was quarrelsome, nervous, passionate and given to extremes of mood. Weingartner thought he lacked the necessary instinct for working in opera and that by devoting his entire attention to the orchestra he ignored his singers; Bülow's 1887 performance of *Carmen* in Hamburg horrified Weingartner with its musical aberrations and excessive rubato. Yet Richard Strauss, a Bülow protégé, had the highest regard for his intellect, analysis of phrasing and grasp of the psychological content of the music of Beethoven and Wagner.

C.F.

Friederike Grün

Friederike Grün was born in Mannheim on 14 June 1836; she died there in January 1917. She studied in Mannheim, joining the Hofoper chorus there in 1857. She was engaged at Frankfurt (1862), Cologne, Kassel, the Berlin Hofoper (1866) and, after further study in Milan, at Stuttgart (1870); she also made appearances in Vienna. Her repertory included Agathe, Norma, Valentine and Elisabeth, which she sang in the Italian première of *Tannhäuser* at Bologna in 1872. Her last engagement was at Coburg (1875–7). Although her voice was a dramatic soprano, she sang Fricka, a mezzo role, in *Das Rheingold* and *Die Walküre*, and created the Third Norn in the first complete *Ring* at Bayreuth (1876).

E.F.

Heinrich Gudehus

Heinrich Gudehus was born in Altenhagen, near Celle, on 30 March 1845; he died in Dresden on 9 October 1909. He studied with Malvina Schnorr von Carolsfeld at Brunswick and with Gustav Engel in Berlin, where he made his début in 1871 as Nadori in Spohr's *Jessonda*. After further study, he reappeared at Riga (1875) as Raoul in *Les Huguenots*. From 1880 to 1890 he was engaged at Dresden, making his début there as Lohengrin. He sang Parsifal at the second performance of Wagner's opera at Bayreuth (1882), returning there as Tristan (1886) and Walther (1888). In 1884 he appeared at Covent Garden, singing Walther, Max (*Der Freischütz*), Tannhäuser and Tristan, and sang at the Albert Hall in the first concert performance in England of *Parsifal*. He made his New York début at the Metropolitan in 1890 as Tannhäuser, also singing Raoul, Lohengrin, John of Leyden (*Le prophète*), Florestan, Walther, Siegfried, Siegmund and Tristan. On his return to Europe he was engaged at the Berlin Hofoper, remaining there until his retirement in 1896. One of the second generation of Wagnerian heroic tenors, he was also much admired in the dramatic French repertory.

E.F.

175

Karl Hill

Karl Hill was born in Idstein im Taunus on 9 May 1831; he died in Sachsenberg bei Schwerin on 12 January 1893. He studied in Frankfurt, making his début in 1868 as Jacob (Méhul's *Joseph*) at Schwerin, where he was engaged until 1890. He sang Alberich in the first *Ring* cycle, at Bayreuth in 1876, and Klingsor in the first performance of *Parsifal* (1882). His repertory included the Dutchman and Hans Sachs as well as Mozart's Count Almaviva, Don Giovanni and Leporello. Signs of insanity forced him to retire from the opera house.

E.F.

Gustav Hölzel

Gustav Hölzel was born in Budapest on 2 September 1813; he died in Vienna on 3 December 1883. The son of an actor-singer, he made his stage début at the age of 16 in Sopron, then sang in Graz, Berlin and Zürich. Engaged at the Vienna Hofoper in 1840, he remained there for more than 20 years. In 1843 at the Kärntnertortheater he created Di Fiesco in Donizetti's *Maria di Rohan*. Dismissed from the Hofoper in 1863 for altering the words of Friar Tuck's song in *Der Templer und die Jüdin*, he appeared at Darmstadt, Nuremberg, the Theater an der Wien and the Munich Hofoper, where he created Beckmesser in *Die Meistersinger* in 1868. In New York he took part in the American première of *Der Schauspieldirektor* (1870). An excellent comic actor, he sang Baculus (*Der Wildschütz*) at his farewell performance in 1877. Other roles included Leporello, Don Basilio and Van Bett (*Zar und Zimmermann*).

E.F.

Ferdinand Jäger

Ferdinand Jäger was born in Hanau on 25 December 1839; he died in Vienna on 13 June 1902. He studied in Dresden, where he made his début in 1865. Engagements in Cologne, Hamburg, Stuttgart and Kassel followed. Recommended to Wagner as a possible Siegfried, Jäger did not sing in the first *Ring* cycle at Bayreuth (1876) although coached in the role by the composer. But he sang Siegfried in both *Siegfried* and *Götterdämmerung* in the Vienna premières (1878–9), at the Munich Hofoper in private performances before King Ludwig II and at the Viktoria Theater, Berlin (1881). He sang Parsifal at Bayreuth (1882), after Winkelmann and Gudehus. Despite his fine voice and a physique perfect for the role, he never quite obtained real success as Siegfried.

E.F.

August Kindermann

August Kindermann was born in Potsdam on 6 February 1817; he died in Munich on 6 March 1891. In 1836 he joined the chorus of the Berlin Hofoper, and in 1839 he was engaged at Leipzig, where he took part in the first performance of Lortzing's *Caramo*. He also created the title role of Lortzing's *Hans Sachs* (1840) and Eberbach in *Der Wildschütz* (1842). In 1846 he went to Munich, where he was engaged at the Hofoper until his retirement in 1889. His very large repertory included Mozart's Figaro and Sarastro, Hidraot in Gluck's *Armide*, Indra (*Le roi de Lahore*) and many of Wagner's baritone and bass roles. He sang Wotan in the first performances of *Das Rheingold* (1869) and *Die Walküre* (1870); his repertory also included King Henry (*Lohengrin*), Fafner, Hunding, Hagen, King Mark and Titurel, which he sang at the first performance of *Parsifal* at Bayreuth (1882). For the 40th anniversary of his engagement at Munich he sang Stadinger in Lortzing's *Der Waffenschmied* (1886). His son and three daughters all became singers, the best known of them being Hedwig Reicher-Kindermann.

E.F.

Hermann Levi

Hermann Levi was born in Giessen, Upper Hesse, on 7 November 1839; he died in Munich on 13 May 1900. He studied with Hauptmann and Julius Rietz at the Leipzig Conservatory (1855–8). After a short stay in Paris he became music director at Saarbrücken (1859), and two years later he was made assistant Kapellmeister of the Mannheim Nationaltheater Opera, on Lachner's recommendation, and Kapellmeister at Rotterdam (1861–4). As Hofkapellmeister in Karlsruhe (1864–72), he became a friend of Clara Schumann (in nearby Baden-Baden) and Brahms, and this led him to produce Schumann's *Genoveva*; he also became interested in Wagner's operas, and in 1869 he gained Wagner's recognition with his performances of *Die Meistersinger* and *Rienzi*. From 1872 to 1896 he was Hofkapellmeister in Munich, and was made general music director of the city in 1894.

A distinguished and serious-minded artist of great personal qualities and musical gifts, Levi was universally recognized as one of the greatest conductors of his time. His modern, flowing, declamatory translations of Mozart's operas (*Le nozze di Figaro*, *Don Giovanni* and *Così fan tutte*), to which he also made alterations in the score, were great successes. But it was at Bayreuth that he made his strongest mark; he must be ranked with Richter, Mottl and Seidl as one of the greatest of the first generation of Bayreuth conductors. Cosima Wagner regarded him as 'a most excellent person, with real delicacy of feeling', and for Wagner he was 'the ideal *Parsifal* conductor'. However, Wagner had made a clumsy and unsuccessful attempt to convert Levi to Christianity, and his attitude, especially in connection with the idea of a Jew conducting *Parsifal* with its representation of the central Christian mystery, compounded by an anonymous letter complaining of this and also accusing Levi of being Cosima's lover, drove Levi to attempt to withdraw from conducting the work. Eventually Wagner, largely at King Ludwig's insistence, made peace with Levi, who conducted the première on 26 July 1882. In 1888 Cosima replaced Levi as *Parsifal* conductor with Mottl, but

Levi was recalled for the performances in 1889–94. He retired in 1896 but was persuaded to conduct again in 1897; however, the effort precipitated a nervous breakdown, and he was by that time mortally ill.

The 'spiritual' quality of Levi's interpretations was widely admired, and the economy of his gestures, as well as his masterly technique, exercised an influence on a number of conductors of the following generation, especially Weingartner.

F.B.

Mathilde Mallinger

Mathilde Mallinger [née Lichtenegger] was born in Zagreb on 17 February 1847; she died in Berlin on 19 April 1920. After studying at the Prague Conservatory with Gordigiani and in Vienna with Loewy, she was engaged at the Hofoper, Munich, where she made her début in 1866 as Norma. While at Munich she sang Elsa, Elisabeth (*Tannhäuser*) and Eva at the first performance of *Die Meistersinger* (1868). She was then engaged at the Hofoper, Berlin, making her début as Elsa (1869) and remaining there until her retirement in 1882. She took part in the first Berlin performances of *Die Meistersinger* (1870) and *Aida* (1874), and her repertory also included Leonore, Agathe, Sieglinde, Valentine (*Les Huguenots*) and Mozart's Pamina, Donna Anna and Countess Almaviva. Her voice, essentially a lyric soprano, was not large but so well schooled that she could sing heavier, dramatic roles without strain.

E.F.

Therese Malten

Therese Malten [Müller] was born in Insterburg, Prussia, on 21 June 1855; she died in Neuzschieren, near Dresden, on 2 January 1930. After studying with Gustav Engel in Berlin, she made her début in 1873 as Pamina at the Dresden Hofoper, where she was engaged for the next 30 years. Wagner heard her as Senta there in 1881 and invited her to Bayreuth the following summer to share the role of Kundry with Materna and Brandt in the first performance of *Parsifal*. She also sang Kundry at Munich in the private performances given for King Ludwig and at the Albert Hall, in the first concert performance in London (1884). She had previously made her London début at Drury Lane in 1882 as Leonore (*Fidelio*), a role she repeated in Munich. At Dresden she sang Isolde, Brünnhilde and many other roles in French, Italian and German operas, ranging from Gluck's *Armide* to *Cavalleria rusticana*. Returning to Bayreuth she sang Isolde (1886), Eva (1888) and Kundry for the last time in 1894. She also took part in the *Ring* cycles presented by Angelo Neumann in St Petersburg and Moscow (1889). Her voice was notable for its extensive compass; its middle register was rich and powerful with the higher and lower notes equally strong and pleasing.

E.F.

Amalie Materna

Amalie Materna(-Friedrich) was born in St Georgen on 10 July 1844; she died in Vienna on 18 January 1918. She made her début in 1865 at Graz and then appeared in operetta at the Carltheater, Vienna. In 1869 she first sang at the Vienna Hofoper, as Sélika (*L'Africaine*), and was engaged there for 25 years. She sang Amneris in the first Vienna performance of *Aida* (1874) and created the title role of Goldmark's *Die Königin von Saba* (1875). Her voice grew to be immensely powerful, but never lost its youthful bright timbre and was ideal for Brünnhilde, which she sang in the first complete *Ring* cycle at Bayreuth (1876), in the first Vienna performances of *Die Walküre* (1877) and *Siegfried* (1878), and in the first Berlin *Ring* at the Victoria Theatre (1881). In 1882 she sang Kundry at Bayreuth in the first performance of *Parsifal*, repeating the role there at every festival until 1891. She made her début at the Metropolitan in 1885 as Elisabeth (*Tannhäuser*), and also sang Valentine (*Les Huguenots*), Rachel (*La Juive*) and Brünnhilde (*Die Walküre*). She gave her final performance in Vienna as Elisabeth in 1894.

E.F.

Hans von Milde

Hans (Feodor) von Milde was born in Petronell, near Vienna, on 13 April 1821; he died in Weimar on 10 December 1899. A baritone, he studied in Vienna and with the younger Manuel García in Paris. From 1845 to 1884 he was engaged at the Hofoper, Weimar, where in 1850 he sang Telramund in the first performance of *Lohengrin*, conducted by Liszt. He also sang the Dutchman and, later, Hans Sachs and Kurwenal. He took part in the revival of Berlioz's *Benvenuto Cellini* (1852), created the title role of Cornelius's *Der Barbier von Bagdad* (1858) and Ruy Diaz in the same composer's *Der Cid* (1865). He sang the High Priest in the first stage performance of *Samson et Dalila*, at Weimar (1877).

E.F.

Anton Mitterwurzer

Anton Mitterwurzer was born in Sterzing, in the Tyrol, on 12 April 1818; he died in Döbling, Vienna, on 2 April 1876. He studied in Vienna, making his début in 1838 at Innsbruck. From 1839 until his retirement in 1870 he was a member of the Dresden Hofoper, where he made his début as the Hunter in Conradin Kreutzer's *Das Nachtlager in Granada*, took part in the première of Marschner's *Kaiser Adolf von Nassau* and created Wolfram in *Tannhäuser* (1845). He also sang Kurwenal in the first performance of *Tristan und Isolde* (1865, Munich). His repertory included Aubry in *Der Vampyr*, Bois-Guilbert in *Der Templer und die Jüdin* and the title role of *Hans Heiling*. An intelligent singer with a powerful voice, he was also an excellent actor.

E.F.

Albert Niemann

Albert Niemann was born in Erxleben, near Magdeburg, on 15 January 1831; he died in Berlin on 13 January 1917. He made his début in 1849 at Dessau, singing small roles. After studying with Schneider and Nusch, in 1852 he was engaged at Halle. Two years later he moved to Hanover, where the king paid for him to study further with Duprez in Paris. Having already sung Tannhäuser, Lohengrin and Rienzi, he was chosen by Wagner to sing in the first Paris performance of *Tannhäuser* in 1861. After the fiasco of the three performances, Niemann returned to Hanover.

In 1864 he made a guest appearance in Munich, singing Tannhäuser, Lohengrin, Faust and Manrico. From 1866 until his retirement in 1889, he was engaged at the Hofoper, Berlin, where he sang in the first local performances of *Die Meistersinger* (1870), *Aida* (1874) and *Tristan and Isolde* (1876), also taking part in a gala performance of Spontini's *Olympie* (1879). He sang Siegmund in *Die Walküre* during the first complete *Ring* cycle at Bayreuth (1876) and in the first cycle given in London, at Her Majesty's Theatre (1882). It was also as Siegmund that he made his New York début at the Metropolitan (1886). During his two seasons there he sang in the first New York performances of *Tristan und Isolde* (1886), Spontini's *Fernand Cortez* and *Götterdämmerung* (1888). His last appearance in Berlin was as Florestan (*Fidelio*) in 1888. Of immense physical stature, with a powerful, heroic voice, Niemann was unrivalled as Siegmund and Tristan during his lifetime.

E.F.

Theodor Reichmann

Theodor Reichmann was born in Rostock on 15 March 1849; he died in Marbach on 22 May 1903. He studied in Berlin, Prague and with Lamperti in Milan, making his début in 1869 at Magdeburg. After singing at Rotterdam, Strasbourg and Hamburg, he appeared for the first time in Munich in 1874 in *Guillaume Tell*, and the following year began a permanent engagement there in Marschner's *Hans Heiling*. He sang Amonasro in *Aida* (1877), the Wanderer in *Siegfried* (1878) and the title role of Nessler's *Der Rattenfänger von Hameln* (1881), all first Munich performances. He sang Amfortas at all 16 performances of *Parsifal* at Bayreuth in 1882, returning to the festival in that role regularly until 1902, as Hans Sachs in 1888–9 and as Wolfram in 1891. He made his London début in 1882 as Wotan in the second and third *Ring* cycles presented by Angelo Neumann at Her Majesty's Theatre. He first sang at Covent Garden in 1884 as Telramund, the Dutchman and Hans Sachs and returned in 1892 to sing Wotan (*Siegfried*, then *Die Walküre*) in the *Ring* cycles conducted by Mahler. From 1883 to 1889 he was engaged at the Vienna Hofoper, where he sang Iago in the first Vienna performance of Verdi's *Otello* (1888). He made his Metropolitan début in 1889 in *Der fliegende Holländer*, and during his two seasons there he sang 16 parts, which included Don Giovanni, Count di Luna, Renato, Solomon (*Die Königin von Saba*), Amonasro, Werner (*Der Trompeter von Säkkingen*), Nélusko (*L'Africaine*) and Escamillo, as well as his Wagner roles. Then he returned to Vienna. He made his final appearance in Munich at the Prinzregententheater as Hans Sachs in 1902, when the resonance of his magnificently warm and even voice was said to have been as powerful as at the beginning of his career.

E.F.

Emil Scaria

Emil Scaria was born in Graz on 18 September 1838; he died in Blasewitz, near Dresden, on 22 July 1886. He studied in Vienna and made his début in 1860 at Budapest as Saint-Bris (*Les Huguenots*). After further study with Garcia in London, he sang at Dessau; in 1863 he was engaged at Leipzig and in 1865 at Dresden. His repertory then included Dulcamara, Nicolai's Falstaff and Peter the Great (*Zar und Zimmermann*). Although his powerful voice had the dark colouring of a true bass, its enormous range allowed him to sing baritone roles with equal success. From 1873 until his death Scaria was engaged at the Vienna Hofoper. He sang Wotan in the first Berlin *Ring* cycle, at the Viktoria Theater (1881), and also in the first London cycle, at Her Majesty's Theatre (1882), where during *Die Walküre* he suffered a breakdown; although he sang in *Siegfried* two nights later, he did not appear in the second and third cycles. Scaria sang Gurnemanz in the first performance of *Parsifal* at Bayreuth (1882) and joined Angelo Neumann's touring company in Germany, Belgium, the Netherlands and Italy, singing Wotan and Rocco (*Fidelio*). During 1883 he sang King Mark at both Berlin and Vienna, and returned to Bayreuth as Gurnemanz, which he sang in the first concert performance of *Parsifal* in London, at the Albert Hall (1884). In 1886 he again suffered a mental breakdown and soon after died insane.

E.F.

Max Schlosser

Max [Karl] Schlosser was born in Amberg, Bavaria, on 17 October 1835; he died in Utting am Ammersee on 2 September 1916. After singing in Zürich, St Gallen and Augsburg, in 1868 he was engaged at the Hofoper, Munich, where he remained until 1904. He sang David in the first performance of *Die Meistersinger* (1868) and Mime in the first performance of *Das Rheingold* (1869). He also sang Mime in *Siegfried* at Bayreuth in the first complete *Ring* cycle (1876). In 1882 he accompanied Angelo Neumann's Wagner tour of Europe, singing Mime in the first London performance of the *Ring*, at Her Majesty's Theatre. His repertory included Almaviva (*Barbiere*), Tonio (*La fille du régiment*), Lyonel (*Martha*) and Max (*Der Freischütz*). Towards the end of his career he sang baritone roles, including Beckmesser and the Nightwatchman (*Die Meistersinger*), which he sang at his farewell performance in Munich, in his 70th year.

E.F.

Ludwig Schnorr von Carolsfeld

Ludwig Schnorr von Carolsfeld was born in Munich on 2 July 1836; he died in Dresden on 21 July 1865. While still a student at the Leipzig Conservatory he was engaged by Eduard Devrient for the Karlsruhe Hofoper, making his first solo appearances in 1854–5 in *Norma* and *Der Freischütz*. He became principal tenor of the company in 1858 and two years later moved to Dresden, where he quickly made a reputation in lieder, oratorio and opera, especially as Tannhäuser and Lohengrin. He began studying Tristan, but his fears about the demands of the role led him to abandon it. Then in 1862 at Biebrich he and his wife, the soprano Malvina Garrigues, sang Tristan and Isolde to Wagner, who was much moved by Schnorr's singing and praised his artistic sympathy and quickness of understanding. The couple were, with Bülow, primarily responsible for the success of the première on 10 June 1865. It was largely the strain of the experience that caused Schnorr to develop a feverish chill. His last public appearance was in Munich as Erik in *Der fliegende Holländer* (9 July 1865), though he sang excerpts from the *Ring* and *Die Meistersinger* before Ludwig II on 12 July. Returning to Dresden, he rehearsed *Don Giovanni* on the 15th, but on the 16th developed what he termed a 'rampant gout' that began in his knee and led to delirium. He burst into song on his deathbed, calling repeatedly on Wagner's name.

A powerfully built man, with baritone colour in his tenor voice, Schnorr was praised for his smoothness of line, his portamento, and his 'elegiac, somewhat veiled' tone (Prölss). Wagner regarded him as inferior vocally to Tichatschek but greatly superior in dramatic power and intelligence; his death affected Wagner profoundly, on both personal and artistic grounds.

Schnorr's wife, Malvina Garrigues (born Copenhagen, 7 December 1825; died Karlsruhe, 8 February 1904), studied in Paris with the younger Manuel García and sang in Breslau (1841–9), making her début in *Robert le diable*, then in Coburg, Gotha, Hamburg and (from 1854) in Karlsruhe. She was praised for her powerful, ringing soprano and her fluent technique. After her husband's death she was unable to continue her career.

J.W.

Wilhelmine Schröder-Devrient

Wilhelmine Schröder-Devrient [née Schröder] was born in Hamburg on 6 December 1804; she died in Coburg on 26 January 1860. Her father, Friedrich Schröder (1744–1816), was the first German Don Giovanni. She made her début at the Kärntnertortheater as Pamina (20 January 1821), when the freshness and confidence of her singing made a great impression. She followed this with Emmeline (Weigl's *Die Schweizerfamilie*) and Marie (Grétry's *Raoul Barbe Bleu*, in German); she also sang Agathe on 7 March 1822 with Weber conducting. Her greatest triumph, and the performance that laid the foundations of her international fame, was as Leonore on 3 November 1822. She first sang in Dresden that year, and in 1823 was given a two-year contract at the Hoftheater; she remained associated with Dresden until 1847.

Schröder-Devrient impressed audiences everywhere with the dramatic power of her performances, especially as Donna Anna, Euryanthe, Reiza, Norma, Romeo, Valentine and Rossini's Desdemona. She had an outstanding success in Berlin in 1828, though she offended Spontini by refusing to sing the title role of *La vestale* (she sang it a year later in Dresden). In Paris in May 1830 she made triumphant appearances as Agathe and Leonore. She returned to sing Italian opera in 1831–2, appearing with Malibran in *Don Giovanni* and *Otello*. From May to July 1832 she also appeared at the King's Theatre in London 30 times, in *Fidelio*, *Don Giovanni* and Chelard's *Macbeth*. In the following season she was heard in *Der Freischütz*, *Die Zauberflöte*, *Euryanthe* and *Otello*, less successfully owing to the rival attractions of Taglioni and Fanny Elssler. After Malibran's death she was encouraged to return to London in 1837, and sing in *Fidelio*, *La sonnambula* and *Norma*. From that time a decline in her vocal powers was noticeable. She seemed tired of the stage and inclined to drag the tempo and to declaim rather than sing; but she continued to have successes in Germany, creating Adriano (*Rienzi*, 1842), Venus and Senta (both 1845) in Dresden, and also singing Gluck's Iphigenia (*Aulide*). Her last appearance was at Riga on 17 December 1847.

In an age when few singers matched their vocal prowess with equal dramatic skill, Schröder-Devrient impressed audiences especially with her interpretation of Leonore; many reports give details of its dramatic effect. Weber thought her the best of all Agathes, and to have disclosed more in the part than he had believed was there; however, on hearing her sing Leonore in 1822 he discerned the deficiencies that later (1842) disturbed Berlioz, who deplored her exaggerated acting, her vehement declamation and her failures of style. According to Chorley, 'Her voice was a strong soprano . . . with an inherent expressiveness of tone . . . Her tones were delivered without any care, save to give them due force'. However, he praised her acting, despite her increasingly exaggerated characterization. It was her Leonore that roused the 16-year-old Wagner to his sense of vocation as a dramatic composer; in *Über Schauspieler und Sänger*, dedicated to her memory, he gave a moving and detailed critical evaluation of her art. Her vocal deficiencies were partly due to shortcomings in her training; as a singer who brought new dramatic powers to the art of opera she was influential on the course of German Romantic opera.

J.W.

Gustav Siehr

Gustav Siehr was born in Arnsberg, Westphalia, on 17 September 1837; he died in Munich on 18 May 1896. He studied in Berlin, making his début in 1863 at Neustrelitz as Oroveso. After singing in Göteborg, Prague and Wiesbaden, in 1881 he was engaged at the Munich Hofoper, where he remained until his death. At Bayreuth he sang Hagen in the first *Ring* cycle (1876), Gurnemanz in *Parsifal* (1882–9) and King Mark (1886). His wide repertory included Sarastro, the Commendatore, Caspar (*Der Freischütz*), Bertram (*Robert le diable*), Daland and Pogner.

E.F.

Sophie Stehle

Sophie Stehle was born in Sigmaringen on 15 May 1838; she died in Schloss Harterode, Hanover, on 4 October 1921. She studied in Augsburg and Munich, where she made her début at the Hofoper in 1860 as Emmeline in Weigl's *Die Schweizerfamilie*. During the next 14 years she sang a wide variety of roles, including Marguerite, Agathe, Rachel (*La Juive*), Pamina, Amazili (Spontini's *Fernand Cortez*), Sélika (*L'Africaine*), Anna (Marschner's *Hans Heiling*), Senta, Elisabeth and Elsa. She sang Fricka in the first performance, in Munich, of *Das Rheingold* (1869) and Brünnhilde in *Die Walküre* (1870). She made her farewell in 1874 as Gretchen in Lortzing's *Der Wildschütz*.

E.F.

Joseph Tichatschek

Joseph (Aloys) Tichatschek [Josef Tichá ček] was born in Ober-Weckelsdorf (now Teplice, near Broumov) on 11 July 1807; he died in Blasewitz, near Dresden, on 18 January 1886. He had lessons with Ciccimarra while studying medicine in Vienna, and in 1830 he joined the chorus of the Kärntnertortheater. He soon progressed to comprimario parts, and sang as a principal in Graz in 1837. He sang in Vienna that year and made his Dresden début on 11 August in the title role of Auber's *Gustavus III*; the following year he was appointed to the Dresden Hofoper. With Wilhelmine Schröder-Devrient and Anton Mitterwurzer, Tichatschek helped the company set new standards of singing. In 1841 he sang at Drury Lane (as Adolar, Tamino and Robert le diable) and elsewhere in England. He was pensioned in 1861 but continued to appear until 1870, his voice being remarkably well preserved. His repertory included the principal tenor role's in *Idomeneo*, *Die Zauberflöte*, *Fernand Cortez*, *I Capuleti e i Montecchi*, *La muette de Portici* and *La dame blanche*. His range included lyric and dramatic tenor parts, but he was also the prototype of the Wagner Heldentenor, creating the title roles of *Rienzi* in 1842 and *Tannhaäuser* in 1845.

Opinions agree on the beauty and brilliance of Tichatschek's voice. Sincerus praised his range of expression, even production, intonation, and enunciation, although he had reservations about his coloratura. In 1840 Nicolai called him the greatest German tenor, and Cornelius was deeply moved by his Lohengrin in 1867. Berlioz described him in the role of Rienzi as 'brilliant and irresistible . . . elegant, impassioned, heroic, his fine voice and great lustrous eyes marvellously effective'; Wagner, however, while admiring his 'glorious voice and great musical talent', found him unable to portray the character's 'dark, gloomy, demonic strain'. Tichatschek's simple devotion to his voice, appearance and costumes was exclusive of any fuller dramatic perception, and he horrified Wagner at the première of *Tannhäuser* by addressing his outburst in praise of Venus with great passion to Elisabeth.

J.W.

Georg Unger

Georg Unger was born in Leipzig on 6 March 1837; he died there on 2 February 1887. He first studied theology, but made his opera début in Leipzig in 1867 with such success that he was soon engaged in other cities. Hans Richter heard him in Mannheim and recommended him to Wagner to create Siegfried at Bayreuth (1876). In 1877 Unger went to London for the series of Wagner concerts in the Albert Hall, but his frequent failure to appear caused the composer to take a dislike to him; he returned to Leipzig that year, singing at the Opera there until 1881. He is an early example of the Wagnerian Heldentenor.

Heinrich Vogl

Heinrich Vogl was born in Au, Munich, on 15 January 1845; he died in Munich on 21 April 1900. He studied with Lachner and made his début in 1865 as Max (*Der Freischütz*) at the Hofoper, Munich, where he was engaged for 35 years. Having already sung Lohengrin (1867) and Tristan (1869), he created the roles of Loge in *Das Rheingold* (1869) and Siegmund in *Die Walküre* (1870), and at Bayreuth he sang Loge in the first complete *Ring* cycle (1876). He sang Siegfried in the first Munich performances of *Siegfried* and *Götterdämmerung* (1878); Loge and Siegmund in the first Berlin *Ring* cycle, as well as both Siegfrieds in the second cycle (1881, Victoria Theatre); Loge and Siegfried in the first London *Ring* cycle (1882, Her Majesty's Theatre); and took part in the early part of Angelo Neumann's European Wagner tour (1882). He returned to Bayreuth as Tristan and Parsifal (1886), and made his Metropolitan début as Lohengrin (1890), also singing Tannhäuser, Tristan, Loge, Siegmund and both Siegfrieds. In Munich he sang in Ritter's *Faule Hans* (1885), *Otello* (1888), *Benvenuto Cellini* (1889), Franchetti's *Asrael* (1892), *Pagliacci* (1893), *Dalibor* (1894), Berlioz's *La prise de Troie* and Cornelius's *Der Cid* (1895). He created Baldur in his own opera *Der Fremdling* (1899) and made his last appearance as Canio (1900), four days before his death.

Vogl's voice was powerful and his stamina legendary (he sang Loge, Siegmund and both Siegfrieds in some *Ring* cycles on four consecutive days without apparent strain). Walther was the only major Wagnerian tenor role that he never sang.

E.F.

Therese Vogl

Therese Vogl [née Thoma] was born in Tutzing on 12 November 1845; she died in Munich on 29 September 1921. She studied in Munich, making her début (as Therese Thoma) in 1865 at Karlsruhe as Casilda in Auber's *La part du diable*. In 1867 she was engaged at the Munich Hofoper, where she remained for 25 years. The following year she married the tenor Heinrich Vogl and in 1869 sang Isolde to her husband's Tristan. She sang Sieglinde in the first performance of *Die Walküre* (1870), and Brünnhilde in *Siegfried* (1878) and *Götterdämmerung* (1879). She sang Brünnhilde in the first London performance of *Der Ring des Nibelungen*, at Her Majesty's Theatre in 1882, and took part in Angelo Neumann's tour of the *Ring* around Europe. Her repertory included Elsa, the title role in *Fidelio*, Agathe, Eglantine (*Euryanthe*) and Gluck's Alcestis.

E.F.

Johann Michael Wächter

Johann Michael Wächter was born in Rappersdorf on 2 March 1794; he died in Dresden on 26 May 1853. A baritone, he sang in various church choirs in Vienna and made his stage début in 1819 at Graz as Don Giovanni. Engagements at Bratislava, Vienna and Berlin followed; then in 1827 he joined the Dresden Hofoper, where he remained for the rest of his career. His roles included Mozart's Figaro, Sherasmin (*Oberon*), Mikéli (Cherubini's *Les deux journées*) and Brian de Bois-Guilbert (Marschner's *Der Templer und die Jüdin*). He sang in three Wagner premières, as Orsini in *Rienzi* (1842), as the Dutchman (1843) and as Biterolf in *Tannhäuser* (1845). Berlioz, who heard *Der fliegende Holländer* in Dresden, considered Wächter's baritone 'one of the finest I have ever heard, and he uses it like a consummate singer. It is of that rich and vibrant timbre that has such a wonderful power of expression, provided that the artist sings with soul and feeling, which Wächter does to a high degree' (*Mémoires*). His wife, the mezzo Thérèse Wächter-Wittman (born Vienna, 31 August 1802), also sang at Dresden; she created Mary in *Der fliegende Holländer*.

E.F.

Johanna Wagner

Johanna Wagner [Jachmann-Wagner] was born in Seelze, near Hanover, on 13 October 1826; she died in Würzburg, on 16 October 1894. She was the adopted daughter of Richard Wagner's elder brother, Albert. Through the influence of her uncle, she made her début at Dresden in 1844 as Agathe. She created Elisabeth in *Tannhäuser* (1845) and also sang in Auber's *Le maçon*. After studying in Paris with the younger Manuel García, she sang in Hamburg (1849) and was then engaged at the Hofoper, Berlin (1850–61), where she took over the part of Fidès (*Le prophète*) from Pauline Viardot. She made her London début in 1856 at Her Majesty's Theatre as Rossini's Tancredi, also singing Lucrezia Borgia and Romeo (*I Capuleti e i Montecchi*). She sang Elisabeth in the first Berlin performance of *Tannhäuser* (1856) and Ortrud in the first Berlin performance of *Lohengrin* (1859). Early in the 1860s she lost her singing voice and appeared for a decade as an actress. Her voice recovered, she sang Schwertleite and the First Norn in the first complete *Ring* cycle at Bayreuth (1876). Her voice was powerful throughout its range, clear and bright in the upper register, round and full in the lower; she had a magnificent stage presence as well as considerable dramatic ability.

E.F.

Hermann Winkelmann

Hermann Winkelmann [Winckelmann] was born in Brunswick on 8 March 1849; he died in Vienna on 18 January 1912. He studied singing in Paris and with Koch in Hanover before making his début in *Il trovatore* at Sondershausen in 1875. After appearances throughout Germany, in 1878 he settled in Hamburg where he sang in the local premières of *Das Rheingold* (as Loge, 1878), *Götterdämmerung* (1879), Rubinstein's *Nero* (1879) and *Tristan und Isolde* (1882). In 1882 he sang with the Hamburg company under Richter at Drury Lane, his roles including Lohengrin, Tannhäuser and Tristan. Following Richter's recommendation, Wagner chose Winkelmann to create Parsifal at Bayreuth in 1882. The next year he was engaged by the Vienna Hofoper, where he became the city's first Tristan and remained a favourite until his retirement in 1906. During this period he continued to sing at Bayreuth, and in 1884 appeared at Theodore Thomas's Wagner festivals in New York, Boston, Philadelphia, Cincinnati and Chicago. Besides Wagner his repertory included Gluck's *Alceste* and *Armide*, *Fidelio*, Auber's *La muette de Portici*, Verdi's *Otello*, Marschner's *Der Vampyr* and, in 1897, Smetana's *Dalibor* under Mahler's direction.

Winkelmann was a leading figure in the first generation of Wagner singers, and was coached by the composer. Although he possessed the ample, sonorous voice of a true heroic tenor, his fluid lyrical delivery stood in marked contrast to the declamatory style of many Bayreuth performers during the era of Cosima Wagner's hegemony.

Ludwig Zottmayr

Ludwig Zottmayr was born in Amberg, Bavaria, on 31 March 1828 and died in Weimar on 16 October 1899. A bass-baritone, he made his début in 1855 at Nuremberg and was then engaged at Hamburg, Hanover and, in 1865, at the Munich Hofoper, where he remained until 1880. He sang King Mark in the first performance of *Tristan und Isolde* (1865) and his repertory included Mozart's Figaro, Don Giovanni, Hans Heiling, William Tell and Luna, as well as bass and baritone Wagner roles.

E.F.

Glossary,
Index of Role Names
and
Suggested Further
Reading

Glossary

Act One of the main divisions of an opera, usually completing a part of the action and often having a climax of its own. The classical five-act division was adopted in early operas and common in serious French opera of the 17th and 18th centuries, but in Italian opera a three-act scheme was soon standard, later modified to two in *opera buffa*. From the late 18th century, operas were written in anything from one act to five, with three the most common; Wagner's ideal music drama was to consist of three acts.

Air French or English term for 'song' or 'aria'. In French opera of the 17th and 18th centuries it was applied both to unpretentious, brief pieces and to serious, extended monologues, comparable to arias in Italian opera.

Apoggiatura (It.) A 'leaning note', normally one step above the note it precedes. Apoggiatura were normally introduced by performers, in recitativevs and arias in 18th-century opera, to make the musical line conform to the natural inflection of the words an (in arias) to increase the expressiveness.

Aria (It.) A closed, lyrical piece for solo voice, the standard vehicle for expression on the part of an operatic character. Arias appear in the earliest operas. By the early 18th century they usually follow a da capa pattern (*A-B-A*); by Mozart's time they took various forms, among them the slow-fast type, sometimes called rondò. this remained popular in Italian opera during most of the 19th century (the 'cantabile-cabaletta' type); even longer forms, sometimes in four sections with interruptions to reflect changes of mood, appear in the operas of Donizetti and Verdi. The aria as a detachable unit became less popular later in the century; Wagner wrote none in his mature operas, nor Verdi in *Otello* or *Falstaff*; in Puccini, too, an aria is usually part of the dramatic texture and cannot readily be extracted. Some 20th-century composers (notably Stravinsky, in the neo-classical *Rake's Progress*) have revived the aria, but generally it has been favoured only where a formal or artificial element has been required.

Arietta (It.)**, Ariette** (Fr.) A song, shorter and less elaborate than a fully developed aria or air.

Arioso (It.) 'Like an aria': a singing (as opposed to a declamatory) style of performance; a short passage in a regular tempo in the middle or at the end of a recitative; or a short aria.

Baritone A male voice of moderately low pitch, normally in the range *A–f'*. The voice became important in opera in the late 18th century, particularly in Mozart's works, although the word 'baritone' was little used at this time ('bass' served for both types of low voice). Verdi used the baritone for a great variety of roles, including secondary heroic ones.

Bass The lowest male voice, normally in the range *F–e'*. The voice is used in operas of all periods, often for gods, figures of authority (a king, a priest, a father) and for villains and sinister characters. There are several subclasses of bass: the *basso buffo* (in Italian comic opera), the *basso cantante* or French *basse-chantante* (for a more lyrical role) and the *basso profundo* (a heavy, deep, voice).

Bass-baritone A male voice combining the compass and other attributes of the bass and the baritone. It is particularly associated with Wagner, especially the roles of Wotan (the *Ring*) and Sachs (*Die Meistersinger*).

Bel Canto (It.) 'Fine singing': a term loosely used to indicate both the elegant Italian vocal style of the 18th and early 19th centuries and the operas (especially those of Bellini) designed to exploit that style.

Coloratura Florid figuration or ornamentation. The term is usually applied to high-pitched florid writing, exemplified by such roles as the Queen of the Night in Mozart's *Die Zauberflöte*, Violetta in Verdi's *La traviata* or Zerbinetta in Strauss's *Ariadne auf Naxos*, as well as many roles by Rossini and other early 19th-century Italian composers. The term 'coloratura soprano' signifies a singer of high pitch, lightness and agility, appropriate to such roles.

Comic opera A musico-dramatic work of a light or amusing nature. The term may be applied equally to an Italian *opera buffa*, a French *opéra comique*, a German Singspiel, a Spanish zarzuela or an English opera of light character. It is also often applied to operetta or *opéra bouffe* and even musical comedy. Most non-Italian comic operas have spoken dialogue rather than continuous music.

Contralto (It.) A voice normally written for the range *g–e"*. In modern English the term denotes the lowest female voice, but the term could also denote a male falsetto singer or a castrato.

In opera, true contralto (as distinct from mezzo-soprano) roles are exceptional. They occurred in the 17th century for old women, almost invariably comic, but in the 18th century composers came to appreciate the deep female voice for dramatic purposes. In Handel's operas several contralto roles stand in dramatic contrast to the prima donna, for example Cornelia in *Giulio Caesare*, a mature woman and a figure of tragic dignity. Rossini's important contralto (or mezzo) roles include Cinderella in *La Cenerentola*, Rosina in *Il barbiere di Siviglia* (original version), and the heroic part of Arsaces in *Semiramide*. In later opera, contraltos were repeatedly cast as a sorceress-like figure (Verdi's Azucena and Arvidson/Ulrica, Wagner's Ortrud) or an oracle (Wagner's Erda) and sometimes as an old women.

Duet (It.) An ensemble for two singers. It was used in opera almost from the outset,

often at the end of an act or when the principal lovers were united (or parted). Later the duet became merged in the general continuity of the music (Verdi, Puccini etc) or dissolved into a musical dialogue in which the voices no longer sang simultaneously (later Wagner, R. Strauss etc). The love duet had become characterized by singing in 3rds or 6ths, acquiring a mellifluous quality of sound appropriate to shared emotion. Often the voices are used singly at first and join together later, symbolizing the development described in the text.

Festa teatrale (It.) A serenata-type genre of the high baroque period, cultivated especially in Vienna; typically the subject matter was allegorical and the production part of a celebration of a court event.

Finale (It.) The concluding, continuously composed, section of an act of an opera. The ensemble finale developed, at the beginning of the second half of the 18th century, largely through the changes wrought in comic opera by Carlo Goldoni (1707–93), who in his librettos made act finales longer, bringing in more singers and increasing the density of the plot.

Grand opéra A term used to signify both the Paris Opéra and the operas performed there. Later it tended to be applied more narrowly to the specially monumental works performed at the Opéra during its period of greatest magnificence, including Rossini's *Guillaume Tell* and several operas composed to librettos by Eugène Scribe by Meyerbeer and others during the 1830s (including *Les Hugenots*). The term also applies to operas by Donizetti, Gounod, Verdi and Massenet.

Handlung für Musik (Ger.) 'Action in music': term used by Wagner in the libretto for *Lohengrin*.

Heldentenor (Ger.) 'Heroic tenor': a robust tenor voice of clarion timbre and unusual endurance, particularly suited to Wagner's heroic roles (Tannhäuser, Tristan,

Siegmund, Siegfried); it was an extreme manifestation of the new dramatic tenor that appeared in the 1830s and 1840s. The term has become standard in the Wagner literature though not used by the composer himself.

Interlude Music played or sung between the main parts of a work.

Key The quality of a musical passage or composition that causes it to be sensed as gravitating towards a particular note, called the keytone or the tonic.

Leitmotif (Ger. *Leitmotiv*) 'Leading motif': a theme, or other musical idea, that represents or symbolizes a person, object, place, idea, state of mind, supernatural force or some other ingredient in a dramatic work. It may recur unaltered, or it may be changed in rhythem, intervallic structure, tempo, harmony, orchestration or accompaniment, to signify dramatic development, and may be combined with other leitmotifs. The concept is particularly associated with Wagner, who used it as a basis for his musical structures, but the idea was older.

Libretto (It.) 'Small book': a printed book containing the words of an opera; by extension, the text itself. In the 17th and 18th centuries, when opera houses were lit, librettos were often read during performances; when an opera was given in a language other than that of the audience, librettos were bilingual, with parallel texts on opposite pages.

Melisma A passage of florid writing in which several notes are sung in the same syllable

Mezzo-soprano Term for a voice, usually female, normally written for within the range $a–f\sharp''$. The distinction between the florid soprano and the weightier mezzo-soprano became common only towards the mid-18th century. The castrato Senesino, for whom Handel composed was described as having a 'penetrating, clear, even, and pleasant deep soprano voice (mezzo Soprano)'. The distinction was more keenly sensed in the 19th century, although the mezzo-soprano range was often extended as high as a $b^\flat''$. Mezzo-sopranos with an extended upper range tackled the lower of two soprano roles in such operas as Bellini's *Norma* (Adagisa) and Donizetti's *Anna Bolena* (Jane Seymour). Both sopranos and mezzo-sopranos sing many of Wagner's roles.

The mezzo-soprano was often assigned a Breeches part in the era immediately after the demise of the Castrato, such as Arsace's in *Semiramide*; at all periods they have taken adolescent roles such as Cherubino (*Le nozze di Figaro*) or Oktavian (*Der Rosenkavalier*). The traditional casting however is as a nurse or confidante (e.g. Brangäne in *Tristan und Isolde*, Suzuki in *Madama Butterfly*) or as the mature married woman (e.g. Herodias in Strauss's *Salome*). Saint-Saëns's Delilah is an exception to the general rule that the principal female role (particularly the beautiful maiden) is a soprano.

Modulation The movement out of one key into another as a continuous musical process. It is particularly used in opera as a device to suggest a change of mood.

Motif A short musical idea, melodic, rhythmic, or harmonic (or any combination of those).

Music drama, Musical drama The term 'Musical drama' was used by Handel for *Hercules* (1745), to distinguish it from opera and Sacred Drama. In more recent usage, the meanings attached to 'music drama' derive from the ideas formulated in Wagner's *Oper und Drama*; it is applied to his operas and to others in which the musical, verbal and scenic elements cohere to serve one dramatic end. In 1869, Verdi distinguished between opera of the old sort and the *dramma musicale* that he believed his *La forza del destino* to be. Current theatrical practice tends to qualify this unity by performing music dramas with the original music and words but freshly invented scenic elements.

Music theatre   A catch-phrase common in the 1960s among composers, producers and critics who had artistic or social objections to traditional grand opera, to designate musical works for small or moderate forces that involve a dramatic element in their presentation. Such works have included small-scale operas, song cycles that are 'staged' and pieces such as Ligeti's *Aventures* and *Nouvelles aventures* that resist precise definition.

Opera buffa (It.)   'Comic opera': a term commonly used to signify Italian comic opera, principally of the 18th century, with recitative rather than spoken dialogue. Though now applied generically, it was one of the several such terms used in the 18th century.

Ostinato (It.)   Term used to refer to the repetition of a musical pattern many times over; the Ground bass is a form of *ostinato* used in early opera.

Overture   A piece of orchestral music designed to precede a dramatic work. By the mid-18th century the Italian type prevailed and the first movement had become longer and more elaborate; there was a tendency to drop the second and the third movements. In serious opera there was sometimes an effort to set the mood of the coming drama as in Gluck's *Alceste* and Mozart's *Idomeneo*; the famous preface to *Alceste* emphasizes the importance of this. In Mozart's *Don Giovanni*, *Così fan Tutte* and *Die Zauberflöte* the overture quotes musical ideas from the opera. Between 1790 and 1820, there was usually a slow introduction. The notion of tying the overture to the opera in mood and theme was developed in France and also appealed to the German Romantics. Beethoven made powerful use of dramatic motifs in his *Leonore* overtures while in Weber's *Der Freischütz* and *Euryanthe* overtures almost every theme reappears in the drama. Composers of French grand opera tended to expand the overture. For Bellini, Donizetti and Verdi the short prelude was an alternative, and it

became normal in Italian opera after the mid-century. Wagner, in the *Ring*, preferred a 'prelude' fully integrated into the drama, as did Richard Strauss amd Puccini, whose prelude to *Tosca* consists simply of three chords (associated with a particular character). In comic operas and operettas the independent overtures lasted longer; the structure based on the themes from the drama became a medly of tunes. The 'medley' or 'potpourri' overture used by Auber, Gounod, Thomas, Offenbach and Sullivan can still be traced in musical-comedy overtures.

Prelude   *see* Overture

Prima donna (It.)   'First lady': the principal female singer in an opera or on the roster of an opera company, almost always a soprano. The expression came into use around the mid-17th century, with the opening of public opera houses in Venice, where the ability of a leading lady to attract audiences became important. Singers who became prima donnas insisted on keeping that title; when conflicts arose, manegerial ingenuity devised such expressions as 'altra prima donna', 'prima donna assoluta' and even 'prima donna assoluta e sola'.

Some prima donnas made it a point of their status to be difficult. Adelina Patti (1843–1919), at the height of her career, stipulated that her name appear on posters in letters at least one-third larger than those used for other singers' names and that she be excused from rehearsals. The need to meet a prima donna's demands shaped many librettos and scores, particularly because her status was reflected in the number and character of the arias allotted to her.

Prologue   The introductory scene to a dramatic work, in which the author explains, either directly or indirectly, the context and meaning of the work to follow. In early opera, an allegorical prologue may pay homage to the author's patron. Prologues were a usual feature in early Baroque opera; in the late 18th century and the early 19th they were rare. Wagner's *Das Rheingold* may be seen as a prologue to the *Ring* since it represents the background to the plot. There are significant prologues to Gounod's *Roméo et Juliette*, Boito's *Mefistofele* and Leoncavallo's *Pagliacci* (the last modelled on those of ancient drama and with an exposition of the theory of *verismo*). In the 20th century various kinds of literary prologue have preceded operas, as in Stravinsky's *Oedipus rex*, Prokofiev's *Love for Three Oranges* and Berg's *Lulu*.

Quartet An ensemble for four singers. Quartets appear as early as the 17th century; Cavalli's *Calisto* ends with one and A. Scarlatti wrote several. There are quartets in Handel's *Radamisto* and *Partenope*. They appear in many *opéras comiques*. In *opera buffa* of the Classical era, when ensembles are sometimes used to further the dramatic action, quartets sometimes occupy that role: examples are the Act 2 finale of Mozart's *Die Entführung aus dem Serail*, where the sequence of sections shows the consolidation of the relationships between the two pairs of lovers, and in Act 1 of his *Don Giovanni*, where 'Non ti fidar' draws together the dramatic threads. The quartet in the last act of *Idomeneo* is however more a series of statements by the characters of their emotional positions, as is the quartet for the 'wedding' toast in the finale of *Così fan tutte*. Another canonic quartet is 'Mir ist so wunderbar' from Beethoven's *Fidelio*. Verdi wrote a quartet in *Otello*, but his best-known example is the one from *Rigoletto*, an inspired piece of simultaneous portrayal of feeling.

Quintet An ensemble for five singers. Quintets, except within ensemble finales, are rare in the operatic repertory. Notable exceptions are the two in Mozart's *Così fan tutte*. The only substantial ensemble in the sense of a number where the characters sing simultaneously in Wagner's late operas is the famous quintet in *Die Meistersinger von Nürnberg*, a rare moment in his operas where the dramatic action is suspended an the characters take emotional stock.

Recitative A type of vocal writing which follows closely the natural rhythm and accentuation of speech, not necessarily governed by a regular tempo or organized in a specific form. It derived from the development in the late 16th century of a declamatory narrative style with harmonic support, a wide melodic range and emotionally charged treatment of words. During the 17th century, recitative came to be the vehicle for dialogue, providing a connecting link between arias; the trailing off before the cadence (representing the singers being overcome with emotion), leaving the accompaniment to provide the closure, became a convention, as did the addition of an Apoggiatura at any cadence point to follow the natural inflection of Italian words.

By the late 17th century a more rapid, even delivery had developed, a trend carried further in *opera buffa* of the 18th century. Recitative was sung in a free, conversational manner. Plain or simple recitative, accompanied only by Continuo, is known as *recitativo semplice* or *recitativo secco* (or simply *secco*), to distinguish it from accompanied or orchestral recitative (*recitativo accompagnato*, *stromentato* or *obbligato*), which in the 18th century grew increasingly important for dramatic junctures. In France, the language demanded a different style, slower-moving, more lyrical and more flexible.

Recitative with keyboard accompaniment fell out of use early in the 19th century. Recitative-like declamation, however, remained an essential means of expression. Even late in the 19th century, when written operas with spoken dialogue were given in large houses where speech was not acceptable (like the Paris Opéra), recitatives were supplied by house composers or hacks (or the composer himself, for example Gounod with *Faust*) to replace dialogue: the most famous example is Guiraud's long-used set of recitatives for Bizet's *Carmen*. With the more continuous textures favoured in the 20th century, the concept of recitative disappeared (as it did in Wagner's mature works), to be replaced by other kinds of representation of speech. *Sprechgesang* may be seen as an Expressionist equivalent of recitative.

Ritornello (It.) A short recurring instrumental passage, particularly the tutti section of a Baroque aria.

Scene (1) The location of an opera, or an act or part of an act of an opera; by extension, any part of an opera in one location. (2) In earlier usage, a scene was a section of an act culminating in an aria (or occasionally an ensemble); any substantial (in some operas, any at all) change in the characters on the stage was reckoned a change of scene, and the scenes were numbered accordingly.

Septet An ensemble for seven singers. Septets are rare in the operatic repertory; a famous example is 'Par une telle nuit', from Berlioz's *Les troyens*, based on a text from Shakespeare's 'On such a night as this' (*The Merchant of Venice*).

Sextet An ensemble for six singers. Sextets are rare in the operatic repertory, except within act finales, but there are two notable Mozart examples: the recognition scene in Act 3 of *Le nozze di Figaro* and the central scene of Act 2 of *Don Giovanni*. The most celebrated operatic sextet is that at the climax of Donizetti's *Lucia di Lammermoor*.

Singspiel (Ger.) Literally, a play with songs; the term was used in 18th-century Germany for almost any kind of dramatic entertainment with music. In operatic usage, Singspiel means a German comic opera of the 18th or early 19th centuries, with spoken dialogue. The genre was particularly popular during the late 18th century in Vienna and Northern Germany (especially Leipzig). In its early days it was influenced by the English ballad opera. The most significant examples are Mozart's *Die Entführung aus dem Serail* and *Die Zauberflöte*.

Soprano (It.) The highest female voice, normally written for within the range *c′–a″*; the word is also applied to a boy's treble

voice and in the 17th and 18th centuries to a castrato of high range. The soprano voice was used for expressive roles in the earliest operas. During the Baroque period it was found to be suited to brilliant vocal display, and when a singer achieved fame it was usually because of an ability to perform elaborate music with precision as well as beauty. The heroine's role was sung by the most skilful soprano, the prima donna; to her were assigned the greatest number of arias and the most difficult and expressively wide-ranging music. The highest note usually required was *a* and little merit was placed on the capacity to sing higher.

The development of the different categories of the soprano voice belongs to the 19th century, strongly foreshadowed in the variety of roles and styles found in Mozart's operas (although type-casting was not at all rigid: the singer of Susanna in 1789 created Fiordiligi the next year). It was a consequence of the divergence of national operatic traditions and the rise of a consolidated repertory. Italian sopranos of the age of Rossini and Bellini developed a coloratura style and the ability to sustain a long lyrical line (the coloratura soprano and the lyric soprano); later, in Verdi's time, with larger opera houses and orchestras, the more dramatic *spinto* and *lirico spirito* appeared. In Germany the dramatic or heroic soprano was already foreshadowed in Beethoven's Leonore and Weber's Agathe; Wagner's Brünnhilde, demanding great power and brilliance, was the climax of this development. French *grand opéra* developed its own style of lyric-dramatic soprano. The operetta too produced a light, agile voice of its own.

Strophic Term for a song or an aria in which all stanzas of the text are set to the same music. The term 'strophic variations' is used of songs where the melody is varied from verse to verse while the bass remains unchanged or virtually so. The form was popular in early 17th-century Italy; 'Possente spirito', sung by Monteverdi's Orpheus, is an example, and Cavalli occasionally used the form.

Tenor The highest natural male voice, normally written for within the range *c–a'*. Although the tenor voice was valued in early opera – a tenor, Francesco Rasi (1574–after 1620), sang Monteverdi's Orpheus (1607) – heroic roles in middle and late Baroque opera were assigned to the castrato. Tenors took minor roles, such as the old man (sometimes with comic overtones), the lighthearted confidant, the mischievous schemer or the messenger, or even a travesty role of the old nurse. By the 1720s, important roles were occasionally given to tenors, and by the Classical era the voice was more regularly used in central roles. Such roles as Mozart's Bassilio, Ottavio, Ferrando and Titus – comic, docile lover, more virile lover, benevolent monarch – define the scope of the voice at this period.

A creation of the early 19th century was the *tenore di grazia*, a light, high voice moving smoothly into falsetto up to *d''*, called for by many Rossini roles. With the increasing size of opera houses, and the changes in musical style, the *tenore di forza* was called for. The tendency continued as, with Verdi's operas, the *tenore robusto* developed. For the German heroic tenor roles of the 19th century, especially Wagner's, a more weighty, durable type was needed, the Heldentenor. The lighter tenor continued to be cultivated for the more lyrical French roles. Many of the great tenors of the 20th century have been Italians, and made their names in Italian music, from Enrico Caruso (1873–1921) to Luciano Pavarotti; to these the Spaniard Plácido Domingo should be added.

Terzet, Trio An ensemble for three singers. Terzets or trios have been used throughout the history of opera. there is an example in Monteverdi's *L'incoronazione di Poppea*; Handel used the form several times, notably in *Tamerlano*, *Orlando*, and *Alcina*, and Gluck wrote examples in the closing scenes of his Italian reform operas. Mozart's include three (one in *Don Giovanni*, two in *La clemenza di Tito*) which are akin to arias with comments from two subsidiary characters. There are two in Weber's *Der Freischütz* and several for very high tenors in Rossini's serious operas. The form was much used by the Romantics, among them Verdi, who wrote three examples in *Un ballo in maschera*.

Through-composed Term for an aria in which the music for each stanza is different.

Tonal Term used for music in a particular key, or a pitch centre to which the music naturally gravitates. The use of tonalities, or the interplay of keys, can be an important dramatic weapon in the opera composer's armoury.

Trio *see* Terzet

Vorspiel (Ger.) 'Prelude': The term appears frequently in German operatic scores from Wagner's *Lohengrin* onwards. *See* Overture. The Prologue to Act 1 of *Götterdämmerung*, marked 'Vorspiel', embraces two extended scenes, and may have been influenced by the opening of Marschner's *Hans Heiling*, where a Vorspiel consisting of choruses flanking a solo for Heiling, precedes the overture.

Index of role names

213

Index of role names

Helmwige (soprano)	*Die Walküre*
Herald (bass)	*Lohengrin*
Herrmann, Landgrave (bass)	*Tannhäuser*
Hunding (bass)	*Die Walküre*
Irene/Irène (soprano)	*Rienzi*
Isabella (soprano)	*Das Liebesverbot*
Isolde (soprano)	*Tristan und Isolde*
Klingsor (bass)	*Parsifal*
Kothner, Fritz (bass)	*Die Meistersinger von Nürnberg*
Kundry (mezzo-soprano)	*Parsifal*
Kurwenal (baritone)	*Tristan und Isolde*
Lohengrin (tenor)	*Lohengrin*
Magdalene (soprano)	*Die Meistersinger von Nürnberg*
Mariana (soprano)	*Das Liebesverbot*
Mark, King/König Marke (bass)	*Tristan und Isolde*
Mary (alto)	*Der fliegende Holländer*
Melot (tenor)	*Tristan und Isolde*
Mime (tenor)	*Das Rheingold, Siegfried*
Moser, Augustin (bass)	*Die Meistersinger von Nürnberg*
Nachtigal, Konrad (bass)	*Die Meistersinger von Nürnberg*
Nightwatchman (bass)	*Die Meistersinger von Nürnberg*
Norns (alto)	*Götterdämmerung*
Orsini, Paolo (bass)	*Rienzi*
Ortel, Hermann (bass)	*Die Meistersinger von Nürnberg*
Ortlinde (soprano)	*Die Walküre*
Ortrud (mezzo-soprano)	*Lohengrin*
Parsifal (tenor)	*Parsifal*
Pogner, Veit (bass)	*Die Meistersinger von Nürnberg*
Raimondo, Cardinal (bass)	*Rienzi*
Reinmar von Zweter (bass)	*Tannhäuser*
Rienzi, Cola (tenor)	*Rienzi*
Rossweisse (alto)	*Die Walküre*
Schwarz, Hans (bass)	*Die Meistersinger von Nürnberg*
Schwertleite (alto)	*Die Walküre*
Senta (soprano)	*Der fliegende Holländer*
Shepherd (tenor)	*Tristan und Isolde*
Siegfried (tenor)	*Siegfriend, Götterdämmerung*
Sieglinde (soprano)	*Die Walküre*
Siegmund (tenor)	*Die Walküre*
Siegrune (mezzo-soprano)	*Die Walküre*
Steersman (tenor)	*Der fliegende Holländer*
Steersman (baritone)	*Tristan und Isolde*
Tannhäuser (tenor)	*Tannhäuser*

Suggested further reading

The New Grove Dictionary of Opera, edited by Stanley Sadie (London and New York, 1992)

*

ANTHOLOGIES, OTHER EDITIONS
C. Dahlhaus, ed.: *Wagners Ästhetik* (Bayreuth, 1972; English translation, 1972)

CORRESPONDENCE
S. Spencer and B. Millington, eds: *Selected Letters of Richard Wagner* (London, 1987) [English translation of 500 letters, with orig. texts of passages omitted from existing printed edns]

C.F. Glasenapp, ed.: *Familienbriefe von Richard Wagner 1832–1874* (Berlin, 1907; English translation, 1911, enlarged J. Deathridge, 1991)

PERSONAL ACCOUNTS, REMINISCENCES
P. Cook, ed.: *A Memoir of Bayreauth: 1876* (London, 1979) [Carl Emil Doepler's account of the first Bayreuth Festival; incl. his costume designs]

PRINCIPAL BIOGRAPHIES
E. Newman: *The LIfe of Richard Wagner* (London, 1933–47)

R.W. Gutman: *Richard Wagner: the Man, his Mind, and his Music* (New York and London, 1968)

C. von Westernhagen: *Wagner* (Zürich, 1968, enlarged 1978; English translation, 1978)

R. Taylor: *Richard Wagner: his Life, Art and Thought* (London, 1979)

D. Watson: *Richard Wagner: a Biography* (London, 1979)

M. Gregor-Dellin: *Richard Wagner: sein Leben, sein Werk, sein Jahrhundert* (Munich, 1980, 1983; English translation, abridged, 1983)

J. Deathridge and C. Dahlhaus: *The New Grove Wagner* (London, 1984)

B. Millington: *Wagner* (London, 1984, 1992)

OTHER BIOGRAPHICAL AND RELATED STUDIES
E. Newman: *A Study of Wagner* (London, 1899)

E. Newman: *Wagner as Man and Artist* (London, 1914, 1924)

G. Skelton: *Richard and Cosima Wagner: Biography of a Marriage* (London, 1982)

E. Magee: *Richard Wagner and the Nibelungs* (Oxford, 1990)

B. Millington, ed.: *The Wagner Compendium* (London, 1992)

G. Skelton: *Wagner at Bayreuth: Experiment and Tradition* (London, 1965, enlarged 1976)

P. Turing: *New Bayreuth* (London, 1969, 1971)

C. Osborne: *The World Theatre of Wagner* (Oxford, 1982)

B. Millington and S. Spencer, eds: *Wagner in Performance* (New Haven, CT, 1992)

LITERARY AND PHILOSOPHICAL STUDIES

B. Magee: *Aspects of Wagner* (London, 1968, enlarged 1988)

P.L. Rose: *Wagner: Race and Revolution* (London, 1992)

M.A. Weiner: *Richard Wagner and the anti-Semitic imagination* (Lincoln, NE, 1995)

D.J. Levin: *Richard Wagner, Fritz Lang and the Nibelungen: the dramaturgy of disavowal* (Princeton, NJ, 1998)

ANALYSIS AND CRITICISM: GENERAL STUDIES

P. Bekker: *Richard Wagner: das Leben im Werke* (Stuttgart, 1924; English translation, 1931)

E. Newman: *Wagner Nights* (London, 1949); as *The Wagner Operas* (New York, 1949)

T.W. Adorno: *Versuch Uuber Wagner* (Berlin and Frankfurt, 1952; repr. in *Gesammelte Schriften*, xi, 1971; English translation, 1981)

S. Spencer, ed.: *Wagner 1976: a Celebration of the Bayreuth Festival* (London, 1976)

P. Burbidge and R. Sutton, eds: *The Wagner Companion* (London, 1990)

C. Osborne: *The Complete Operas of Richard Wagner* (London, 1990)

ANALYSIS AND CRITICISM: INDIVIDUAL STUDIES

J. Deathridge: *Wagner's Rienzi: a Reappraisal based on a Study of the Sketches and Drafts* (Oxford, 1977)

N. John, ed.: *The Flying Dutchman* (London, 1982) [ENO opera guide]

N. John, ed.: *Tannhäuser* (London, 1988) [ENO opera guide]

Der Ring des Nibelungen

R. Donington: *Wagner's 'Ring' and its Symbols: the Music and the Myth* (London, 1963, enlarged 1974)

D. Cooke: *I Saw the World End* (London, 1979)

P. McCreless: *Wagner's Siegfried: its drama, History, and Music* (Ann Arbor, MI, 1982)

N. John, ed.: *Die Walküre* (London, 1983); *Siegfried* (London, 1984); *The Rhinegold* (London, 1985); *Twilight of the Gods* (London, 1985) [ENO opera guides]

D.A. White: *The Turning Wheel: a Study of Contracts and Oaths in Wagner's 'Ring'* (Selinsgrove, PA, 1988)

C. Wintle: 'The Numinous in *Götterdämmerung*', *Reading Opera*, ed. A. Groos and R. Parker (Princeton, NJ, 1988)

H. Richardson, ed.: *New Studies in Richard Wagner's 'The Ring of the Nibelungen'* (Lewiston, NY, 1992)

W. Darcy: *Wagner's 'Das Rheingold'* (Oxford, 1993)

Wagner's 'Ring of the Nibelung', a companion ([the full German text with a new translation by Stewart Spencer and commentaries by Barry Millington *et al.*], London, 1993)

Tristan und Isolde

N. John, ed.: *Tristan and Isolde* (London, 1981) [ENO opera guide]

R. Bailey, ed.: *Richard Wagner: Prelude and Transfiguration from 'Tristan and Isolde'* (New York, 1985) [Norton Critical Score]

A. Groos: 'Appropriation in Wagner's *Tristan* Libretto', *Reading Opera*, ed. A. Groos and R. Parker (Princeton, NJ, 1988)

Die Meistersinger von Nürnberg

N. John, ed.: *The Mastersingers of Nuremberg* (London, 1983) [ENO opera guide]

J. Warrack: *Richard Wagner, 'Die Meistersinger von Nürnberg'*, (Cambridge, 1994)

Parsifal

L. Beckett: *Richard Wagner: Parsifal* (Cambridge, 1981)

N. John, ed.: *Parsifal* (London, 1986) [ENO opera guide]

WAGNERISM

T.W. Adorno: *Versuch über Wagner* (Berlin and Frankfurt, 1952; English translation, as *In Search of Wagner*, 1981)

B. Magee: *Aspects of Wagner* (London, 1968, 1988)

S. Martin: *Wagner to 'The Waste Land': a Study of the Relationship of Wagner to English Literature* (London, 1982)

D.C. Large and W. Weber, eds: *Wagnerism in European Culture and Politics* (Ithaca, NY, 1984)

WIELAND WAGNER

G. Skelton: *Wagner at Bayreuth: Experiment and Tradition* (London, 1965, enlarged 1976)

G. Skelton: *Wieland Wagner: the Positive Sceptic* (London, 1971)

W.S. Wagner: *The Wagner Family Albums* (London, 1976)